Michael Veitch is well known as an author, actor and former ABC television and radio presenter. His books include the critically acclaimed accounts of Australian pilots in World War II, *Heroes of the Skies*, *Fly*, *Flak*, *44 Days*, *Barney Greatrex* and *Turning Point*. *The Battle of the Bismarck Sea* is his tenth book. He lives in the Yarra Valley, outside Melbourne.

T0385213

Also by Michael Veitch

44 Days: 75 Squadron and the fight for Australia

*Barney Greatrex: From Bomber Command to the French
Resistance – the stirring story of an Australian hero*

*Turning Point: The Battle for Milne Bay 1942 – Japan's first land
defeat in World War II*

THE BATTLE OF THE BISMARCK SEA

THE FORGOTTEN BATTLE THAT SAVED THE PACIFIC

MICHAEL VEITCH

hachette
AUSTRALIA

hachette
AUSTRALIA

Published in Australia and New Zealand in 2021
by Hachette Australia
(an imprint of Hachette Australia Pty Limited)
Level 17, 207 Kent Street, Sydney NSW 2000
www.hachette.com.au

 A catalogue record for this
work is available from the
NATIONAL
LIBRARY National Library of Australia
OF AUSTRALIA

ISBN: 978 0 7336 4589 1 (paperback)

Cover design by Luke Causby, Blue Cork Designs
Cover photographs courtesy of the Australian War Memorial (plane image 128005, ship image 141996)
Author photograph courtesy Gina Milicia
Typeset in Simoncini Garamond by Kirby Jones
Printed and bound in Australia by McPherson's Printing Group

Contents

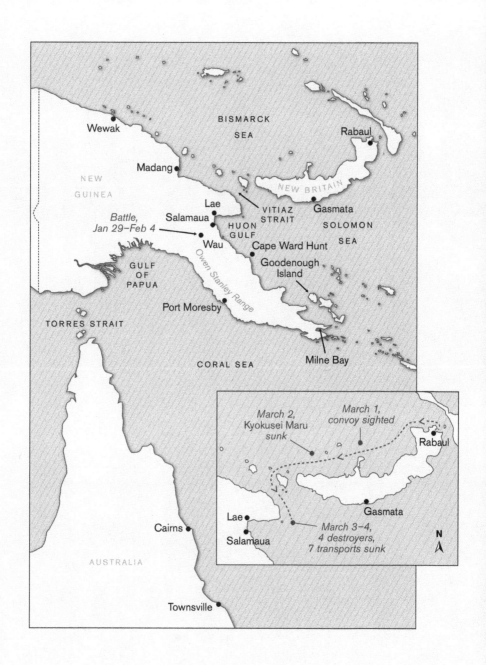

Wewak

BISMARCK
SEA

Rabaul

Madang

NEW
GUINEA

NEW BRITAIN

Lae

VITIAZ
STRAIT

Gasmata

Salamaua

Battle,
Jan 29–Feb 4

HUON
GULF

SOLOMON

Wau

Cape Ward Hunt

SEA

Owen Stanley Range

Goodenough
Island

GULF
OF
PAPUA

Port Moresby

TORRES STRAIT

Milne Bay

CORAL SEA

March 2,
Kyokusei Maru
sunk

March 1,
convoy sighted

Rabaul

Cairns

Lae

Gasmata

Salamaua

March 3–4,
4 destroyers,
7 transports sunk

N

AUSTRALIA

Townsville

PART ONE

CHAPTER 1
THE MIRACLE OF WAU

Finally, the weak grey light began to edge its way across the featureless tropical sky. Soaking wet, the men huddled behind their haphazard defences, strung along the creek.

'Take a look, everyone,' said a quiet voice – a sergeant, perhaps, or just one among this hotchpotch few dozen who last night were told to find a rifle and make their way down to the perimeter of the base, quick smart.

Taking their eyes – for a moment – off the rows of dark green foliage stretching out in front, a couple of the men checked to see who had joined them during this night of rain and fear and confusion. The most senior officer present seemed to be some bloke from the transport section. Then there were clerks, batmen, drivers, even the cook, wide-eyed and clutching a .303 a little too tightly, licking the sweat off his top lip.

'So what's for breakfast?' someone snorted in his direction.

A few men laughed. The cook didn't seem to hear it.

3

They could start to make it out now, this coffee plantation, with its neat lines of wet, serrated leaves and berries turning red. A few days before, you could walk right through it, easy as you like. Not now.

Now, lurking somewhere out there, were the Japanese.

'Careful, fellas,' muttered another voice.

Maybe the enemy was still up in the hills, on one of those impossible ridges which flew like green buttresses across the interlocking mountain spurs, all now obscured by this thick wet curtain of grey mist which clung to everything it touched.

Worryingly, it also obscured that long, clear strip of green up behind them – the airfield.

No planes would be landing at Wau today.

•

The night before last, a few miles away, the Imperial Japanese Army's forward units had burst like crazed chimeras out of the jungle into a small crossing above a village called Wandumi. That had shocked everyone. For a week or so now the Allies had known the Japanese had pushed out from Salamaua, their base on the coast nearly 40 miles away as the crow flies, and were reportedly heading to Wau to grab its precious high-altitude airstrip.

But where were they now?

The commando boys had sent patrols up the Black Cat and Crystal Creek tracks that wound their tortuous way through the jungle to Mubo but had found nothing. Too late, the Australians realised they'd been outfoxed. Somehow the Japanese had discovered a *third* track, unmarked on any map, partially hacked out by the Germans – the *Germans*, for Christ's sake – thirty years before. And now here they were, just a few miles away, tantalisingly close to their prize.

If it wasn't for the fog you could see the runway standing out up behind the men, the only levelled patch of this part of the Bulolo Valley: surely one of the most peculiar airstrips in the world.

One hundred and fifty miles to the northwest of Port Moresby, the old gold-mining village of Wau sits some 3000 feet above sea level at the end of a vast valley cupped on three sides by vertiginous mountains. 'Weird, fantastic country', as a wartime newsreel film described it.

Built by half-crazed miners back in the twenties, the two-thirds of a mile–long airstrip features a tricky 300-foot height differential from one end to the other, south being the only possible direction of approach.

In order to land, pilots have to bank steeply to avoid hitting one of the dozens of surrounding mountain tops – 'rocks in clouds', they called them – then level out before touching down on the uphill runway, all while maintaining sufficient engine power to pull the plane up the slope, but not so much as to slam into the huts and houses at the far end, not to mention any other parked aircraft which had been lucky enough to make it into this impossible airstrip in one piece.

Even before the war, landing at Wau had been hard enough for the tough bush pilots with thousands of flying hours in their logbooks, flying their old Dornier transports, bringing in the miners and their dredging equipment to harvest this gold-rich alluvial valley. Now it was the turn of the Americans and Australians – teenagers, some of them – straight out of flying school, pushing their brand new Dakota transports above the 14000-foot Owen Stanley Range, knowing there was no chance of a turnaround if they got it wrong.

When they finally reached Wau all they could do was line up, lower their flaps, and hold their breath.

It was the sound of just such an approaching aircraft that the men waiting in the creek bed on this January dawn in 1943 longed to hear. Looking up at the thick wet sky, however, they knew there was bugger-all chance of that.

'Kanga Force' they'd called them, this ad hoc collection of soldiers sent to defend the Wau base. So named, as some wit explained, because the only way to get up there was to hop in a bloody aeroplane. These couple of thousand misfits were grouped into two independent commando companies and joined by the New Guinea Volunteer Rifles, who had been there for years as civilians before the war. Hardly the most military of outfits, but they knew the place backwards. Try telling them anything about this place, or any part of New Guinea, they didn't already know.

Reconnaissance had been Kanga Force's initial brief: just keep an eye on the Japanese to the north at Lae, 40 miles away. This soon evolved into guerrilla hit-and-run missions, slithering up through the jungle to surprise the enemy.

One such raid in June 1942 had been one of the first offensive actions conducted by the Australians in the entire war. Seventy-eight men slipped quietly into the Japanese base at Salamaua like phantoms in the night and unleashed bloody mayhem. One hundred enemy were killed – shot where they slept, blown to pieces when hand grenades flew through the open windows of their dormitories and onto their cots, or knifed or bayoneted when they tried to flee. Some of them died quickly, but not all.

In addition to the human tally, a store of equipment and intelligence was captured, all for the cost of only three 'lightly wounded' Australian casualties who were able to traipse back to Wau beside their mates in high spirits. No one was kidding themselves, though, that the Japanese would take the insult lightly.

They would soon be planning their revenge.

•

Bill Sherlock was a good-looking bloke, square-jawed, tall and athletic; bit of a toff, rowed for a fancy school – Geelong Grammar, someone had said. He'd already been over in the desert at Bardia and Tobruk and now here he was, closer to home but up against a very different enemy in a very different kind of war. They'd put Bill and his men on a ridge guarding the approaches to the Wau airstrip, but nobody had expected the Japanese to get this close. However, two days earlier they'd screamed out of the jungle in their hundreds and slammed into Sherlock's under-strength A Company with machine guns and mortars.

Sherlock surveyed the valley and airstrip below, then the jungle ahead, and knew that this was where he would remain. 'We can't let 'em through, fellas,' he said quietly, and for two crucial days he was true to his word. Two thousand feet below, the men in the creek bed heard the muffled sounds of the shooting.

At first the Japanese were amused by this show of defiance so close to their goal of a ready-made mountain airstrip which they would take over and use to protect their bases of Lae and Salamaua, and to prevent the sort of deadly raid that had taken 100 or so of their number back in June. Finally, the Australians had decided to put up a fight! After being stopped by the surprisingly fierce initial barrage of rifle and Thompson machine-gun fire from Sherlock and his men, they began taunting the Australians with their usual choruses of 'Aussie, we're coming over!' and 'Time to give up, Aussie!'

But here on this mountain track of kunai grass in the hills above Wau, Bill Sherlock decided that the enemy would proceed no further. Outnumbered ten to one, and with a dense, low cloud which offered no chance of air cover, his men sought what protection they could in the grass and behind hastily dug earthworks, forcing back every attempt the Japanese made to push, shoot or slither their way through. Thwarted by terrain chosen specifically to deny them the chance to employ their trademark tactic of outflanking and encirclement, the light-hearted taunts of the Japanese soon turned to screams of fury.

For a day and a night, Sherlock held the line. Not only did he block the Japanese, he organised quick and savage counter-attacks – some with hand grenade and bayonet – throwing them off their guard. Refusing, initially, to yield an inch, the young captain eventually retreated some way down the mountainous switchbacks to one of the dozens of terraces. There, enfilading fire could be thrown into the path of the enemy.

Hour after hour, the Japanese advance was repulsed, but Sherlock and his men were weakening. Ammunition became scarce. Men's throats begged for water. *Things very hot here, any help sent may be too late* was the signal he sent down to Kanga Force HQ. Still, he insisted his men counterattack, though in ever-decreasing numbers. At one stage A Company was down to forty men, then later just eighteen. In the late afternoon reinforcements arrived, but more and more Japanese were seen advancing from the ridges above.

In the fading light, Sherlock's left flank was breached.

Again he withdrew, and again he held.

Don't think it will be long now, he signalled early the next morning. *Enemy close up to front and flank. About 50 yards in front.* At dawn, several hundred Japanese gathered to attack across the slopes of a small pimple on a ridge being held by Sherlock and his remnant of A Company. Sherlock waited till they were close, then called calmly to his men, 'Let 'em have it!' The last of their magazines were emptied and their final grenades hurled.

To their astonishment, the Japanese stopped in their tracks.

Suddenly, the awful crump of mortar fire began to land among them and again Sherlock's flank was broken. Finally ordered to withdraw, he gathered his remaining men, telling them that they were already partly surrounded and that they would have to shoot their way out back down the hill. Oh, and good luck.

Some would take days to get back down, seeking the cover of the jungle, dodging patrolling Japanese soldiers wherever they could.

Around 3 a.m., Sherlock and a small group of men reached the Bulolo River, where a large fallen tree marked a crossing point beyond which they could reasonably expect to be safe. Hearing voices somewhere in the jungle ahead, he challenged with an 'Are you an Aussie?' which, after a pause, was met with the distinctive slow-firing burst of a Japanese 'woodpecker' machine gun.

'I'll give you Japanese, you bastards!' he then shouted before rushing forward. Some of his men following said he hurled a grenade towards the enemy position, destroying it, only to be cut down when a second position opened fire. Several Australian soldiers were wounded but managed to roll over the log and head downstream to a safer crossing point.

Not so for Captain Bill Sherlock. Killed instantly within reach of safety, the mettle of his heroism can scarcely be measured. His actions in holding up the Japanese advance that day, in full knowledge of the likelihood of his own destruction, unquestionably saved the base at Wau. The critical thirty-six hours during which he frustrated, then blunted, the Japanese attack was time they would never get back.

Sherlock's leadership and sacrifice, deserving as they were of at least the Distinguished Service Order (DSO) were in the end rewarded by the army with a paltry Mentioned in Despatches, *posthumous*.

•

Down at Big Wau Creek, the men on the perimeter of the base looked out over the coffee plantation and – now that they could make them out – the native gardens beyond, seeking any sign of movement. Nothing. Still the grey mist lay thick on the ground, crushing every outline in a dismal monochrome. If a battle was coming, it would be akin to one fought between two blind men, probing and stabbing their way towards each other in the gloom.

Then came the unmistakeable sound of patrolling fighters making wide circles above the cloud, the throb of their motors receding and returning like a tide. The Kittyhawk and Wirraway pilots of the Royal Australian Air Force (RAAF) were up there somewhere, though in this cloud there was little they could do but hope for a break in the weather.

Someone managed to produce some tea – hot and sweet – which was gratefully accepted. 'Keep the bloody noise down,' urged a voice up the line. Then, just on 7 a.m., the sky suddenly lightened and a patch of blue prised apart two great banks of cloud, which quickly and indignantly evaporated. More gaps in the sky appeared and then, in a burst, the sun broke through, its fierce tropical heat instantly warming the men's clammy skin. A piece of tin under which some were sheltering popped and buckled, and behind them steam began to rise from the surface of the runway. The weather, which in this place never behaved but with a will of its own, was finally lifting.

A few thousand feet above, the Australian pilots noted the dissolving cloud layer. Pausing just a few seconds more to make sure what they were seeing was real, they hit their radios. Within seconds, the message was received at No 4 Fighter Sector at Port Moresby and copied hurriedly onto a piece of dispatch paper: *Wau – weather clearing – runway visible to 5000 feet.* After a moment's consultation, the excited radio operators passed the order to the American controller at Ward's airstrip, just 2 miles north of the town: *Proceed – Wau – immediate.*

The handful of ageing Dakotas left to the US No 374 Troop Carrier Group had, just a few days before, been replenished by the arrival of fifty-two brand new machines – still smelling of paint – direct from the factory at Long Beach, California.

'It's on!' went the call as Australian soldiers raced to their allotted aircraft, their kitbags already stowed under the long bench seats which ran the length of the fuselage. With the whine of a starter motor, the engines roared into life.

Half an hour later, to tears of relief, the first bass note of a mass of approaching aircraft could be heard. For three anxious days and nights the 2/7th Infantry Brigade had been waiting beside their aircraft at Port Moresby, fretting for a gap in the weather. Increasingly bitter at their forced exclusion from the battle, they'd pleaded with their officers to take them aloft, to 'stuff the bloody weather and just get going!'. The pilots had nodded their sympathy, looked to the sky and shrugged their shoulders.

Now, finally, they could set out to relieve their mates.

The first of the grey-green Dakota transports moved slowly up the long valley before touching down, the sound of their gunning engines echoing in report. Stopping at the top of the slope of green, their doors opened, instantly disgorging lines of men in khaki, ready for battle.

'Move, move now, you bloody Diggers!' exhorted a sergeant, while a lieutenant shepherded them clear of the still-spinning prop towards defensive positions around the base. Like a river of green, the men, in slouch hats and with rifles over their shoulders, poured into Wau. 'Christ, am I glad to see you bastards!' muttered every man they passed.

Several miles away, the Japanese had likewise observed the blanket of cloud evaporate – and with it their chances of taking the airfield. As the Dakotas touched down, a few of the Japanese forward elements raced desperately into sniping positions in the surrounding gardens and slaughter yards. Though at the edge of their range, they managed to land a few pot shots as the men disembarked; some of those soldiers, now wounded, were forced to return to Port Moresby in the very same aircraft which had just delivered them.

All that day – 29 January 1943 – no fewer than fifty-seven troop-carrying Dakotas would touch down at Wau, bringing in 814 men. Some pilots made the round trip several times, shuttling back and forth from Port Moresby like taxis. Some men arrived in aircraft only recently pressed into military service from their former lives as civilian airliners for ANA (Australian National Airways). The men stowed their rifles in the luggage racks, bemused by the padded seats, barley sugars and travel brochures still in the seat pockets.

All day the young Australian and American pilots touched down and disgorged their cargo, keeping their engines running before twisting around on the impossibly small turning area – ably assisted by manpower hauling at the tail – then roaring downhill to take off again and make room for the next aircraft.

One anxious pilot braked too hard and sent his plane up on its nose, forcing others to taxi around as they came in. One of these carried the pieces of two 25-pounder field guns which, with burred hands, the artillerymen of the 2/1st Field Regiment assembled, sighted, and made ready for action in just two hours. With each arrival, the Allies' Wau garrison grew stronger.

The following day, just as the Japanese were gathering the bulk of their forces for a massed assault on the airfield, the Beaufighters of 30 Squadron arrived, their dark shapes racing up the valley, sleeve-valve engines roaring like great prowling cats. Four hundred Japanese soldiers emerged onto a road which led up to a plantation known as Leahy's Farm. The Allied artillery was waiting, having ranged on the area the day before, and opened up. In a brief paroxysm of slaughter, the Japanese were torn to pieces, shells falling among them as the Beaufighters fired cannon from above. As instructed, the pilots strafed on the smoke laid down by the soldiers' mortar bombs. In half an hour some 22 000 rounds of cannon and machine gun had been fired.

Perhaps the luckiest men that day were sergeants Ron Downing and Danny Box flying Beaufighter A19-53. Lining up on his target, pilot Downing roared over the heads of the airstrip's defenders and pressed his firing button just as a shell landed on the same target, which turned out to be a large ammunition dump. A massive blast of flame and smoke filled Downing's vision and the aircraft was pelted and buffeted like a tin can in a hailstorm. Somehow, he managed to keep his throttle open and his aircraft aloft. The explosion was seen and heard for miles, killed a large number of Japanese and flattened around fifteen nearby native huts. Returning to Port Moresby, the riggers counted fifty-eight holes in the skin of the Beaufighter. The paintwork was scorched. Whether it was his cannon fire or the artillery that had set off the explosion was to be the source of inter-service rivalry for some time.

Two months later, Downing and Box would test their luck again in the frenzied battle over the Bismarck Sea.

Sergeant Norrie Jones, one of the 2/1st Field Regiment's gunners, described walking through the carnage of the Japanese positions:

> ... a farmhouse blew up. It was 550 metres away from us and the blast knocked us off our feet. A mushroom cloud formed over it ... the farmhouse had been filled with explosives and one of our shells had set it off. In the fire area, gutters and on the road the bodies of 430 Japanese were found after the battle. Many had been close to the huge blast and had been atomised. The surviving Japanese had also collected a lot of their dead and packed them into two pyramids ready for cremation. The base of the pyramids was 7 metres square and ... 3 metres high. But the survivors had been driven off, leaving the masses of decomposing bodies. No one counted those bodies but we estimate that there were 200 in each pyramid.

In a few days, the newly reinforced Wau garrison would push the Japanese back up the hills and along the foetid jungle tracks towards the coast from where they had come.

•

Though defeated, the Japanese knew the battle for Wau had been the closest of calls. Nor were they shaken in their belief that this isolated jungle outpost and its airstrip remained theirs for the taking. As they skulked back along the dank and spongy jungle track towards their base at Salamaua, they brooded on the bad luck which had snatched away victory. But they had learned, and whatever mistakes had been made would not be made again. Despite the best efforts of the American and Australian airmen, the convoy that had delivered the Japanese from Rabaul to Lae had been modest in size. The next would be considerably larger, and would determine once and for all the outcome of the Battle for New Guinea.

CHAPTER 2
JAPAN REJUVENATED

In the first week of 1943, twenty-four days before Bill Sherlock's heroic stand in the hills above Wau, a Japanese convoy designated 'Operation 18' by General Hatazo Adachi's 18th Army Command steamed out of Rabaul bound for Lae. It consisted of five transports ranging in size from the nearly 6000-ton *Brazil Maru* to the *Myoko Maru* at just over 4000 tons. There was also the *Clyde Maru*, Japanese-built but oddly named after the famous shipbuilding river bank in Scotland, as well as the more than twenty-years-old and thoroughly clapped-out steamer *Nichiryu Maru*; by comparison, the *Myoko Maru* was barely two years old. Operation 18 would be protected by an escort of destroyers: the *Maikaze*, *Hamakaze*, *Hanikaze*, *Tanikaze*, and the flagship, *Urakaze*, all under the command of 45-year-old Captain Masayuki Kitamura.

Distributed across the holds of the ships of Operation 18 were the men and equipment of the Okabe Detachment, so described in accordance with the Japanese habit of naming certain military units after their commander, in this case Major General Toru Okabe. Okabe had begun his career in the Imperial Japanese Army in training divisions in the late thirties, before transferring to the elite Kwantung Army Group in China in September 1941 to lead a regiment in the Battle of Changsha. There, along with much of the Japanese army in this important engagement of the Sino–Japanese War, he was defeated. The retreat seemed not to blunt Okabe's career, however, and after being promoted he was awarded another command of three battalions of the 51st Division's 102nd Infantry Regiment which would now bear his name. Departing from the expanse of Rabaul's Simpson Harbour for the two-day voyage to Lae on 5 January 1943, the 4000 men under his command felt confident in their ability to achieve the task they had been set: a landing at Lae followed by a speedy overland trek to capture the Australian airfield at Wau.

The fact that Japan was even capable of launching such an offensive in early 1943 speaks volumes to their unlikely strength and confidence at this juncture of the war in the South West Pacific. Despite what many had assumed to be a debilitating series of defeats; despite having been repulsed at Milne Bay and Kokoda; their carrier force wiped out at the battles of the Coral Sea and Midway; having been dragged and blasted out of Guadalcanal; their New Guinea bases of Buna, Gona and Sanananda about to be overrun by a joint Australian–American campaign launched the previous November, the Japanese nevertheless felt New Guinea to be well within their grasp. There was, in truth, much to justify this belief. The war in early 1943 was far from over, and Japan far from defeated.

Although Midway and defeat in the Solomons had abruptly halted the expansion of the new empire Japan had seized for herself in the hundred-day Blitz unleashed in December 1941, she was still a formidable force over a year later. Among the natural resources swept up in her orgy of conquest of far eastern European colonies was 80 per cent of the world's rubber, more than half of its tin, and 20 per cent of its tungsten, as well as vast quantities of oil, manganese and iron ore. All this being courtesy of the mines, wells and plantations of the Dutch East Indies and the British territories of Malaya and Singapore.

The decision in June 1942 to expand the defensive perimeter of Japan's initial conquests – south to the Solomons, east to Midway and north to the Aleutians in faraway Alaska – had perhaps been rash, and defeats there had been bitter, but the crux of Japan's initial gains remained intact. Although her carrier fleet had been annihilated at Midway, her navy was still formidable, particularly in the use of smaller ships such as destroyers, which at Guadalcanal had performed a brilliant series of operations – largely at night – managing to evacuate most of her defeated forces to fight another day. These fast and agile ships racing out of the darkness like torpedo-spewing speedboats confounded the slower Allied ships, and had already broken the backbone of the Royal Australian Navy. At the Sunda Strait the previous March, they had dispatched the *Perth*, then six months later at Savo Island it was the turn of the heavy cruiser *Canberra* to be sent to the bottom. Along with the catastrophe of the *Sydney* – lost to a German merchant raider in 1941 – Australia's navy had by early 1943 been reduced to virtual impotence as a fighting force.

Also around this time, Allied reconnaissance photographs revealed to astonished American and Australian intelligence officers that, despite her losses, Japan was nevertheless able to cram into Rabaul Harbour no fewer than ninety ships – twenty-one warships and sixty-nine merchant vessels – representing an aggregate 300000 tons. Further north at Truk, Japan's great naval base in the Caroline Islands, the presence of a full combat fleet had been discovered, lurking just three days' sailing from New Guinea. Even closer to Australia, warships and accompanying destroyers had been making regular forays to Wewak Harbour, and similar activity was reported around the Aru and Kai islands off New Guinea's south-west coast – a direct and unimpeded line to Darwin, just 434 nautical miles away.

In terms of land forces, it was estimated that Japan still had no fewer than eighty-six divisions in all theatres, of which fifteen were considered a 'floating force' which could be deployed at short notice. Even in the midst of its defeats, the Imperial Japanese Army in late 1942 managed to send both the 2nd and 38th Divisions to Rabaul, which were in turn bolstered by the arrival of the 6th Division in the new year. The 5th Division, in the meantime, had been sent to the island of Ambon, and the 48th deployed to Timor. On the New Guinea coast, the 20th and 41st Divisions remained dug in around Wewak and Madang representing, even without resupply, over 20000 Japanese fighting men. Fourteen full-strength fighting divisions, it was thus estimated, were in place defending the southern and western perimeters of Japan's 'Greater East Asian Co-prosperity Sphere'. These could be quickly reinforced via a direct route from Japan through her Philippines citadel. Her industries, although not vast, were nonetheless considerable and as yet unassailable to any enemy ground or air power, and her 70 million plus population dwarfed that of Australia by more than ten to one.

Furthermore, unlike the Allies, Japan was not hampered by her resources being split in two by another theatre of war entirely, one which was considered a far higher priority than the South West Pacific – namely, Europe. Despite Japan's conquests, the Americans still considered the Pacific a backwater, with the supply of men and equipment remaining modest compared to the materiel flowing into the European/African campaign. In vain, US Pacific generals and commanders pleaded for more support but were met with their government's unshakeable policy of 'Europe first'. In fact, the Japanese threat ranked as low as sixth out of seventh on the list of Allied strategic priorities, with only the defeat of the German U-boats and the retaking of Burma considered less important.

In early 1943, General George C Kenney, the new commander of American air power in the South West Pacific, estimated that his fleet of 537 aircraft – 200 of which were at any time under repair – was outnumbered by the Japanese by at least 150. Of his fighter force of 330 aircraft, only eighty were the brilliant new Lockheed P-38 Lightning, the only fighter then capable of matching the formidable Japanese Zero. The remainder consisted mainly of the P-39 Airacobra and P-40 Kittyhawk, unwanted cast-offs considered inadequate for the European theatre, and incapable of matching the Zero in a dogfight.

The Japanese, meanwhile, were in a race to rebuild their strategic air weapon, with the Allies in New Guinea, according to historian Peter Thompson, facing the prospect of enemy airfields 'spawning along the north coast all the way east to Lae'.

Reconnaissance in the first weeks of 1943 likewise reported intense enemy activity across the arc of occupied islands to Australia's north-west. From Java to Bougainville, sixty-six Japanese airfields were reported to be in operation, including both the expansion of older strips and the establishment of new ones. Intelligence estimated they were capable of holding 1380 aircraft (even if, at least for the present, roughly half that number were, in fact, deployed).

Exhibiting the characteristic bluntness that made his superiors in government wince, AIF Commander-in-Chief General Thomas Blamey publicly stated that this Japanese-held archipelago contained no less than 200 of the enemy, a figure which was later revised upwards to 230000.

In November 1942, in the very nadir of her setbacks, Japan conjured an entirely new army – the 18th – three divisions strong, its sole purpose being to restart the conquest of New Guinea. Its newly appointed head, General Hatazo Adachi, was a competent veteran of the war in China, where he had ruthlessly enacted Japan's scorched-earth policy.

Correspondingly, from his Eighth Area Command headquarters in Rabaul, Lieutenant General Hitoshi Imamura decreed that 6000 or so of those men would be sent to reignite the battle for New Guinea. Fresh, well-trained and experienced, they would tear open a new front in the Lae–Salamaua sector, luring in the weary Australian and American units whose ranks were already exhausted by the long and bloody Kokoda and Buna/Gona campaigns, decimated by months of fighting, heat and tropical illness.

The Japanese forces would then advance and finally secure the airfield at Wau, which would become the crucible of the new Japanese front in New Guinea.

The tip of the rejuvenated spear of this new offensive would be the men of the Okabe Detachment, travelling within the hulls of the ships of the convoy designated Operation 18.

CHAPTER 3
THE FIRST CONVOY

Late in the morning of Thursday, 7 January 1943, 1st Lieutenant Len Nicholson took off from the tiny Reid River airstrip near Townsville at the controls of his fast Martin B-26 Marauder bomber. With several other aircraft from the US 408th and 22nd Bombardment squadrons, he headed due north out to sea. In a few hours, he would be over Lae. His orders were to attack the ships of a Japanese convoy that was making its way there from Rabaul. Over the aircraft intercom Nicholson and his co-pilot, 1st Lieutenant Jack Childers, checked in with their crew of seven, reminding each soldier to keep his eyes open, especially as they approached the misty green horizon of New Guinea.

Around the same time, at the controls of a larger and slower B-17 E Fortress, Lieutenant Ray Dau lifted off the metal mesh runway at Port Moresby's Jackson Airfield with his crew of nine. Dau was flying with the 56th Bombardment Squadron. They had a far shorter distance to fly, and as they headed into the grey tropical gloom Dau reflected that this was his thirteenth mission.

The crews of both aircraft – along with the several dozen others tasked with attacking the Operation 18 Lae convoy that day – had little reason to be optimistic about their chances of success or, indeed, their safe return. Throughout the year in which the US Army Air Forces had been fighting the Japanese in New Guinea, the results had been – in the words of one official postwar study – 'pitiful'.

In a single day the previous July, Japan's Major General Tomitaro Horii had landed nearly half his 11 000 troops earmarked for the first stage of the coming Kokoda campaign at the mission stations of Buna and Gona on Papua's north coast without so much as being touched. Despite the absence of Japanese fighter aircraft, twenty American bombers – a mix of B-26 Marauders, B-25 Mitchells and B-17 Fortresses – had managed just a single hit on one solitary Japanese transport ship. Disgorging their bomb loads from 25 000 feet, the disembarking Japanese soldiers watched the 250- and 500-pounders create harmless white plumes in the sea. A handful of American fighters, as well as one frustrated B-25 pilot, ventured down to sea level to attempt to strafe the Japanese on the beaches. But they had little success and most of the Japanese soldiers made it ashore safely.

The following month, intelligence officers of the US 3rd Bomb Group, having pored over the target photographs in their bases around Townsville, broke the news to the flight crews that out of 434 bombs dropped in August, only nineteen hits had been recorded – a 4.4 per cent strike rate.

September was even worse, when just nine hits were scored from 425 bombs dropped, reducing the strike rate to a dismal 2.1 per cent. The sole Allied success in September had been the sinking of one small Japanese cargo vessel.

Nor had their support of the troops on the ground during the subsequent recapture of Buna and Gona six months later been anything to write home about, with the same report describing US air performance during this costly and withering two-month campaign as 'spotty, and anything but decisive'.

Part of the problem was exhaustion. The US air forces operating in Australia in early 1942 were formed from the shattered remnants of the Far East Air Force, which had been based in the Philippines and all but wiped out when the Japanese attacked on 8 December 1941, the day after Pearl Harbor. Later that month, just fourteen B-17s and a handful of P-40 fighters managed to limp south to Darwin, carrying 143 personnel. This rump was further decimated when it mounted a valiant but doomed attempt to stem the Japanese advance into Java in March.

Many of the US aircraft were old, outdated, and barely able to bring the fight to the Japanese. The hero of Midway – the Douglas SBD Dauntless – was obsolete and outmoded even then, and was now getting mauled by the slowest of Japanese fighters. As powerful as the industries of the United States were, the newer, faster aircraft disgorged by the factories of the 'Arsenal of Democracy' were earmarked almost exclusively for the European theatre.

In August 1942, the 3rd Bomb Group's 89th Bombardment Squadron received a long-awaited shipment of A-20 Havoc medium bombers, known as 'Bostons' by the Australians. The bombers' nose fixtures could accommodate four forward-firing .30-calibre machine guns, perfect for ground assault against Japanese jungle positions and tearing up the decks and bridges of supply ships. To the dismay of the aircraft fitters, however, the guns themselves were *not* included in the shipment. In addition, the Havoc's combat range of 520 miles meant it could only strike the closest enemy targets. In its present state, the men and machines of the 89th Bombardment Squadron weren't going anywhere.

Another problem facing the Allied forces was geography. When General George C Kenney took command in September 1942 he found his components to be dispersed, disorganised and nowhere near the enemy they were supposed to be fighting. Only one of his three fighter and five of his bombardment groups were currently based in Port Moresby, the rest being scattered across airfields from Darwin to Townsville. The 19th Bombardment Group, incorporating four individual bomber squadrons, operated, at least nominally, from Mareeba near Cairns, but its forces had been so battered by their experience in the Philippines that they were still listed as 'unoperational'. Kenney's own headquarters were anchored in faraway Brisbane, an insistence of his ultimate master, General Douglas MacArthur, who was loath to allow any aspect of his forces to slip from his control.

Not surprisingly, when Kenney arrived in Australia he found morale was dangerously low.

•

For two days the men of the Okabe Detachment, crammed onboard the vessels of the Operation 18 convoy, had had a dream run. On the stroke of midday on 5 January, Captain Kitamura had led his ten ships in a procession out of Rabaul's Simpson Harbour, past Blanche Bay, before turning south into St George's Channel between New Britain and New Ireland. They then followed the long coast of New Britain southwest and eventually crossed the 185-mile gap of the Huon Gulf to Lae on the Papuan coast. If all went to plan, they would time their arrival to begin unloading under cover of darkness. The journey was meant to take no more than two and a half days, and so far it had gone well.

The tropical blanket of wet mist which clung to the masts and superstructures of the vessels provided a shield just as potent as that of any air cover. In this grey cloak of invisibility the convoy proceeded, passing Wide Bay without detection, then leaving Jacquinot Bay likewise in their wake. As they watched on deck and from the bridge, the men's anxious ears were attuned to the sound of approaching aircraft, and eyes to the first signs of a break in the cloud cover which might reveal their position to the enemy above.

To the surprise of the Japanese, however, no Allies seemed to be waiting for them.

Then, late in the morning of 5 January, after almost a full 24 hours at sea and passing the southern town of Gasmata, the slow throb of aerial engines was at last detected in the gloom above. More lookouts were posted, anti-aircraft guns were manned, and the escorting destroyer captains prepared to throw their ships into the wild manoeuvres which would hopefully evade the Allies' bombs. But soon after the initial alert, the skies over the ships carrying the Okabe Detachment once again fell silent.

High above, an RAAF 11 Squadron Catalina flying boat was nearing the end of its patrol range and could only radio in its position before swinging south and heading back to its base in faraway Cairns, having just managed to glimpse a series of ships' wakes through a gap in the cloud. At 2 p.m. two other Catalinas were dispatched, one each from 20 and 11 squadrons, piloted by Squadron Leader Thomas Stokes and Flight Lieutenant Dave Vernon respectively. Being nearly twelve hours' flying time away, however, the Japanese convoy could be anywhere by the time they arrived.

After refuelling in Milne Bay, the Catalinas reached the seas to the south of New Britain late in the afternoon of 6 January, but, with no real idea of where to look, each took up positions a hundred miles distant and began searching the long and lonely corridors of open water. American Marauders from Port Moresby, they had been told, would also be in the area, patrolling and dropping flares, but there was no sign of them either.

Just after 10 p.m., south of the gap between the western tip of New Britain and Finschhafen on New Guinea's Huon Peninsula, Stokes's navigator excitedly called over the radio that images resembling ships had started to appear on his small cathode radar screen, dead ahead. Descending to 1000 feet, Stokes pushed through a barrier of thick cloud, and in the weak moonlight could just make out the outlines of a series of ships steaming due west. Now, he thought, would be a good time for one of the American aircraft to drop a flare, but the darkness persisted.

With four 250-pound bombs slung under the Catalina's enormous single wing, Stokes wasted no time in ordering them armed. He then proceeded to line up on the first vessel he could identify: a medium-sized transport. It was a hurried approach, but Stokes had no intention of giving the ship's anti-aircraft gunners any extra time to bring their weapons to bear on his slow flying boat. Lying flat in the nose, the observer pressed the bomb release mechanism. Normally, the sudden release of hundreds of pounds of bombs pulled the aircraft upwards as if on a spring, but straightaway Stokes knew something was wrong.

Cursing, the observer reported that two bombs had fallen harmlessly into the sea astride the Japanese transport, while the remaining two were still firmly attached to the wing. It was a dismal situation. Pulling away, their position now exposed, Stokes contemplated a difficult flight back to Cairns with 500 pounds of ordnance still stubbornly clinging to the aircraft. He radioed Dave Vernon to come in and try his luck.

Patrolling several hours away to the east, Vernon's aircraft, A24-1, was the first Catalina to have been delivered to Australia from the United States back in February 1941. It had been in constant service ever since. With no Japanese ships in sight, Vernon had taken advantage of the fading afternoon light to wreak some havoc on the small Japanese airstrip at Gasmata, right in the centre of New Britain's southern coast. In a low pass, he released a series of 20-pound fragmentation bombs, and announced over the intercom that any man who would like to get behind one of the .5-inch machine guns was free to do so.

Two parked Zero fighters were soon riddled with bullets.

Vernon's spontaneous strike damaged the Japanese at Gasmata, and was but small justice for the six captured Australian soldiers of Lark Force who had been executed on that same beach the previous March, adding another to the long list of war crimes committed by the Japanese in their conquest of the South West Pacific.

Upon receiving Stokes's message, Vernon swung his Catalina around to the west and put on power, just as his flight engineer, with a furrowed brow, reminded him that the aircraft was well overdue for her major 240-hour service. Vernon didn't need the reminder: he could feel it in the vibration of the engines, which seemed to fly rougher every hour.

Just after 4 a.m. on 7 January he arrived over the Japanese convoy, but the eastern sky was yet to offer any light. Every set of eyes on board peered down into the gloom.

Then, from out of nowhere, a flare – distant but effective enough – dropped by an American aircraft lifted the darkness enough for Vernon to make out the grey shapes of five Japanese merchant vessels steaming in a line with three naval escorts, one leading and one abeam on each side. Vernon's navigator, Flight Lieutenant George Leslie, agreed that the group of ships represented a formidable anti-aircraft screen, particularly for their slow Catalina.

Nevertheless, Vernon believed he could risk a single pass without exposing himself and his crew. Leslie agreed the attack should be made – low – from the rear of the convoy, where a number of targets would present themselves. Bringing the Catalina around in a long, wide arc, Vernon approached the vessels – strung out as if on a string – line astern. To his surprise, no ship challenged his approach, nor was any evasive action taken. Vernon told his crew that, having come this far, they might as well make their daring count for something.

George Leslie watched the first ship line up perfectly in his sight but was in fact aiming for the second. He paused, then pressed the release. Vernon's luck was indeed better than Stokes's, and two 250-pound high-explosive and two anti-submarine bombs dropped from their racks under the Catalina's wing.

Two went wide, but two hit home, illuminating the darkness in great orange flashes.

They'd struck the 6000-ton *Nichiryu Maru*, which immediately fell out of her position in the convoy, doomed.

Over the intercom, the crew observing in the back excitedly described a further series of explosions, leading one of them to suggest, incorrectly, that they'd hit a munitions ship. In fact, the *Nichiryu Maru* was carrying two companies from the 3rd battalion of the Okabe Detachment's 102nd Infantry Regiment, many of whom were killed in her crowded holds as the bombs exploded.

Even now, however, no trails of anti-aircraft fire made their way towards Vernon as he wheeled around past the stricken vessel. Instead searchlights illuminated the scene as one of the escorting destroyers, the *Maikaze*, inexplicably turned on her lights. Vernon's gunners were quick to react and sent a hail of fire down into the night, prompting the destroyer to quickly return to darkness. His bombs spent, at the end of an active patrol, and with the light of the dawn now rising on his left, Dave Vernon headed south towards Milne Bay.

The *Nichiryu Maru* went down quickly, but the warm tropical water and proximity of the *Maikaze* allowed 739 of her 1100 men to be rescued by the speedy destroyers which immediately appeared alongside. The remainder of Operation 18 steamed on. It would now be the turn of American airmen to attempt to stop the convoy reaching Lae.

CHAPTER 4
DISASTER IN THE AIR

Though flying off adjacent airstrips in Port Moresby, bomber pilots Len Nicholson and Ray Dau had never met. Their fates, however, would bear a striking symmetry on this dismal January day for the Allies in the skies above New Guinea.

Flying into ever-worsening weather as he approached Lae, Dau had been comforted by the familiar sight of the 63rd Squadron's B-17 *Panama Hattie* flying off his starboard wing, with her distinctive nose art of a luxuriously busty dame appearing to lean suggestively from the cockpit. Ray knew Captain William Thompson, an experienced and capable pilot, was at the controls. A third B-17 had already turned back to Jackson Airfield, leaving just Thompson and Dau, who had been detailed to attack the ships of Operation 18 – and warned to expect resistance.

Around midday, the two aircraft broke through the clouds above Lae. They were disheartened to find the Japanese ships not only already there but well underway unloading their stores and men. Moments after they took in the situation, fierce anti-aircraft explosions erupted around Dau's aircraft. 'Oscars!' shouted one of his gunners as several enemy fighters roared past him.

Guns from the ships, guns from the shore and guns from escorting Japanese fighters all converged on Dau, who ordered the aircraft bomb doors opened, even as the perspex bubble of the nose shattered then disappeared altogether. Lloyd Dumond in the top turret cursed, and Henry Bowen on the rear gun position shouted out in pain.

Another explosion in the space between the two port engines caused them to both vibrate sickeningly, followed by a sudden drop in revs. Now smoke was filling the aircraft and Dau knew the B-17 would soon be unflyable. Ahead of him, at the controls of *Panama Hattie*, Thompson was heading for the target. Dau followed as best he could, then ordered the bombs jettisoned. Using rudder and elevator, he flew his crippled aircraft inland on an angle south from the coast and began looking for a place to put her down. All he could see were mountains, razorbacks and endless jungle.

'We were headed up a small valley and couldn't get over the mountains,' Dau recalled fifty years later. 'I knew it was just a matter of time, so I began looking for a soft place to set her down.' Lack of a landing area was only one of Dau's problems, however, as clusters of Japanese Zero and Oscar fighters, sensing a lame duck, pursued the stricken aircraft down. A half-hour running battle began.

Now Dau could neither climb nor turn. Every man who could operate a gun did so, unleashing streams of .5-inch bullets towards any Japanese fighter that ventured close. Though fast and nimble, the Japanese Zero was pitifully light on armour, lacking both protective windshield glass for the pilot and even self-sealing fuel tanks. A single round from one of the American gunners could be fatal. After several passes the Japanese pilots, convinced the bomber was doomed, broke off and returned to Lae.

Passing to the east of Wau, the men of the mountain garrison stood still and watched the big bomber struggling to maintain altitude before disappearing from view below a ridge, the sound of its engines still reverberating down the Markham Valley.

Then, behind a ridge, immediately below Dau, a long expanse of grass appeared. Dau put the nose down but, with limited controls and flaps, knew he was coming in dangerously fast. However, with only two working engines he dared not risk a stall by lowering the flaps. 'We glided in on the side of a mountain at about 110 miles an hour,' he recalled, 'and as luck would have it there were no trees – nothing but nice soft grass – so we slid along into a crash landing.'

A rescue party from Wau reached the crash site at dawn the next morning. Two of the aircraft's gunners, sergeants Bob Albright and Henry Bowen, were wounded and had to be carried on litters back to the base. There, with the rest of the crew, they were loaded onto an RAAF Hudson and taken to Australia.

Both men died in hospital in Darwin a few days later.

The bleached bones of Dau's B-17 remain on the grassy New Guinea hillside on which it crash landed in 1943, now known to the locals as 'The Grey Ghost'.

•

In his smaller and faster twin-engine Martin B-26 Marauder, 1st Lieutenant Len Nicholson had barely arrived over the target zone when he was swarmed by nine Zeros patrolling almost directly above their base at Lae. As with Dau minutes earlier, anti-aircraft fire from the ships below began exploding in great percussive bursts. The aircraft's hydraulic pressure collapsed, and a shell slammed into Nicholson's port engine with a terrible grating sound of metal against metal while another exploded just behind him in his navigator's compartment, slicing through the leg of 1st Lieutenant Norman De Freese.

His battle over before it had even begun, all Nicholson could do was point the nose of his battered aircraft downwards, pick up some speed and get away from Lae before his Marauder gave out altogether. With skill, and a little luck, he might just be able to determine where this would be. Bolting south-east down along the New Guinea coast as fast as his one engine would take him, he made it to a small inlet named Hercules Bay before hitting the water.

Badly holed, the Marauder began to sink.

Radio operator Staff Sergeant Joe Papp and bombardier Sergeant Jack Mosley were trapped in the fuselage and drowned as it went under. Norman De Freese, already suffering with a virtually severed leg, was pulled ashore by three of the remaining crewmen but died on the beach shortly after. Nicholson, along with his co-pilot 1st Lieutenant Jack Childers, gunner Corporal Tom Moffit, and flight engineer Staff Sergeant Will Brown, decided to continue along the beach, where they hoped to be spotted by a friendly aircraft or taken in by a sympathetic native, presuming the Japanese did not capture them first. Thirsty, hungry and in shock, the men wandered for a while, then found shelter for the night.

Early next morning, they were woken by the sound of an approaching aircraft. Waving their yellow life jackets, they caught the attention of a patrolling 30 Squadron RAAF Beaufighter, piloted by Flight Sergeant Bob Cummins, with navigator Allan Kirley. Unable to land, the Beaufighter circled the waving Americans, bundled up some rations and a map with their position marked, and threw it down. Back at their base at Ward's airstrip they reported the stranded airmen's position, and hoped their ordeal would soon be over.

Sadly, it was not to be.

The next morning, while moving along the beach, shots were fired at the small party and Will Brown was killed. The others scattered into the scrub. Believing they were being pursued by the Japanese, they split up. In fact, a New Guinea native patrol – mistaking the Americans for Japanese – had opened fire, before reporting proudly that they had killed one of a group of enemy before the others had fled.

A few hours later, as an increasingly desperate Jack Childers continued south along the beach a mile from the mouth of the Mambare River, two more Beaufighters approached, one of them piloted by 30 Squadron's Bob Brazenor with Fred Anderson as his observer. In his logbook Anderson would later describe the forlorn figure of Childers, alone and in 'poor physical condition'.

As accurate a description as this was, Childers nonetheless had the wherewithal to quickly scratch in the sand a simple but urgent request: SHOES, MAPS, FOOD, MATCHES. As Brazenor circled he consulted with Anderson, who removed his flying boots and stuffed them into a canvas bag along with a canteen of water, two ration packs and a medical kit. On his small navigator's table, he pencilled a hurried map and a brief note – *You are one hour's walk from the Japanese. An enemy patrol is close at hand* – then hurled the lot from the open observer's hatch down to a grateful Jack Childers. With a waggle of their wings for luck, they were gone.

With the aid of Fred Anderson's map, Childers found his way to a deserted Papuan village. Two days later, a passing native took him via canoe a day up the Mambare River to an outpost of the New Guinea Volunteer Rifles. To his relief, Childers was informed by an Australian army officer that Moffit and Nicholson had already passed through a couple of days earlier and were now safe in Port Moresby. After being taken on to the small airstrip at Ioma, Childers was picked up by an RAAF Hudson and also flown to Port Moresby. A week later the three airmen would be reunited in Townsville Hospital, the last survivors of the seven-man crew of 1st Lieutenant Len Nicholson's Martin B-26 Marauder.

The stories of both these crews illustrate the conditions faced by Allied airmen in the South West Pacific. Fighting above empty oceans or battling through some of the thickest jungle in the world, their area of operations was one of the most hostile on earth. To survive at all was lucky. Scores of airmen who had bailed out of their stricken aircraft, and were seen by their comrades drifting down towards the ocean of green jungle canopy, were never heard of again. One can only speculate on their torturous ordeals far from home, alone in an utterly alien world.

The loss of both Nicholson's B-26 and Ray Dau's B-17, along with five more American bombers which attempted to strike at the Operation 18 convoy in January 1943, would ultimately be for nothing. Over two days aircraft such as theirs, or small groups of three or four, were sent into battle as soon as they became ready, then thrown piecemeal against the enemy's defences, resulting in drawn-out, uncoordinated actions which played into the hands of the concentrated Japanese defenders.

•

Meanwhile, at Rabaul, another chaotic episode was playing out, further underscoring the lack of Allied cohesion. Brigadier General Kenneth Walker, a career Army Air Corps aviator, had been sent from Washington the previous July to take charge of the US bomber wing currently operating from Australia and New Guinea.

He was shocked by what he found.

A driven and determined man and a zealous advocate for high-level strategic bombing, Walker had calmly announced at his farewell lunch that he had little expectation of returning. 'I doubt I'll be back,' he had said coolly, 'I've made a terrible mess of things here.' (Walker already had two broken marriages behind him.) Upon his arrival in New Guinea weeks later, he was struck by the poor morale among his airmen, and concertedly attempted to raise it. Not content with just lining up with his soldiers in the 'chow line', Walker began to lobby for improvements in their conditions and, in order to learn as much as he could about the Japanese and how to fight them, began personally flying and leading combat missions. While this earned him the undoubted respect of his airmen – as well as the Silver Star for bravery – General George Kenney was aghast to learn that a high-ranking officer was risking his neck in combat, and immediately ordered him to desist flying.

In Kenney's forthright and exhaustive postwar autobiography, *General Kenney Reports*, he recalled the incident:

> I told Walker that from then on I wanted him to run his command from his headquarters. In the airplane he was just extra baggage. He was probably not as good in any job on the plane as the man already assigned to it ... I would hate to have him taken prisoner by the Japanese. They would have known that a general was bound to have access to a lot of information and there was no limit to the lengths they would go to [to] extract that knowledge ... I told Walker that frankly I didn't believe he could take it.

Walker would ignore Kenney's order completely.

The vessels of Operation 18 had not gone unnoticed by Allied codebreakers as they gathered in Rabaul Harbour in the last days of December 1942. Seizing on what he believed to be a unique chance to strike a blow before the convoy departed, General Kenney ordered Walker to organise his bombers into a dawn attack on 5 January – when he hoped the Japanese defences would be unprepared.

Walker demurred.

A dawn attack, he argued, would mean a night departure from Port Moresby and a rendezvous with a formation arriving from Queensland. He doubted his pilots could pull it off and instead suggested a midday attack when he could concentrate his forces.

Kenney strongly disagreed:

> The Nip fighters were never up at dawn, but at noon they would not only shoot up our bombers but would ruin our bombing accuracy. I would rather have the bombers not in formation for a dawn attack than in formation for a show at noon which was certain to be intercepted.

Much to Kenney's annoyance, Walker argued the point and refused to back down, leading Kenney to suspect that the strain of the tropics, as well as an over-association with his men, was affecting Walker, and that he'd need to send him home at the end of the month.

Then, after clinging to his argument, Walker suddenly reneged, assuring Kenney he would comply as ordered.

•

Six B-17s and six B-24 Liberators were to be joined by another group of B-24s flying from Iron Range in Queensland, but sudden heavy rain saw this last group scrubbed from the mission at the eleventh hour. This left just the original dozen, which would depart from Jackson Airfield at Port Moresby, a force barely sufficient to carry out the attack.

Whether it was this last-minute change or simply his own stubbornness which prompted Walker's second change of heart can never be known. Perhaps he had intended to ignore Kenney all along. Twenty-four hours later Kenney was shocked to learn the raid had been launched – not under the agreed protection of dawn but into the full face of prepared Japanese defences, at high noon.

Worse was to come.

Kenney then learned that Walker had also ignored his earlier order, not only deciding to fly the mission himself, but lead it, usurping the role from the 64th Squadron Commanding Officer, Major Allen Lindberg. Walker duly signed himself onto the crew list of the 64th Squadron B-17, *San Antonio Rose I*, an aircraft already piloted by Lindberg, as well as yet another valuable officer, Lieutenant Colonel Jack Bleasdale, the Executive Officer for the entire 43rd Bombardment Group.

Also flying that day was Captain Fred Wesche, who later recalled his foreboding at the morning briefing:

When this was announced that it was going to be done in broad daylight at noontime, as a matter of fact, at low altitude, something like 5000 feet over the almost most heavily defended target in the Pacific ... most of us went away shaking our heads. Many of us believed that we wouldn't come back from it ...

Alerted, the Japanese anti-aircraft gunners opened up with a fierce barrage on the approaching American formation, which Walker was attempting to direct over the radio by standing in the Perspex astrodome behind the pilot, with headphones and a microphone. Peppered with anti-aircraft fire, the American airmen then looked down to see defending Zeros taking off from the Rabaul runway. Using their formidable rate of climb, the Zeros tore into the bombers.

As Wesche described it:

All of us got attacked. I was shot up ... we had to break formation over the target to bomb individually and then we were supposed to form up immediately after crossing the target, but no sooner had we dropped our bombs and my tail gunner says, 'Hey, there's somebody in trouble behind us.' So we made a turn and looked back and here was an airplane, one of our airplanes, going down, smoking and on fire ... with the whole cloud of fighters on top of him. There must have been about fifteen or twenty fighters ... he disappeared into a cloud bank and we never saw him again. It turns out it was the general. General Walker was onboard. He actually had a pilot, but he was the overall air commander for the operation. To put all those officers on the one plane ... many of us thought it was foolhardy to tell you the truth.

For Kenney, the nightmare scenario of three of his senior air officers being captured and interrogated by the Japanese was unfolding before him. Adding insult to injury, the late arrival of the Americans meant they missed the departure of the

Japanese convoy by several hours. Although one small, empty and ageing freighter, the *Keifuku Maru*, was straddled by near misses and sunk, no other significant damage was recorded.

Kenney's diary entry was terse. 'Walker off late. Disobeyed orders by going along as well as not starting his mission when I told him.' In the forlorn hope that Walker and his crew might be found floating on dinghies in the sea, further US aircraft that could otherwise have been deployed to attack Operation 18 were diverted to look for them.

By 9 January, the search was called off, and Walker was pronounced 'missing, presumed killed'. Nine men, including the squadron CO Major Lindberg were killed in the crash of the *San Antonio Rose*, while the Group XO, Lieutenant Colonel Jack Bleasdale, was one of two who managed to bail out, only to be taken prisoner by the Japanese. Contrary to Kenney's fears, however, no significant information seems to have been extracted from Bleasdale, and he is reported to have died in Japanese captivity in early 1945.

Earlier, while complaining to MacArthur about several of his senior officers, Kenney had railed against Walker and his foolhardiness in insisting on flying combat missions.

'Don't worry,' said MacArthur, 'if he doesn't come back, I'll recommend him for the Medal of Honor.' MacArthur was good for his word, and Brigadier General Kenneth Walker became World War II's forty-third recipient of the Congressional Medal of Honor. His citation read in part:

For conspicuous leadership above and beyond the call of duty ... Kenneth N Walker led an effective daylight bombing attack against shipping in the harbor at Rabaul, New Britain, which resulted in direct hits on nine enemy vessels …

It wouldn't be the first or the last time American successes in the Pacific were exaggerated. Upon receiving MacArthur's request for the award, the US Adjutant General asked, 'Is it considered above and beyond the call of duty for the commanding officer of a Bomber Command to accompany it on bombing missions?'

As far as is known, the query remained unanswered.

•

After the destruction of the *Nichiryu Maru* on 7 January, the Allied mission soon petered out into a debacle of mini attacks in which airmen were, as at Rabaul, made to face the full fury of the Japanese defences individually. As Lieutenant Donald Sanxter, who flew several missions with General Walker, recalled, even when flying as a unit, American aircraft at this stage of the Pacific War operated on their own: 'Pilots tended to think more as single-plane units rather than elements. When it came to enemy fighters, the mindset was that pilots could handle the situation themselves and escape destruction.'

There were, however, a number of notable displays of courage and determination, particularly from one formation of twelve B-25 Mitchell bombers from the US 405th Bombardment Squadron under the command of another, albeit future, Congressional Medal of Honor recipient, Major Ralph Checi.

Hours after Australian pilot Dave Vernon's lone success against the *Nichiryu Maru*, Checi led his men off the runway at Durand airstrip, one of a rapidly expanding complex airfields situated 17 miles south of Port Moresby. Checi climbed into the cloud then headed out over the formidable hump of the Owen Stanleys. Just before 8 a.m., he found the convoy still at sea. Checi alerted his crew then made a pass over the Japanese vessels and released his bombs.

Hardly had his attack begun when it was broken up by an escorting formation of Oscar fighters.

Damage was, however, inflicted to the steering mechanism of the *Myoko Maru*, a cargo vessel which would be forced to beach itself the next day at Malahang just east of Lae, though not before safely transferring almost all its cargo and crew to other vessels.

On 8 January, 146 bombs were dropped by a variety of aircraft for the paltry result of three claimed hits and three near misses, nearly all of which were later discounted. The following day was even more of a debacle when 258 bombs were dropped – again for no result – and enthusiastic American gunners and P-38 Lightning pilots claimed great successes against escorting Japanese fighters. But while the RAAF Kittyhawks and US Lightnings indeed accounted for some of the Japanese Oscars and Zeros, it was nowhere near the dubiously optimistic sixty-eight claimed.

Checi's and Vernon's early successes would be the only victories of the two-day effort against the Japanese Operation 18. Some claims of ships 'damaged' were mounted, but as eight of the ten vessels later returned safely to Rabaul without having had to endure any subsequent attack, such claims must be regarded as doubtful. For the Allies, there was little to show for 416 individual sorties and the loss of six American bombers to anti-aircraft fire, fighters, or aircraft ditching in the sea for lack of fuel.

Cloudy tropical weather admittedly played into the hands of the Japanese, resulting in many Allied aircraft failing to locate their targets, and no question can be raised as to the bravery of individual airmen.

The real problem with the Allied attack against Operation 18 was one of organisation.

With a few exceptions, the piecemeal attacks involved small groups of one or two aircraft which – if they managed to find the target at all – appeared in a convenient procession, allowing the Japanese to concentrate their defences. As historian Lex McAulay writes, 'What had been lacking were suitable tactics and the application of one of the principles of war: concentration.'

Across a multitude of Allied airfields around New Guinea, other factors contributed to the inability to assemble a potent and effective striking force: poor transportation, poor communication between commands, and even poorly thought-out airfield design where bomb dumps and ordnance-handling facilities were situated nowhere near the aircraft that were supposed to carry them.

Not only that, airfield construction – despite Herculean efforts on the part of US construction battalions – was often slow and carried out in the most trying of tropical conditions. Mud, particularly in the wet season, hampered movement and machinery, leading to a shortage of basics such as bomb-handling and refuelling equipment. Telephone lines failed or were unreliable. Living conditions, even for the Americans – who were better supplied than the Australians – were difficult and demoralising. Tropical diseases such as malaria and gastroenteritis were rife; food was poor and monotonous. And a series of airstrips on the north coast close to Buna Mission – taken by the Japanese initially but wrenched back during a long and costly campaign which dragged on for months – needed to be made fit for Allied use but were nowhere near completion.

•

Despite the losses of the *Nichiryu Maru* and *Myoko Maru*, Operation 18 was regarded by the Japanese Imperial Army as a significant and uplifting success. Not only had the American and Australian air forces been unable to halt them at Rabaul, or later at sea, they had also failed to impede the vital disembarkation process in Lae. Here, a well-rehearsed system was enacted whereby soldiers in full kit clambered down rope nets thrown over the ships' sides, into speedy motorised Daihatsu barges. They'd then be whisked to shore, where marshals would urge them to clear the beach quickly and disperse into the jungle or to well-hidden and prepared campsites.

The unloading of Japanese ships had likewise been finely tuned. Soldiers and sailors alike were required to handle the many tons of food, fuel and ammunition, lined up like worker ants passing it up from the ships' holds, before hurling the goods into the waiting barges below. Padded cotton bags cushioned the drop of food and ammunition from the decks above to speed the process, and drums of fuel were tied on long ropes that were then towed to shore on great floating chains.

The 3000 men of Major General Toru Okabe's detachment would waste little time at Lae. Within a day or two they would head off into the jungle to begin the long, slow climb into the highlands to battle the Australians at Wau. For the prospect of the prize of the mountain airstrip and a much-needed victory against the Australians of Kanga Force, the Japanese were more than happy to have sacrificed just two ships and a few hundred sons of the Emperor.

This, reported the Eighth Area Army Commander at Rabaul to the Imperial General Staff in Tokyo, *will send chills through our conceited enemy.*

CHAPTER 5
THE HOMECOMING HERO

Wing Commander Garing Returns! Corryong Flyer Given a Wonderful Reception! declared the front page of the *Corryong Courier* on 3 April 1941. The photograph of the nuggety young officer, confident and smiling in his RAAF dark blue with the ribbon of the Distinguished Flying Cross (DFC) sewn onto his tunic, told the story of a true hero. It was a proud day for the small rural Victorian town.

Since September 1939, William Garing had seen plenty of combat flying. If he'd wanted it, he could reasonably have expected to be granted permission to sit the remainder of the war out. But for the ambitious and pugnacious Bill Garing – whose moniker would soon become the highly fitting 'Bull' – this would have been the last thought to enter his head.

Bred in rugged mountain country in north-east Victoria, Garing would walk the 6 miles to and from his small rural school every day. At age four he was given responsibility for tending twenty head of cattle, a task he was expected to carry out barefoot. 'The Alps really made you a tough little bloke,' he would later recall in interviews about his long and eventful life.

Garing's father, George, a formidable figure as well as a drinker with a 'frighteningly bad temper', insisted the child be brought up in the arcane tradition of 'breeching', whereby the youngster was dressed as a girl for his first few years, ostensibly to 'confuse the devil'. Garing's mother, Amy, who would bear eight children – four of whom died in childbirth or soon after – would be subject to violent rages by her husband, into which young Bill would insert himself, usually resulting in him receiving a beating of his own.

One day, when finally big enough, Garing gave as good as he got. His father never laid a hand on him or his mother again.

'The two men never liked each other,' says Garing's son, Robert, 'and Dad got out of there as soon as he could.'

Tragically, Amy Garing died when her son was just fourteen.

Enrolling in a technical college in Melbourne, Garing studied electrical engineering, but after seeing an aeroplane passing overhead, harboured thereafter but one burning ambition: to fly with the Royal Australian Air Force. Joining the RAAF Reserve, he discovered he adored military life and asked his instructor, a squadron leader, how he might apply to join the permanent air force. Sizing up the eager young man, the officer told him that he would first have to join the army. Garing hated the idea. 'Join the army, go to Duntroon, and then reapply for the air force. They're the only officers the Air Board are accepting at the moment,' the officer said. 'Oh, and by the way, I hate Duntrooners.'

For several miserable years, under the designation Special Air Cadet, Garing endured the Royal Military College at Duntroon – which he regarded as a complete waste of time – before transferring at the first possible instant to the RAAF. Shortly after, he was accepted into the Central Flying School at Point Cook in Victoria.

From the start, Garing proved a brilliant, albeit instinctive, pilot. 'He may have been educated, but he had no real idea of what he was doing or how things worked,' says Rob Garing. However, an innate seat-of-the-pants ability, combined with a photographic memory, saw him marked out as a rising star, particularly in regard to his prodigious skill in astronavigation. As his career progressed, he heard about actual combat directly from the heroes of the old Australian Flying Corps (AFC), men like Harry Cobby, the AFC's top-scoring ace of the Great War, and Frank McNamara, a living legend and Australia's only air recipient of the Victoria Cross.

In November 1938, having been sent to Britain to study advanced navigation, Garing entered the record books when he became the first ever recipient of the First Class Aircraft Navigator's Certificate of Competency No. 1. Unlike many pilots who craved to fly fast and glamorous fighters, Garing instead gravitated towards slow and steady flying boats, a squadron of which he came to command at Point Cook. It was a role which suited his gritty and determined character, as well as his skills in air navigation.

With war appearing to be inevitable, Australia in the late thirties began a belated program of rearmament, including the formation of a brace of new RAAF squadrons, some of which were established in such haste that no aircraft were yet available to equip them. One of these was 10 Squadron, a maritime unit formed at Point Cook in July 1939 for which only a dilapidated collection of time-expired machines could be found. It was decided that six brand new Short Sunderland flying boats would be bought and delivered to Australia from Britain, a task for which no one would be better suited than the men who would be flying them. In late 1939, selected personnel of the newly formed 10 Squadron RAAF departed on board Qantas Empire flying boats for the week-long haul to Britain.

During the several weeks' familiarisation with the Sunderland before the long trip home, Garing grew to love the United Kingdom, as well as the magnificent aircraft he was to fly. Late one Sunday morning in September, while at lunch with a former governor of Victoria, Lord Huntingfield, a hush descended on the dining room. The exhausted voice of Prime Minister Neville Chamberlain announced over the radio that war with Germany had just been declared.

'Well, young man,' said Lord Huntingfield without looking up from his lemon sole, 'I suppose you'd best go and join your regiment.'

Weeks later, the Australian government gave permission for 10 Squadron to remain in Britain under the command of the RAF and to fight their war there, thus earning the double distinction as the first Australian military unit to see action in World War II and the only one to be operational on both the first and last days of the six-year conflict.

Unlike many squadrons formed in wartime with hurriedly trained airmen, 10 Squadron was manned by professional

THE HOMECOMING HERO • 55

pilots, some of them former Qantas flying-boat captains with hundreds of hours' flying time already logged. 'We were all-weather pilots,' Garing said later. 'We used to be given jobs to fly in weather that was just unreal. The zero visibility, frightful weather and temperatures of minus thirty and forty degrees. Even the sea water on the coast of England froze on the beaches in that year so you can imagine what it was like.'

No 10 Squadron began its long war, undertaking exhausting patrols over the North Atlantic, protecting shipping and hunting U-boats. It was tedious and difficult work, with boredom and the atrocious weather proving opponents as formidable as the Germans. Week in, week out, Wing Commander Garing and his crew of eleven would take off from the waters of the base at Mount Batten in Plymouth to watch over a slow-moving convoy of ships. He would circle like a watchful shepherd, or follow a monotonous grid over a patch of grey-green Atlantic at 1500 feet, his wireless operator glued to the green glow of an ASV Mark II radar screen for the telltale 'blip' of a U-boat. Hours later, and with his exhausted eyes barely able to register anything at all, he'd be relieved by the next operator and the cycle would begin again.

Flying concentric ellipses of up to 50 nautical miles out from the convoy, every available eye would scan the water for signs of the enemy and the skies for approaching aircraft, but they never travelled too far from the ships themselves. Except in extreme cases, radio silence was strictly maintained and all communication was done by the Morse flashes of the Aldis lamp. Sometimes the only exchanges with the rest of the world were a 'hello' or 'goodbye and good luck' signalled to the convoy's commodore at the beginning and end of a patrol.

In the Battle of the Atlantic, World War II's longest campaign, Coastal Command would frequently put up patrols which lasted for more than a day of nonstop flying. 'From the time we reported to be briefed in the morning or night or whatever, until we got back for debriefing, it was as much as twenty-seven hours,' recalled Garing.

Given the variability of the Atlantic weather, particularly in winter, there was no guarantee of returning to the same port from which they had departed. 'We always carried a spare bag of clothing – socks, underclothes and so on,' said Garing. 'We never knew if we'd be returning to our home base. And any man who forgot to pack that bag of clothing would get a terrible rocket!'

Despite the dangers, and given the vastness of the ocean over which they patrolled, many Coastal Command flying-boat crews reported not a single U-boat sighting. Garing's tour was not nearly so dull, and at least one of his trips involved an element of cloak and dagger.

As France collapsed in June and July 1940, Garing was ordered to spirit Lord Lloyd, the leader of the House of Lords and Secretary of State for the Colonies, on a clandestine trip to Bordeaux in a last-ditch attempt to persuade the defeatist French to fight on. After a fruitless day's negotiating, an exhausted Lloyd climbed onboard and dejectedly asked Garing to take him back to England. Lloyd had brought along a case of Champagne in the hopes of celebrating a successful outcome. Instead, he passed it around to Garing and his crew, wishing them better luck in this war than he had so far encountered.

A few weeks later, Garing was escorting an armed merchant vessel called the *Mooltan*. He knew the former P&O ship well, having made practice attacks on her in Port Phillip Bay during her regular runs between Britain and Australia in the thirties.

On this day, however, both Garing and the *Mooltan* were a very long way from home.

As the *Mooltan* approached the English Channel west of Land's End, a German Junkers 88 appeared several thousand feet above and headed straight for her, seemingly untroubled by the presence of Garing's flying boat. Somewhat affronted, Garing wheeled the Sunderland around and flew straight at the Junkers 88, ordering his crew to open up with every weapon they had – and not let up for a moment.

Thus began an extraordinary thirteen-hour running battle in which Garing, in his words, 'turned the Sunderland into a four-engine fighter'. With every one of the aircraft's eleven machine guns rattling away furiously, the astonished German pilot had to swerve to avoid both the stream of fire and the flying boat itself. After depositing two wildly inaccurate bombs off the *Mooltan*'s stern, the Junkers 88 turned sharply to the south and hightailed it back to France, though not before radioing in the position of the merchant vessel and its pugnacious escort.

Sure enough, a few hours later two more Junkers 88s appeared on the horizon, but Garing was just as happy to take on two enemies as one. Charging straight for the Germans, he repeated his order to 'let them have it' and the front and dorsal turrets – four Browning machine guns in all – rattled away aggressively. The only man denied some of the action was Corporal Doherty in the rear turret. As the skipper piloted his aircraft like an enraged bull straight towards the enemy, Doherty, denied a decent angle of attack, pleaded over the aircraft intercom: 'For Christ's sake, Skip, turn around and give me a bloody go at them!'

Like in the earlier encounter, the second German attack was broken up and confused, as was yet another later in the afternoon involving two more Junkers 88s. Such German bombs that managed to be hurled at the *Mooltan* failed to find their mark.

For his resourcefulness and outstanding courage, Bull Garing was awarded a Distinguished Flying Cross, with the citation in the *London Gazette* attesting to the Australian officer's 'coolness, gallantry and devotion to duty'.

He would later state that even the German propaganda made much of the incident, with the English traitor and Nazi broadcaster William Joyce, aka 'Lord Haw-Haw', dubbing the Sunderland and its many guns *The Flying Porcupine*, a name which stuck indelibly to the Sunderland legend.

•

At dawn on 27 September 1940, Garing began an uneventful six-hour patrol over HX-73, a large convoy of forty-three ships entering Britain's Western Approaches after a two-week voyage from the Canadian port of Halifax. No sign of German submarine activity was detected, and at 1 p.m. Garing handed over to a relieving RAF Sunderland and headed to Oban to refuel. But just thirty minutes into the return flight Garing's wireless operator called urgently over the radio: 'Radar's picked something up ahead, Skip – 10 miles due north.' Garing swung the aircraft around, ordered depth charges run out on the racks under the wings, and the crew to battle stations. They were told to keep their eyes peeled for a German submarine running on the surface. If they were lucky, they might catch it unawares.

What greeted them at half a mile distant, however, was something quite unexpected: a mast, and the small unmistakeable wooden hull of a lifeboat. As the Sunderland passed over it Garing saw, to his astonishment, that the lifeboat was full of people. Some waved listlessly; all appeared exhausted. At the rear of the lifeboat, a lone signaller stood with flags in each hand and spelled out letters in semaphore. As the watching crew translated, a rush of horror and excitement swept over them.

'Good God,' said Garing, 'they're from the *City of Benares*.'

Two weeks earlier, one of the most tragic and controversial episodes of the Atlantic War had begun when the elegant and relatively new passenger steamer *City of Benares* had set sail from Liverpool on 13 September with just over 400 souls on board – ninety of them children – destined to be resettled in Canada by the Children's Overseas Reception Board. Some in government had cast doubts on the wisdom of sending so many children into the waters of the Atlantic in wartime, but the urgency brought on by the London Blitz convinced the authorities that British children must be removed from harm's way.

As part of a fleet of nineteen ships with the designation OB-213, *City of Benares* took her position as the lead vessel in the convoy's central column. On her fourth day at sea, she was spotted by one of the most brilliant U-boat aces of the war, Korvettenkapitän Heinrich Bleichrodt. In patrol after patrol Bleichrodt would terrorise Allied shipping lanes, sinking an astonishing twenty-five merchant and naval vessels, and be awarded the Knight's Cross with Oak Leaves. Even more remarkable, he would survive the war.

In command of the boat U-48 that fateful day in September, however, this was his first foray into the Atlantic.

Just before midnight, some 434 nautical miles west of Ireland and having shadowed the liner for several hours, Bleichrodt let loose a brace of torpedoes towards the liner, but all missed. Fifteen minutes later he tried again, and a single torpedo slammed into the *City of Benares*' stern, tearing it open and sending her to the bottom in less than half an hour, taking over 200 of her passengers, including more than seventy of the children, with her.

In poor weather, some of the ship's lifeboats were launched, and about half the passengers were rescued by an escorting destroyer. But, due to a miscount, one lifeboat was overlooked and, unbeknown to all, left to drift in the merciless North Atlantic.

The loss of the *City of Benares* was met by shock then anger in Britain, many railing at the obvious risk of sending children into war zones. Even the Germans expressed their horror, though they defended Bleichrodt's actions by pointing out – not without some justification – that the presence of children onboard could not possibly have been known. The blame was hurled back at the British.

After the war, Bleichrodt was tried as a war criminal for sinking the *City of Benares*, but his plea of innocence was accepted. When asked if he was prepared to apologise to the victims' families, he refused.

Garing and his crew had heard about the catastrophe and had shared the revulsion felt across the country at the loss of so many innocent lives. When, therefore, the figure standing at the rear of the lifeboat spelled out the name of the lost ship, their astonishment was palpable, especially as they knew they'd been at the mercy of the elements for more than a week.

The depth charges were pulled back inside the hull and Garing prepared his crew, not for an act of war but of mercy. A rough headcount was made of the passengers in the lifeboat and all agreed that it was around forty-five. 'Can we take that many?' Garing asked. His men were keen and said the extra space could be found at a pinch. Three times Garing lowered the Sunderland to wave height and three times he was forced to ascend once again. The chop was simply too rough, reducing the chances of alighting on the water safely, let alone getting off again, to virtually nil.

Cursing, he consulted his navigator. 'Do we have fuel enough to make it back to the convoy then home?' After a pause the navigator responded, albeit with less confidence than Garing would have liked, 'Er … yes … if all goes well.'

Garing ordered emergency packs of food and fresh water – wrapped in Mae West life jackets – be dropped to the lifeboat as he flew as low and as slow as he dared. He then turned and headed towards convoy HX-73, trusting in his navigator's ability to find it again. His luck held this time, and the RAF pilot was surprised to see Garing's aircraft return, then come alongside.

Under strict radio silence, Garing ordered the most perfunctory of messages to be tapped out on the Aldis lamp: *follow me.* The Sunderland complied, and both aircraft headed back to the lifeboat. Upon sighting it the RAF Sunderland waggled its wings, then returned to the convoy, signalling the commodore, who sent the destroyer HMS *Anthony* to pick up the passengers.

Garing prepared to head home, but when calculations were checked he realised their base at Oban was barely within range. The alternative was Northern Ireland, but if their fuel ran out beforehand, and they were forced to set down anywhere in the neutral Irish Republic, they could expect to be interned for the duration of the war.

A quick conference ensued among the crew and various possibilities were presented. All decided the risk to get home was worth it.

Running the aircraft as lean as possible, Garing set his course for Oban. Again, luck once more intervened in the form of an unexpected tailwind which, in Garing's words, 'literally blew us back to Scotland'. After landing, two of the four engines spluttered and cut out just as they approached the mooring buoy. When the ground crew inspected the aircraft's tanks, they were virtually dry.

It had been a very close call.

As his understanding of ships and aircraft expanded, Bull Garing would reach the end of his tour with the proud distinction of having had just one of the hundreds of ships under his protection, over dozens of convoys, torpedoed while on his watch. Even in this incident, however, Garing was able to claim a level of mitigating circumstances.

Flying towards a convoy to begin patrol one day, he passed over an upturned merchant vessel, her crew already pulling away in lifeboats as their ship disappeared behind them. As soon as he could, Garing alerted the commodore to alter course as the convoy was heading straight for the U-boat's patrol area.

'I warned him,' said Garing in later years, 'and he took no notice.'

Sure enough, several hours later, the ships were attacked, and another merchant ship carrying vital supplies for the United Kingdom was sent to the bottom.

At a subsequent admiralty inquiry at which Garing gave evidence, he witnessed an admiral giving the convoy leader 'the most tremendous ticking off I've ever heard in my life. This admiral was a VC winner in World War I, and I tell you, he could swear.'

His tour completed, Garing returned to Australia in early 1941 onboard a slow New Zealand ship, the *Awatea*, along the coast of America and the Panama Canal. Feted as a celebrity, he readily posed for the cameras for his hometown newspaper in Corryong, besides many others. However, he was not the same airman who had left two years earlier. Higher in rank and with a DFC ribbon on his dark blue tunic, he had a wealth of experience and hundreds of hours of combat flying under his belt. His eyes were harder, his jaw firmer, and he understood as much about the nature of ships, aircraft and modern war as anyone alive.

Soon, however, it would be not the United Kingdom but his own country that would come under attack from a ghastly new enemy.

Bull Garing's war was far from over.

CHAPTER 6
ENTER GENERAL KENNEY

Like many megalomaniacs who in a later age would be described as suffering from a narcissistic personality disorder, General Douglas MacArthur liked to surround himself with bullies and sycophants. In his Chief of Staff, General Richard K Sutherland, he managed to find both. Although only partway along the path of derangement which, a decade later in Korea, would finally consume his career, MacArthur's arrival in Australia in March 1942 to take charge of all Allied operations in the South West Pacific Area was already characterised by the hallmarks of a man seriously deluded by his own sense of greatness.

In the vast pantheon of MacArthur's bizarre characteristics, perhaps the most telling was his habit of referring to himself, like the emperors of old (the reincarnation of whom he no doubt believed himself to be), in the third person. Many were the witnesses granted an audience to the great man who would attest to suddenly glancing around in confusion when, apropos of nothing, he would begin sentences with, 'General MacArthur believes ...', or 'General MacArthur would prefer ...' and so on, thinking for a moment that some *other* General MacArthur had just walked into the room.

Save for a few hand-picked devotees from his staff in the Philippines (a post which he had hastily abandoned after a disastrous defence in which he had refused to believe any assessment of the enemy which did not match his own), MacArthur hated everyone. His superiors, his subordinates, even the presidents under whom he served, were the subjects of his jealousy and scorn. It was for good reason that Franklin D Roosevelt, hearing of the general's ambitions for the White House, dubbed him 'the most dangerous man in America'.

Sent to the backwater of Melbourne, MacArthur remained steadfastly contemptuous of Australia and Australians. But his deepest loathing was reserved for the brave and competent officers and men who had distinguished themselves in combat and who therefore threatened to diminish the dazzling orb of his own genius. In *American Caesar*, the great biographer William Manchester recounted that of the first 142 press communiqués issued by MacArthur pertaining to the progress of the war, 109 mentioned no individual other than himself.

Obsessed with his public image, MacArthur insisted on vetting all related press – both American and Australian – rejected photographs that failed to capture his 'good side' or which showed his bald spot, and even insisted photographers descend to their knees to shoot from an angle which would further exaggerate his already six-foot frame.

Vanity aside, MacArthur also ignored intelligence that contradicted his own often flawed views of Japanese intentions, and spilled his first untruth the moment he stepped off the train in Melbourne, recounting a lurid story of his bomber fending off Japanese fighters as it approached Garbutt Airfield after its long journey from the Philippines.

All of it was nonsense, and others on the flight attested to the trip being without incident.

MacArthur quickly made his feelings known about those fellow officers he saw as 'outsiders', telling the commander of Allied air forces, General George Brett, that he did not wish him to accompany him from Melbourne's Spencer Street Station to his luxury suite at the Windsor Hotel. MacArthur would soon make Brett's life hell, ordering him to conduct pointless bombing missions to an already surrendered Philippines with a handful of clapped-out B-17s which could, in any case, barely make the distance.

Within a few weeks, Brett was manoeuvred out of his position.

As his replacement, MacArthur was offered two names. The famous James 'Jimmy' Doolittle had recently led a daring raid on Japanese forces from the pitching deck of the USS *Hornet*, capturing headlines around the world. For his courage and leadership, he'd been elevated two ranks to brigadier general and awarded the Medal of Honor. MacArthur, loath to share the limelight with a genuine hero, wanted nothing to do with him and chose instead the second person on the list: the virtually unknown George C Kenney.

•

'Your bad boy's outside,' drawled Kenney's secretary with a wry smile, before ushering a terrified young airman into the general's office one bright July morning. For the next few minutes, standing rigidly at attention, the airman dared not look at the older man as he was loudly bawled out. Kenney noted with satisfaction that the young airman's eyes occasionally flicked to the stack of paperwork – placed strategically on his desk – detailing his misdemeanour.

A couple of days earlier, one of the new Lockheed P-38 Lightning fighters had apparently put on an impromptu lunchtime aerobatics display for the citizens of San Francisco, including a couple of tight circles around the Golden Gate Bridge and a buzz down Market Street at such a height as to enable the pilot to wave to some pretty stenographers hard at work on the lower levels of one of the government buildings. In Oakland, a woman had her laundry blown off the line, prompting her to write that she didn't in fact need any help from fighter pilots in removing her washing, unless of course they'd like to do it on the ground. As entertaining as the ladies of San Francisco may have found the improvised display of air power, this, thundered Kenney now, simply would not do.

'Have you any idea of the trouble you've caused me?' he yelled at the young airman. 'Do you realise I'm now going to have to grovel to the governor, the mayor, the chief of police, and God knows what other prominent citizens who already think the air force is just a bunch of irresponsible airplane jockeys?' Wielding a sheaf of paper, he reminded the young man that he was in all likelihood facing a court martial, and that his flying career could well be already over.

His initial anger vented, Kenney then paused to take in the young lieutenant, becoming distracted, he would later admit, by his boyish, even cherubic face.

> I suspected that he was not over eighteen and maybe even younger. I doubted if he was old enough to shave. He was just a little blond-haired Norwegian boy about five feet six with a round, pink baby face and the bluest, most innocent eyes – now opened wide and a bit scared.

In the face of the young airman's obvious contrition, Kenney – a former combat pilot himself – admitted his amazement at how the kid had actually managed to do what he did in the first place. By the way, he ventured in a quieter tone, wasn't the air pretty rough down in that street around the second-storey level? At this point the young man became animated, free at last to speak about his passion, flying.

'Well, yes sir, it was' he said, looking at Kenney directly for the first time. 'It was kind of rough, but it was easy to control the plane. You see, the aileron control is good on the P-38 and if you have enough ...'

And so the spell was broken.

For the next half-hour, the pair discussed all aspects of flying, Kenney fascinated to get the lowdown of the characteristics of the P-38 – an aeroplane in which he had placed great hopes – from someone who truly knew. More and more impressed with the young pilot, Kenney quickly decided not only to tear up his court martial report, but to earmark him for transfer to any active command he might be given. This was just the sort of man, he decided, he wanted on his team.

After again imploring the boy to refrain from such foolishness in the future, Kenney picked up a handwritten letter on his desk and issued one final instruction: the following Monday the airman was to visit the lady in Oakland and help her with her washing. And if the lawns needed mowing, he was to do that too. And he was to do the job properly, not just plonk the washing in the basket but fold it neatly, and if he dropped it on the ground he was to pick it all up and wash it again, himself.

'I want that woman to think we are good for something besides annoying people. Now get out of here quick before I get mad and change my mind!'

'Yes, sir!' said the young man crisply, and saluted.

Kenney was still smiling when the red light on his telephone flashed, indicating a priority call. His secretary put through General 'Hap' Arnold, supremo of the entire US Army Air Corps, who told Kenney that by the end of the week he'd be on his way to Australia to take charge of all Allied air forces in the South West Pacific Area, operating directly under the command of General Douglas MacArthur.

Leaving the building that day, the young man who dreamed of combat flying – and who had so nearly seen his career evaporate before his eyes – was 21-year-old Richard Ira Bong, from Superior, Wisconsin, the eldest of nine children born to Swedish immigrant parents. Bong would go on to become the top US fighter ace of all time, shooting down forty Japanese aircraft, all at the controls of the P-38 Lightning. He was also awarded the Medal of Honor.

George Kenney was *definitely* taking him to Australia.

•

The B-24 Liberator bomber, Kenney had been assured as he prepared to climb onboard, had been specially fitted out for passengers. Once onboard, though, he couldn't find anything that resembled comfortable seating or windows, let alone something to dull the roar of the twin Wasp engines. But no matter, the long trip from the American west coast to Australia via Hawaii, Fiji, New Caledonia and finally Brisbane was nearly at an end. Only when standing up behind the pilot could Kenney get a sense of the majesty of the gorgeous blue waters of Australia's east coast. But this was to be no holiday trip.

Even as his aircraft approached the Australian mainland in July 1942, the Japanese had begun landing on the north coast of New Guinea at Buna and Gona to commence the campaign that would be named for a nondescript village nestled on a small plateau high up in the spine of the Owen Stanleys: Kokoda. Kenney was already contemplating the enormity of the task that lay ahead, what he would have to deal with and, more particularly, whom.

He was not MacArthur's first choice to lead the air forces under his command. At age fifty-two, Kenney was the antithesis of the typical American general. Barely five feet six inches tall, he had nothing of the swagger or pomposity of West Point, could count neither senators nor governors among his coterie of dining companions, and did not drink socially with the members of the general staff. Kenney was the son of a carpenter, a practical man with an earthy sense of humour who cared nothing for rank – neither his own nor anyone else's. He had dropped out of MIT, having found it 'kind of boring', before drifting into railroad surveying in Canada. When he joined the Aviation Section, US Signal Corps soon after America's entry into World War I, he found his life's purpose.

Qualifying as a pilot, Kenney went into action in France in early 1918 with just twenty flying hours in his logbook. A crash on take-off left him with a broken hand and ankle but, recovering quickly, he wasted no time getting back into the air, now with a new nickname, 'Bust 'em up George'. Having scored his first victory in September 1918, he was pounced upon one morning by six German Pfalz fighters. Wheeling his two-seater French-built Salmson around the sky like a madman, he claimed one German, and drove off the rest, adding the Distinguished Service Cross to the Silver Star he had earned just weeks earlier.

During the great final Allied offensive into the vast Forest of Argonne in north-eastern France, where green American units became lost and separated, Kenney was instructed by no less than Brigadier General 'Billy' Mitchell – the future father of US air power – to conduct 'special missions' at treetop level to spot American uniforms, herding them in the right direction or reporting their positions.

Kenney found this low-altitude flying revelatory. Suddenly, he was safe from much of the German ground fire, flashing over the heads of their gunners before they could get a bearing. Even better, his ability to pinpoint what was beneath him was increased tenfold. Kenney would complete seventy-five missions, many at low level, and coin a phrase that would shape his career: 'attack aviation'.

Kenney was keen to remain in the services after the fighting stopped, applying for several positions in the greatly reduced peacetime Army Air Service, eventually securing a place at an engineering school, then as a test pilot for the Curtiss Aeroplane and Motor Company. Here, he proved himself to be both a brilliant organiser, as well as an innovator, constantly striving for new ways to improve military aircraft and their capabilities, unafraid to tinker, to fiddle, and open to new and original ideas.

His motto became 'Hell, let's try it'.

Remembering how he had been constricted in combat by low rates of firepower from guns synchronised to fire through the propeller arc, in 1922 he began experiments mounting machine guns on aircraft wings, choosing as his platform a bulky but stable ex-army DH-4. After wiring up an improvised firing mechanism, the results were pleasing, but he was ahead of his time, and the Air Service were not interested.

Ruminating on the theory of low-level bombing attacks, he explored the associated problems, such as aircraft being damaged by fragments from their own bombs, and in 1928 conceived the idea of the 'parachute bomb', allowing a slower rate of descent onto the target and pilots to escape their own blasts.

As Kenney's star rose, he made low-level 'attack aviation' his mantra, teaching the tactics – then rewriting the textbook –

at the Air Corps Tactical School in Virginia. Here, however, his brusque self-belief brought him into conflict with the so-called 'Bomber Mafia', a powerful clique that included future generals Carl Spaatz and Curtis LeMay, for whom air power meant only one thing: high-altitude strategic bombing. Their aim, for which they lobbied hard and ruthlessly, was to direct every available resource exclusively into vast fleets of large, self-defending aircraft crewed by up to ten men, and capable – they believed – of winning wars on their own without the support of either escorting fighters or troops on the ground.

Kenney professed the idea to be both absurd and wasteful, advocating instead for smaller, more mobile aircraft which could concentrate their influence tactically in a battlefield situation and at much lower cost of machines and men. Later, as the Allied strategic bombing campaign ground on – at horrendous cost – throughout World War II, early sceptics such as Kenney would be proven correct.

In the mid-thirties, however, taking on the military establishment was a risky business, and Kenney likened himself to General Billy Mitchell, who ten years earlier had been court martialled and driven from the service for accusing a cabal of naval and army officers of incompetence. Nonetheless, Kenney threw himself into acrimonious disputes with the Army General Staff, in 1935 offering his opinions loudly on the Air Corps' decision to purchase more B-17 Flying Fortress bombers, and joining the fight over the establishment of an independent air force, a notion which continued to appal both the army and navy.

To quieten him down, Kenney was transferred to the Fort Benning Infantry School, with a temporary rank of major, where he was required to teach rifle and infantry tactics to young officer cadets, a humiliation he seems to have suffered in dignified silence.

He was then shuffled further away from anything that resembled a command, sent to Paris as Assistant Military Attaché for Air at the US embassy. In Paris he witnessed – albeit from the safe position of a neutral observer – the onslaught of Germany's Luftwaffe in 1940. Shocked by the power of a truly modern air force, he once again antagonised several senior officers by suggesting – possibly not seriously – that America's own comparatively pitiful air force be disbanded and rebuilt from scratch. This outburst saw him hauled back to the United States and given a position far from the public, in engineering. From here, however, he was at least able to implement some urgent technical reforms, such as the self-sealing fuel tanks and the upgrading of aircraft armaments from .30 calibre to the far more powerful .50 calibre.

Still unwilling to risk the outspoken Kenney with a command, the Air Corps gave him the Fourth Air Force, a defence and training organisation based in San Francisco. If not for the deteriorating situation in the Pacific and the unpredictable whims of Douglas MacArthur, Kenney may well have been stuck there for good.

•

Kenney could sense he was getting to the point of not being able to contain his irritation any longer. Surreptitiously glancing at his watch, or out the window at the big clock on the tower of the Brisbane Town Hall, he had lost any notion of how long MacArthur had been ranting. Shuffling in his seat, he could almost no longer bear to watch him pacing back and forth around his large office on the eighth floor of the AMP Building in Queen Street, now requisitioned by the US military.

MacArthur's greeting had been cold enough, but that was only the beginning. The first half-hour had been a dissertation on the nature of war itself – as if this was a foreign concept to Kenney and the gallantry awards on his chest. Then the lecture moved on to the Pacific War in general, followed by complaints about everyone and everything, with particular venom reserved for the air force. Kenney could picture the smile on the face of the man no doubt listening with glee in the next room, MacArthur's sycophantic Chief of Staff, Richard K Sutherland.

Everything, according to MacArthur, had been somebody else's fault. In December 1941 in the Philippines, it had been the air force commander, General Brereton, who had allowed his aircraft to be wiped out on the ground. In fact, the word around Washington – Kenney had heard on the quiet – was that in the days before Pearl Harbor, a skittish MacArthur had refused Brereton permission to send reconnaissance flights to Taiwan, where rows of Japanese bombers readying for action would have been revealed. After the attack, Brereton had begged MacArthur to be allowed to take the initiative and strike those same Japanese airfields, possibly even catching them on the ground. Brereton was told to 'go to his office and await order'. This just allowed the Japanese to inflict exactly this scenario on Americans, destroying eighteen B-17 Fortresses parked neatly at Clark Airfield.

Still, Kenney had been told, a numbed MacArthur did nothing, failing to issue orders for other aircraft to become airborne, or even be properly dispersed, before blaming the airmen themselves for being 'bomb happy', despite many having fought with gallantry against overwhelming odds.

In silence, Kenney listened on.

'The air force were practically useless,' MacArthur thundered, 'an inefficient rabble of boulevard shock troops whose contribution to the war effort was practically nil! I have no use for anyone in the whole organisation from Brett down to – and including – the rank of colonel!' Then, staring at Kenney, he launched a particularly pointed barb delivered quietly but with menace. 'Air personnel,' he said, 'have gone beyond being antagonistic to the point of *disloyalty*.'

The general's mouth was hard, his eyes bitter. Kenney understood full well the depth of the oblique accusation, aimed at officers Kenney knew well and, by implication, himself. Still, he said nothing, but quietly recalled General Marshall's warning before he left the United States, referring to 'certain personality clashes' currently infesting MacArthur's command in Australia.

But when MacArthur said his own staff could take over and run the air force better than the air force themselves, Kenney could contain himself no longer. Rising from the sofa, he looked MacArthur straight in the eye. 'General, I didn't ask to come out here. *You* asked for me.' MacArthur paused. The look on his face told Kenney this was a man entirely unused to being interrupted. Then Kenney played his hand, '... and I think it's one of the *smartest* things you ever did, because I'm the best goddamn air force commander in the world today!'

The only way to impress a man like MacArthur, Kenney reasoned, was to wield a pomposity even greater than his own. He then played straight to the general's insecurities by pledging both his own loyalty as well as that of his subordinates, then pushed his luck by demanding that MacArthur demonstrate the same level of loyalty in return.

'Let's make this thing fifty-fifty,' said Kenney, 'or I'll be calling you from San Francisco and telling you I've quit.'

Kenney half expected to be packed onto the next plane home, but, confronted by a man willing to stand up to him, MacArthur demurred and looked at the man for a long time, studying him as one would a new and exotic creature. The tactic had worked. The conversation reset on Kenney's terms, MacArthur pledged to work with him, even announcing with a hand on Kenney's shoulder as he left the office that they 'should get along with each other just fine'.

None of this, Kenney realised, would please General Sutherland, who had been the bane of Kenney's predecessor's life and would likewise need to be handled carefully. Sutherland guarded access to MacArthur fiercely and had so successfully obstructed General Brett's attempts to meet his commander face to face that after many months in the job Brett could count the number of meetings with MacArthur on the fingers of one hand, and they had been pointless exercises in any case. 'Every endeavour I have made to explain what I was trying to do,' Brett recalled, 'has been lost among lengthy dissertations which I would not take the time to deliver to a second lieutenant.'

Sutherland, whose sole qualification as far as aircraft were concerned was holding a private pilot's licence, had made

Brett's life hell, continually encroaching into his command by issuing orders for bombing attacks, making and dismissing appointments, and interfering in air operations generally. Kenney had been well briefed about his bullying, however, and was ready for it.

At one early meeting in which Sutherland began parroting MacArthur in a tirade against the air force, Kenney listened for a while then suggested the two men get one thing straight. From his briefcase, he pulled out a blank sheet of paper. Unscrewing his pen, he drew a tiny circle in the corner and held it up.

'See this black dot?' he asked. 'This dot represents your understanding of air power. The rest of the sheet of paper represents mine.'

Momentarily stunned by the insult, as well as Kenney's audacity, Sutherland's fury was immediate, but Kenney was not done yet. 'I told him that I was running the air force because I was the most competent airman in the Pacific,' he recalled later, 'and that, if that statement was not true, I recommended that he find somebody that was more competent and put him in charge.' At this point, Sutherland appeared to become 'a little antagonistic' but Kenney upped the stakes: 'Let's go in the next room, see General MacArthur, and get this thing straight. I want to find out who is supposed to run this air force.'

Taking the bait, Sutherland did just that, but Kenney's bluff worked. Having already impressed the general, MacArthur tried to calm his wounded Chief of Staff, reminding him that the job of air force chief was – indeed, after all – not his but Kenney's. The rug thus unexpectedly pulled from under him, a sulky Sutherland backed down.

Kenney had won the day.

From then on, all communication between Kenney and MacArthur would take place directly.

It was a significant early win for Kenney, who – though not entirely sincere in his tactical boast to MacArthur – nonetheless believed that with the right support an air force under his command could turn around its fortunes and achieve great results.

But what, exactly, was the nature of this air force he had been given to command?

Wasting no time, Kenney arranged to borrow General Brett's personal transport to take him directly from Brisbane to Port Moresby, arriving at 11 p.m. the day of his meeting with MacArthur. He'd spend twenty-four hours inspecting what he could, then do the same in Townsville and several of the other American bases in Queensland.

After settling himself into the belly of *The Swoose*, Brett's ageing and somewhat patched-up B-17, Kenney took off from Brisbane airport in the hands of a rather taciturn young pilot who seemed none too pleased at having been given the graveyard shift ferrying around a new general. After a few hours' sleep, Kenney woke to find himself approaching the coastline of New Guinea, with its backdrop of the majestic blue wall of the Owen Stanleys. Landing at Port Moresby's Seven Mile Strip, his nervous pilot immediately took off again for the safety of Horn Island. He was keen to avoid the regular Japanese air raids coming over from Lae, then a daily occurrence.

Almost immediately, Kenney realised that things were not well with the air forces of the South West Pacific. Surveying the rows of Bell P-39 Airacobra fighters, he was informed that most of them couldn't fly for want of spare parts which had stopped arriving weeks ago. Of the 245 fighters listed on his inventory, 170 were grounded. The situation was even worse with the bombers. Of his seventy medium bombers, such as the B-25 Mitchell and A-20 Havoc, only thirty-three were currently airworthy. Of the thirty-six aircraft in his transport fleet – an almost unmaintainable mishmash of nineteen different types – only half were flyable. One entire B-17 Bombardment Group comprising four squadrons and thirty-two aircraft could mount just fourteen machines due to lack of parts, and of his fifty-three light bombers, not a single one was able to fly – though this in fact may have been a blessing as the obsolete A-24 Dauntless/Banshee was a death trap.

Such missions that could be mounted to attack the Japanese were desultory affairs. 'The set-up was really chaotic,' Kenney recalled, as staff officers attempted to untangle the bureaucracy surrounding any air combat operation. Speaking with squadron administration officers on the ground, Kenney's broad shoulders slumped. All combat missions, he learned, were assigned by the Director of Bombardment in Brisbane, the orders for which had to be passed to Townsville, then on to the 19th Bombardment Group in Mareeba, hundreds of miles to the north. What aircraft were available (always far fewer than requested) were sent on to Port Moresby, where they were refuelled and the crews given a weather update and briefing.

'On the average,' Kenney wrote, 'seven to nine bombers usually came up from Australia, and of those, six would probably get off on the raid.' Inevitably, several would return with engine trouble soon after take-off. Kenney noted no cohesion in the attacks. Aircraft often departed individually or in small groups with no designated formation leader, and 'even the matter of assembly of individual planes was ignored'.

Targets were chosen haphazardly, with often no specific aiming point declared, and instructions on how to proceed against targets of opportunity that may present themselves were vague. Far worse was the apparent absence of any sense of fighting spirit. 'If enemy airplanes were seen along the route, all bombs and auxiliary fuel tanks were immediately jettisoned and the mission abandoned,' he recalled. Airmen seemed haunted by the notion that even a single Japanese bullet could detonate an entire bomb load in one great incinerating flash. 'The bombs, of course, were not that sensitive, but no one had explained it to the kids, so they didn't know better.'

Late in the morning, he quietly entered a briefing tent for crews who were attacking Rabaul that afternoon. Looking around at the faces of these disengaged airmen who for their part barely noted his presence, he observed that as far as the mission itself went, 'No particular point was assigned as a target and I found out afterwards that nobody expected airplanes to get that far anyhow.'

The men, devoid of morale, hated being in New Guinea, and for good reason. They had been poorly prepared for the tropics and were terrified of the jungle, with no training in how to survive in it, even for a short time. Living conditions were atrocious; food and sanitation were minimal. Dysentery and malaria were rife and there was no mosquito screening. Men lost a third of their body weight over a tour of just a few months. Some of the officers told Kenney they felt they had been forgotten, with rotation back to Australia long overdue. Some of his 'kids' told Kenney that they had been in combat continually for four or five months.

The problems were not new. Even back in May, during the Coral Sea engagement, the air force had put on a dismal display that did not go unnoticed by the navy. On one occasion at the height of the battle, a gaggle of US bombers accidentally attacked their own warships. But as the US naval commander remarked at the time, 'Fortunately their bombing, in comparison with that of the Japanese formation minutes earlier, was disgraceful.'

On the trip back to Brisbane, Kenney reflected on MacArthur's words, reluctantly admitting the general may have had a point, though wishing he had done more to support the men in the first place.

Kenney decided to take a blowtorch to his new command.

On his initial inspection of his Brisbane headquarters, he was under the impression some event must be taking place because there were so many people in uniform. '[They] seemed to be falling over each other,' he recalled. In a few days he began reducing his bloated headquarters, divesting himself of staff officers enjoying their cushy jobs by transferring them either to New Guinea, or back to the United States. 'Within the first week, I got rid of a couple of major generals and a couple of brigadiers and about forty colonels and lieutenant colonels and one captain.'

Next, he sought to address one of the most urgent complaints the men had raised. Engines, spares, ordnance and even basics such as lubricating oil and aluminium sheeting were in perilously short supply just where they were needed – in the airfields around Port Moresby. Simply to keep aircraft in the air, maintenance teams were having to recycle vital aircraft parts.

As Kenney described it:

There were very few spare instruments, so the kids salvaged them from wrecks and repaired them. There was no aluminum[sic]-sheet stock for repair of shot up or damaged airplanes, so they beat flat the engine cowlings of wrecked fighter planes to make ribs for a B-17 or patch up holes in the wings of a B-25 where a Jap 20-mm. shell had exploded. In the case of small bullet holes, they said, they couldn't afford to waste their good 'sheet-stock' of flattened pieces of aluminum [sic] from the wrecks, so they were patching little holes with scraps cut from tin cans. The salvage pile was their supply source for stock, instruments, spark plugs – anything that could be used by any stretch of the imagination.

Supply processes were mired in red tape. Not only were requisition orders taking over a month to be processed, but most were returned stamped 'Not Available' or 'Improperly filled out'. Kenney could scarcely believe what he was hearing until junior officers showed him filing cases stuffed with slips of paper, each representing a refusal to allow an officer in the field to do his job.

In a system Kenney could not understand and no one could satisfactorily explain, requisitions for supplies and spare parts were submitted via headquarters at Townsville, then forwarded to a depot at Charters Towers. From there they found their way to Melbourne, nearly 1500 miles to the south. Melbourne then forwarded them north again to another depot at Tocumwal on the Victoria–New South Wales border, before somehow returning to Charters Towers before the requested items were – or *were not* – sent to New Guinea. Kenney's air force was choking on paperwork, a situation he was determined to remedy, personally and quickly.

Flying to the newly constructed base at Breddan Aerodrome in Charters Towers, Kenney listened patiently to the colonel in command of the supply depot express his passion for paperwork, proudly informing Kenney that he would frequently return equipment requisitions on which information had been entered on the incorrect line. He had even rejected requests from the 3rd Bombardment Group, currently stationed half a mile away on the other side of the aerodrome. 'It's about time these combat units learned how to do their paperwork properly,' he said, oblivious to the stony-faced general he was addressing. After a pause, Kenney politely instructed the colonel to go immediately to his quarters and pack his things, as he would be on the next plane back to the United States.

For the next few weeks, Kenney rebuilt his air force from top to bottom, clearing out dead wood and offering overdue leave to those who deserved it. He gave talk after talk, reminding his people that they were after all at war, and winning this war would be a twenty-four hours a day, seven days a week job. 'Most of the crowd appreciated what I was talking about. The rest would go home.'

Promotions in non-combat outfits were halted, while battle-weary lieutenants and captains in New Guinea were bumped up to major. Kenney began handing out medals, having been given permission to award anything up to the level of the Distinguished Service Cross. As morale boosting as this may have been for the Americans, the practice somewhat irked the Australian airmen for whom – particularly in the Pacific – such recognition from the far more parsimonious RAAF was almost impossible to obtain. For a single mission against Lae during the botched convoy attacks in January, Kenney awarded no fewer than forty-one Distinguished Flying Crosses and forty Air Medals to a single bombing squadron.

He also ordered for construction of accommodation and office facilities currently underway at Tocumwal to cease, and for the building material to be loaded onto trucks and sent north to bases closer to the action.

Then there was the question of his airmen's flying skills. 'The exhibition I had seen at Port Moresby of six B-17s taking an hour to get off the ground and never assembling into formation before arrival at the target was something that I did not want to see again,' he said. All flying operations against the enemy were henceforth halted and at stations all over Australia and New Guinea aircrew were told to go back to basics, practising take-offs, landings and formations under the direction of a dedicated formation leader, as if they were back at training school. They were to learn to do it quickly and would be required to practise it in their sleep.

All men were to attend demonstrations on the base in which bullets were fired at unprimed bombs, to assure the more skittish among them that the bombs would not detonate if struck by a few stray bullets, Japanese or otherwise. In a week or so, Kenney told them to be ready to conduct what he hoped would be the largest air assault on the Japanese yet carried out in the Pacific War.

•

Much has been made of Kenney's strike against the Japanese stronghold of Vunakanau Airfield at Rabaul, the major enemy base on the eastern tip of New Britain. Constructed by Australian engineers before the war, it was now firmly occupied by the Japanese, and heavily defended. Intelligence had revealed the presence of an unusually large number of Japanese aircraft lined up in the standard Japanese pattern of wing tip to wing tip along both sides of Vunakanau's long concrete runway. Exactly why they persisted in this habit of presenting their aircraft in conveniently assembled rows to any marauding bomber or strafing fighter is unknown. Throughout the Pacific, little emphasis was placed on protecting their precious aerial assets with proper revetments or dispersal systems as in the Allied manner.

Kenney's airmen were in no mood to forgive their enemy's lack of foresight.

He had promised MacArthur a 'maximum effort' of at least twenty B-17s to take part, describing it as 'the heaviest single attack in the Pacific War up to that time'. However, due to the maintenance issues that had long plagued the 19th Bombardment Group, their commander, Colonel Richard

Carmichael, who would be leading the attack himself, could muster only sixteen serviceable aircraft. It would have to do.

Having flown up to Port Moresby's Seven Mile Strip from their base at Mareeba, Carmichael's bombers took off early in the morning of 7 August 1942. One aircraft piloted by a Lieutenant Hillhouse suffered a blown turbocharger on take-off, skidding off the runway and careening into a rock wall, injuring his navigator and reducing the aircraft to scrap, while two others aborted soon after with engine and electrical failures.

This left just thirteen bombers to continue the attack.

Twenty miles from the target, the group was intercepted by fifteen Zeros, then eleven more from two newly arrived Japanese units, one of these being the famous Tainan Kokutai flown by some of Japan's finest aces. The American pilots held their nerve and, despite being woefully out of practice, managed to hold their formation, allowing concentrated defensive fire from their gunners which accounted for three claims of Zeros destroyed in just a few minutes.

Kenney's subsequent report of the attack would paint an ebullient picture of a deadly blow struck against the great Japanese base, and how the 'kids closed up their formation and fought their way to Vunakanau where they dropped their bombs in a group pattern that was a real bull's eye'. Kenney claimed infrastructure was destroyed as well as a bomb and fuel dump, and that 'we shot down eleven of the twenty Jap fighters that participated'.

Much of this was simply wishful thinking.

Bombing from 22 000 feet, the spread bomb pattern stirred up a lot of dust on the airfield but little damage was in fact done either to it or the adjacent facilities. It was claimed that of the 150 Japanese planes lined up, at least seventy-five were destroyed or damaged, but this was untrue. As historian Anthony Cooper concludes in his brilliant analysis of the entire 1942 Pacific air campaign, *Kokoda Air Strikes*:

> Nothing of the sort happened. The 23 Japanese bombers present had already departed on their strike to Guadalcanal, and indeed the returning B-17 crews reported during debriefing that there were 'nil' aircraft on the airfield when they bombed. Kenney's claim was pure fiction ...

Furthermore, a formation of Japanese aircraft returning from Guadalcanal that afternoon managed to do so without incident.

Nor was the raid without cost to the Allies, with a B-17 piloted by Captain Harl Pease lost. This aircraft in reality should not have been flying at all, being so worn out that ground crewmen did not consider it fit for combat. But such was the pressure for the group to put up a 'maximum effort', it was placed on the day's battle order regardless. After dropping their bombs, the American airmen's tight formation broke down under Zero attack. In his slower aircraft, Pease was pounced upon and sent down in flames after doing his best to fight off his attackers. Managing to bail out, Pease and a lone gunner survived, but were soon captured by the Japanese and a month later executed by the sword after being forced to dig their own graves.

Nor, in the final analysis, were the claims of up to eleven Zeros destroyed and several more damaged by the Fortresses' gunners accurate. The Japanese didn't lose a single fighter that day, and the raid produced nothing for the Americans except one precious B-17 lost and several others written off. If not for the equally poor airmanship of the Japanese who could account for no more than a single unescorted bomber destroyed and some more damaged, the raid on Rabaul could have been a disaster.

The fact that the outcome of the mission was not merely exaggerated but to a large extent concocted seems to have little bearing on its viewed 'success' as a mission. Kenney was a man with a keen political instinct and he needed a win. He had to tell MacArthur what he wanted to hear and the attack shored up Kenney's own reputation in comparison with that of his luckless predecessor, General Brett. MacArthur now knew he had an air general upon whom he could rely. And Kenney had secured the necessary support in order to rebuild his air force.

Kenney also saw the story of the gallant Captain Harl Pease's epic bravery in combat as just the tonic to lift the spirits of the men under his command, and requested Pease be posthumously awarded the Congressional Medal of Honor. Amid great publicity, the medal was given to Pease's grieving parents by President Roosevelt on 2 December 1942.

•

Kenney had begun the task of melding and reforming the disparate units under his command, but what his air force now needed was a singular identity. Kenney sent an urgent wire to

Washington, requesting General 'Hap' Arnold to allow his command be grouped under one overarching unit. Arnold informed him that the number five was available and he was welcome to it. Hence, from 18 September 1942 on, Kenney's three bomber and five fighter groups, plus the transport, photographic, maintenance, cargo and troop carrier wings, as well as dozens of ancillary units totalling 1600 officers and 18 000 men – including veterans of the debacles of the Philippines and Java and men just arrived from the United States and yet to see a shot fired in anger – were all now to come under the umbrella of the brand new Fifth US Army Air Force.

Its job would be – finally – to bring the war to the Japanese.

CHAPTER 7
ENTER PAPPY GUNN

There was something about the man in greasy overalls that kept distracting Kenney from the conversation, and an important conversation it was too. After dismissing the well-meaning but misguided stores officer from his post at the supply depot in Charters Towers, Kenney was taken on an inspection of the 3rd Bombardment Group (Light). Under the leadership of a Philippines veteran, Lieutenant Colonel John Davies, the 3rd Bombardment Group had had an inauspicious start to the war, most of its pilots having been diverted to Brisbane after the fall of the Philippines and finding themselves stranded there without any aircraft to fly.

As Davies explained the situation, he raised another issue: the unit's name. Upon arriving in Australia, they had been renamed, and 'Bombardment Group (Light)' was hardly a title about which his eager airmen – now thankfully equipped with B-25s and A-20 Havoc bombers – could become particularly excited. Davies enquired about applying to have their former moniker of 'Attack Group' reinstated. Kenney loved the idea and told Davies not to apply for anything, but just do it. From that moment, the four squadrons under Davies' command went under the banner of the far more warlike '3rd Attack Group'. Davies, and his men, could not have been happier.

Glancing over Davies' shoulder now, however, Kenney couldn't help noticing the overalled mechanic working on the nose section of one of the 89th Squadron's A-20 Havocs. Davies followed his curious gaze. 'Oh, that's Pappy,' he said enthusiastically, 'he can do anything, come over and meet him.' The conversation that then took place in the open at Charters Towers would change the direction of the Pacific air war.

•

For eight months, there had been silence. It was a silence over which he had no control, a silence with no end in sight, a silence which gnawed away at him every moment of every day. The only thing that made life bearable, the sole purpose for which he strove and thought and worked with every fibre of his being, was getting back into the war.

It had been eight months since that terrible day, arriving as the crescendo of the terrible final weeks of 1941, when Manila finally drowned under the Japanese tide; eight months since he pressed a wad of American banknotes into his wife's hands, kissing his four children goodbye, and listened to her assurances to not worry, that they'd be safe until he returned. Then he had left, obeying his orders to pilot a planeload of high-ranking officers – who must not under any circumstances be permitted to fall into the hands of the Japanese – out of Manila to Australia and safety.

His wife's name was Clara, but he had always called her Polly. And for eight months the strength in her eyes had been the last thing he saw at night and the first thing he saw in the morning. Leaving Polly and his kids – Donald, Julie, Nathaniel and Paul – had been by far the hardest thing this hard man had ever done.

Now, 3000 miles away at a dusty aerodrome in Charters Towers, his only communication had been via the Red Cross informing him that, during the sudden fall of Manila, his family had been interned, along with thousands of American and British citizens, in squalid conditions in a former university, now the Santo Tomas Internment Camp. Utterly helpless, his only recourse was to do all he could to shorten the war, and the removed nose section of the Douglas A-20 Havoc bomber in front of him was the best way he knew to do it.

•

Paul Irving Gunn was the most unlikely of war heroes, yet his ad hoc technical innovations were to have a profound effect on the Pacific air war. The quiet son of an Arkansas cop who was killed in a shootout when he was still a kid, in 1917 the teenage Paul was arrested for running moonshine and sent before a local judge. Sympathetic to the boy's plight, the judge strongly hinted that signing up for the navy might be a way of avoiding a stint in custody.

With little education and scant prospects, Gunn agreed, and initially went to work in the navy kitchens. But when his innate mechanical skills were noticed, he was transferred to the motor pool. Here he came to the attention of the chief engineer, who marked him down as an aviation mechanic. And so Gunn's love of flying was born. Learning about aircraft from the ground up, he was so keen to fly he took private lessons at his own expense and purchased a surplus navy seaplane in which to practise. At the end of his enlistment the navy, impressed by the young man's dedication, offered him the chance to re-enlist as a pilot.

He grabbed the opportunity with both hands.

Serving during the interwar period flying fighters off the decks of aircraft carriers, Gunn eventually rose to be an instructor before deciding to go out on his own. In 1939 he moved his family to Hawaii, where he set up a charter flying business. As fate would have it, he was approached by a wealthy Filipino businessman to start his own airline there, flying Beech-18 passenger aircraft.

When the war in the Pacific erupted in December 1941, Gunn was quickly brought back into the service and commissioned as a captain in the Army Air Corps. His handful of passenger planes were painted green and requisitioned for military service. In the drawn-out and chaotic invasion of the Philippines, Gunn flew constantly, making transport flights into the collapsing fronts of Bataan. He worked like a one-man supply line, grabbing medical supplies and ammunition from bases in the yet-to-be-overrun south of the country, and flying in under the noses of the Japanese, trying to stem the inevitable collapse. One dark night, he even risked swooping onto a deserted street close to the Japanese in Manila, hoping to locate his trapped family and spirit them away to safety.

His daring came to nothing.

In March 1942, on his way to Bataan to pick up some airmen in danger of being taken prisoner, he was surprised by a Japanese seaplane which shot out one of his engines. Gunn put his plane down on a beach, luckily uninjured, then set it on fire to trick the Japanese pilot into thinking he had made a kill. He then found his way to Del Monte Airfield on the island of Mindanao, where he discovered a B-17 sitting idle on account of one engine being unserviceable. He quickly repaired the engine, then flew it to Darwin with a couple of dozen rescued airmen who would fly and fight another day.

It was here that Gunn was informed that his family had been interned.

Gunn's war just became personal.

Lumped in with another hundred or so similarly orphaned airmen from the 27th Bombardment Group who had been unceremoniously bundled out of the Philippines, Australia was home for the time being. Initially not attached to any particular unit, Gunn was assigned cargo and troop-carrying flights, but stories attest to him taking anything he could get his hands on for impromptu one-man missions back to the Philippines, taking in supplies, but also conducting lone bombing sorties against Japanese shipping in the Java Sea.

Eventually settling in with the 3rd Attack Group in Charters Towers, Gunn flew regular transport flights around Australia. One afternoon in March while overflying Laverton air base near Melbourne, he noticed a line-up of what appeared to be brand new American B-25 Mitchell bombers sitting idly in a quiet corner of the airfield. Knowing the 3rd Attack Group was desperately awaiting just such a consignment, he landed to enquire as to their provenance, convinced they must be these same aircraft which had somehow gone astray. The station ordnance officer, while assuring him they were indeed brand new machines which had been there a couple of weeks already, said they had nothing to do with the 3rd Attack Group. The officer said they'd been diverted from their intended recipients, the Dutch East Indies Air Force in faraway Java.

Staring at the officer in disbelief, Gunn politely asked if he had considered the reason they had been diverted might just be because Java had already fallen to the Japanese, and that in any case the Dutch lacked aircrews to fly them there, or indeed anywhere else? Meanwhile up at Charters Towers, he pointed out, the men of his Attack Group were sitting on their hands, desperate for aircraft with which to take the war to the enemy. The ordnance officer agreed but, shrugging his shoulders, referred Captain Gunn to the paperwork in his hand.

Fuming, Gunn flew back north and told the stunned 3rd Attack Group CO, Colonel Davies, of his discovery. The pair immediately sat down to hatch a plan.

•

The next day Major General Eugene Eubank, the Far East Air Forces bomber leader, was sitting in his Brisbane office when his adjutant informed him that Colonel Davies had arrived impromptu and had requested to see him immediately. Eubank welcomed in his old friend, who cut right to the chase, explaining the incomprehensible situation at Laverton. Over the next half-hour Eubank, a two-star American general, was persuaded to produce both a letter and acquisition papers – all fake – ordering the B-25s in Victoria to be flown 1500 miles to Charters Towers at the first opportunity.

Although the risk to his reputation and career was considerable, Eubank had been humiliated in the Philippines retreat and was desperate to bring the war back to the Japanese. At the end of the meeting he said, 'What have we got to lose except our necks? And we won't have those anyway if the Nips keep coming on the way they are.'

With a short, silent prayer, Eubank put his name to the letter and joined the conspiracy.

Two days later, Gunn once again touched down in a Dakota transport at Laverton, this time in the company of Colonel Davies, who coolly handed General Eubank's 'order' to the very same ordnance officer Gunn had met a day or two earlier. The officer looked it over a couple of times and mumbled something about it 'all being a bit irregular', but he could find no reason to dispute its validity.

'But in any case,' he asked, 'how are you going to fly them up there?'

Gunn signalled to the couple of dozen pilots he had secreted in the Dakota. He told them to prepare the Mitchell bombers for flight. The ordnance officer was aghast.

'Wait,' he spluttered, 'you're … you're taking them … *now*?'

They certainly were. In the end, the unwitting officer arranged ground crews to warm up the aircraft, check fuel levels, and even provided a hot meal for the pilots for their long flight north. At 6.30 p.m., as the sun set over Melbourne, the last of the 'Dutch' B-25s took off from Laverton and headed north.

The audacious plan would have gone smoothly, but for the ordnance officer bemusedly recalling the episode an hour or so later in the mess at dinner to an incredulous colleague whose face went pale at the news of the twenty-five brand new aircraft which the ordnance officer had blithely allowed to take off under his nose.

'You … did what?' the officer demanded. At this point all hell broke loose. Priority military trunk lines were connected up and down the Australian east coast trying to find the stolen planes.

Of course, Gunn and Davies had foreseen this very scenario. And it was no surprise that while they were refuelling at Archerfield in Brisbane they were greeted by a stern-looking Air Corps major and a squad of well-armed military policemen who were determined to allow them to proceed no further. Ultimately, it came down to a contest of wills – and even a threat of court martial for holding up the war effort.

Gunn and Davies prevailed.

Arriving at Charters Towers the next morning, the 3rd Attack Group mechanics could hardly believe their eyes. Before them were brand new machines still in their factory green livery – even smelling of fresh paint – with working hydraulics and electrical systems which did not have to be butchered from other aircraft. One mechanic approached Gunn, however, with a look of caution on his face.

'Ah, boss,' he said, 'what about the bombsights?'

Gunn's shoulders sagged.

In their glee at the ease of their getaway, they had neglected to secure the vital bombsights, which were always stored away from the aircraft under lock and key.

Within an hour, Gunn was once again heading back to Melbourne.

At Laverton, the pliable ordnance officer had been replaced by a grave and furious Dutchman who foretold of a major diplomatic incident unless the aircraft were returned immediately. What exactly transpired next was something Gunn was forever coy about, but one part of the mythology is that he at some stage produced a submachine gun and aimed it at the man's head. Whatever the truth, next morning he returned to Charters Towers with twenty-five wooden crates containing the bombsights for the B-25s.

Finally, the 3rd Attack Group was ready for action. Gunn himself wasted no time and a couple of days later used one of the fast new Mitchells to bring out some of the last US personnel to leave Mindanao the day before the Japanese arrived, even landing on a Philippines beach to pick up a valuable Japanese double agent and Chinese intelligence officer.

•

George Kenney knew nothing of this when he approached Gunn that crisp morning in August 1942 on the airstrip at Charters Towers in front of a partially dismantled 90th Squadron A-20 Havoc medium bomber. Gunn explained that the Havocs had originally arrived without any .50-calibre machine guns – or any bomb racks, for that matter – but here in Australia there seemed to be plenty of them in storage, plus others retrieved from the wings of wrecked and unserviceable aircraft. In any case, he explained, the Havoc's standard lone forward-firing weapon was completely inadequate, so he was attempting to bolster its firepower.

Gunn drew the general closer and showed him his makeshift arrangement. He'd managed to build four guns into the nose, as well as another two mounted either side of the forward fuselage, each of which could handle 500 rounds of ammunition. He had also dispensed with the bombardier's position and was adding an extra fuel tank. The weight, he said, needed reconfiguring, but he was working on it. He then showed Kenney the added electrical, firing and recoil mechanisms he had installed.

As Kenney listened, he recognised a fellow innovator and liked him more and more by the minute. Gunn's talents, he realised, were too valuable to be confined to one unit. Kenney told him that, effective immediately, he was relieved of his duties with transport flying and would be transferred to his personal staff, tasked with what Kenney vaguely described as 'special duties'. What these would entail was made clear when Kenney asked whether Gunn could adapt more Havocs.

As Kenney recalled, 'I told him I wanted sixteen of them ready in two weeks. Pappy said he would have them. No one else but me believed he could do it, but when I offered to make a small bet on the possibility, I found no takers.'

Kenney also asked whether Gunn could devise racks to hold special fragmentation bombs he'd had shipped out from the States.

Gunn grinned. 'No problem,' he said, adding that he very much liked the idea of dropping fragmentation bombs on the Japanese.

Kenney knew then he had found a partner he could work with.

One thing Kenney remained curious about was the man's age. 'No one knew how old he was but he was probably well over forty, although he looked you straight in the eye and said thirty.' In fact, Gunn was only forty-two, but that still made him one of the oldest men in the group. His ordeal in the Philippines had aged him considerably, leading to the name by which he would be forever known, 'Pappy'.

CHAPTER 8

'FINALLY THEY BEGAN TO SKIP ALONG LIKE FLAT STONES'

From the moment war was declared at 11 a.m. on 3 September 1939, Britain's Royal Air Force took just over twenty-four hours to launch their first strike against Hitler's Germany. But its power to inflict any great damage was severely limited. Although in just a few short years the power of Bomber Command would evolve into a terrible weapon of mass destruction, capable of incinerating an entire German city and tens of thousands of its inhabitants in a single night, the notion of attacking civilian population centres – or even 'private property' such as factories – was, at this early stage of the war, considered abhorrent, an anathema to civilised behaviour, even in time of war.

German shipping, on the other hand, was a legitimate target.

On 4 September, a Wellington pilot conducting the first reconnaissance flight over Germany reported warships at anchor at Wilhelmshaven and several more 20 miles away at Schillig in the Heligoland Bight. The RAF decided to act. In fact, they would have 'acted' somewhat sooner had the pilot been fitted with a functioning wireless and reported his findings immediately. As it was, he had to wait until he returned to his base to relay the news verbally late in the morning.

By 3.45 p.m., twenty-nine Wellington and Blenheim bombers from four squadrons had been readied, their crews in their flying gear, eager to carry out the first British air strike of World War II. Their targets were the German battleships *Gneisenau*, *Scharnhorst* and *Admiral Scheer*.

To mark the occasion, King George VI sent a special message which was read out to the young assembled airmen as they prepared to depart:

> The Royal Air Force has behind it a tradition no less inspiring than those of the older Services, and in the campaign which we have now been compelled to undertake you will have to assume responsibilities far greater than those which your service had to shoulder in the last war. I can assure all ranks of the air force of my supreme confidence in their skill and courage, and in their ability to meet whatever calls may be made upon them.

The attack, despite the King's confidence, turned out to be a bloody and unmitigated disaster.

It set in motion Bomber Command's profligacy with regards to the lives of its brave and committed airmen, nearly 60000 of whom would be killed in action, making flying in Britain's bomber offensive one of the most lethal occupations of World

War II with the death rate averaged over five years reaching a staggering 46 per cent.

The fine weather which had aided the reconnaissance flight early on the morning of 4 September had, by late afternoon, given way to the type of low-cloud squall which probably should have seen the mission scrubbed. As it was, half the pilots failed to find the ships and turned back, leaving fifteen Blenheim crews to face the onslaught of the German naval defences alone. Even worse, it was evident the men were woefully unprepared for war. One Wellington pilot nearly took off without his bombs, sensing the aircraft to be somewhat light when taxiing, before stopping to take a look in the bomb bay and finding it empty. One of the Blenheim pilots asked his gunner to test the aircraft's guns. None were functioning, but the pilot carried on to face the enemy anyway.

The RAF, unwilling to risk any of their bombs falling on the town or harbour lest civilian casualties be incurred, ordered their pilots to approach the ships beam-on at just 100 feet. They would then 'bounce' their four 250-pounders over the water, hopefully having them land on the decks and explode. The German sailors would, they said, be so surprised and terrified by the technique's daring and accuracy they would offer no resistance.

In driving rain, 110 Squadron RAF Bomber Command went in first – led, as it happens, by the first Australian to go into action in World War II, thirty-year-old Wing Commander Ivan McLeod from Victoria. As their airfield at Wattisham was not ready, they had taken off instead from the nearby civilian airport at Ipswich. After their attack, they were to be followed by 107 Squadron. One pilot indeed bombed accurately, his load skidding across the water before slamming into the superstructure of the *Admiral Scheer*. But then, to his dismay, he watched all his bombs sink harmlessly into the sea. Four more such duds would hit the *Admiral Scheer*. Other bombs had their fuses set to explode at an entirely useless eleven-second delay, allowing just enough time for them also to fall into the sea, disturbing nothing but fish at the bottom of Wilhelmshaven harbour.

Another Blenheim then lined up on what turned out to be the cruiser *Emden*, a vessel not even on the target. This particular Blenheim happened to be piloted by Flying Officer Henry Lovell Emden. Tragically, he failed to pull up in time and crashed headlong into his namesake's bow, killing himself, his two crew members and an extra gunner, a leading aircraftsman who had come along for the experience.

With the German gunners alerted, it was the turn of 107 Squadron to make their attack, but the pom-pom anti-aircraft shells fired up at them at point-blank range tore them to pieces. The pilot of one aircraft, Sergeant Albert Prince, became the first Canadian of the war to be killed. Another killed, 21-year-old Flying Officer Brian Lightoller, was the son of the famous second officer of the *Titanic*, and hero of the disaster, Charles Lightoller. Having lost one son in the first month of the war, Charles Lightoller would suffer the cruel fate of losing another, a Royal Navy PT boat commander, in the conflict's final month. Two other airmen would become the first British POWs of the war, when their aircraft was shot down into the harbour intact, and they were picked up by a German navy launch.

One 107 Squadron Blenheim pilot managed to bounce his bombs along the water accurately onto the deck, only to be caught in their explosion as he overflew the ship. Both he and his crew were killed. While others had their bomb fuses set too long, his was set perilously short.

In all, four of the five Blenheims put up by 107 Squadron were shot down, plus another from 110 Squadron. Two Wellingtons mucked up their navigation and ended up dropping bombs 100 miles away on the Danish town of Esbjerg, killing two civilians before they were shot down by German fighters.

In all, thirty highly trained British and Commonwealth airmen had been sacrificed for no gain whatsoever. Australian pilot Ivan McLeod managed to survive the disaster, but his luck would last only another three weeks when, on 28 September, he would be shot down and killed while on a reconnaissance flight over Germany.

Apart from recording Bomber Command's first casualties of the war, the 4 September raid would become noteworthy for another reason: it was the first, albeit wholly unsuccessful, attempt to 'bounce' bombs across the surface of the water. The attack would be studied and analysed, and the technique would be adapted, improved and used – with varying degrees of success – by Coastal Command against German shipping in the Atlantic and Mediterranean.

Two years later in the faraway South Pacific, the idea would be perfected by the pilots of George Kenney's Fifth Air Force. They also came up with a new term for it: 'skip bombing'.

•

At a conference in England in August 1941, overall commander of the US Army Air Force, General Hap Arnold, sat riveted as a bold new concept was discussed by senior RAF officers. Although America was still months away from entering the war, Arnold could already envisage its uses.

> I learned about skip bombing that night. The talk brought out the fact that ... many German ships had been sunk by a new method which the British Coastal Command was using ... the British claimed to have had wonderful success with that method and to have made far more hits than with high-altitude bombing.

Another new concept in air warfare – low-level bombing – was also discussed. Some senior officers were passionately for it, while others dismissed it in favour of the more established high-level strategy. With America still at peace, however, the debate spluttered out inside the bubble of military theory, but Arnold knew America would soon be drawn into the conflict and he had no intention of missing the bus.

Upon his return to the United States in January 1942, just a few weeks after Pearl Harbor, he put together a team to thoroughly examine all aspects of extremely low altitude bombing. Under the strictest secrecy at Eglin Army Airfield in Florida, pilots armed with bombs, and engineering and scientific officers armed with slide rules, went to work. Within a few months they released their *Final Report on Minimum Altitude Attack of Water-Borne Surface Vessels with Aircraft Bombs*, a complex document which distilled what it purported to be the essential theory of low-level bombing against naval targets. Various methods of attack were outlined and described as '... a quartering front attack on armored surface vessels (more than one inch of side armor plate) at maximum level flight speed and one hundred-fifty (150) feet to three-hundred (300) feet altitude, dropping one-thousand (1,000) pound or two-thousand (2,000) pound demolition bombs ...' etc, and it was posited that large aircraft such as the B-17 were ideally suited to the task.

However, the advocates of high-level strategic bombing – a cabal which wielded considerable power – not only remained unconvinced but felt their position under threat.

Not so George Kenney, who had for years been advocating the advantages of low-level bombing, though few had wanted to listen. Since his days as a pilot in 1918 zooming over the treetops of northern France, he had been convinced of the efficacy of low-level aerial warfare. Now, decades later, with his superiors finally starting to show some interest, the opportunity was ripe to develop the idea within his new command in the Pacific.

The fact that he would be far removed from prying eyes in Washington or, indeed, the high-profile air force establishment in Europe was, he felt, even better. On the long trip in the B-24 Liberator to Australia from San Francisco, he wasted not a minute examining low-level bombing from every conceivable (albeit theoretical) angle. He found a willing audience in two of his fellow passengers, Major General Willard Harmon and Kenney's aide, Major William Benn.

Kenney had protested that he was not the kind of man who wanted or needed an aide, but was quietly informed that it was expected that an officer of his standing should have one, if only for the sake of appearances. As it turned out, Kenney would be eternally grateful for the appointment. Forty-two-year-old Benn was both a gifted pilot and passionate advocate of low-level bombing, and, of particular interest to Kenney, he had witnessed firsthand many of the recent low-level trials undertaken in secret at Eglin. Soon after their initial meeting, Kenney advised Benn 'not to buy any more aide's insignia for his uniform' as he would soon be doing far more important work than holding his boss's overcoat.

Major General Harmon was another World War I flyer and a man very much after Kenney's own heart. On the long flight, the three officers transformed the rear fuselage of the big bomber into a classroom, working out on notepaper and exercise books the theory of low-altitude bombing in minute detail. Every conceivable aspect was discussed – from fuse settings to correct angles of attack to altitudes, and the best means for a pilot to avoid being blown to pieces by the blast of his own bombs.

All were of the opinion that the British were mistaken in trying to 'bounce' a bomb onto the deck of a ship. Far more effective, they reckoned, would be to hit the superstructure and bridge. But the idea which particularly enthralled them was dropping a bomb beside a ship's hull moments before it detonated.

'In the few seconds remaining,' Kenney surmised, 'the bomb should sink just about far enough so that when it went off it would blow the bottom out of the ship. In the meantime, the airplane would have hurdled the enemy vessel and would get far enough away so that it would not be vulnerable to the explosion … everyone would be happy except the Japs on board the sinking ship.'

By the time the trio landed at Nadi in Fiji for a scheduled layover, their feet itched sufficiently for them to attempt to put the theory into practice.

The colonel in charge of the airfield in this sleepy hollow was, however, evidently quite unprepared to receive such a dynamic group of officers. Not only did he fail to show up to greet Kenney and his party, but unwisely sent a note via a lowly lieutenant explaining that his absence was due to the fact that he was currently preoccupied sunbathing. General Harmon, expressionless, read the note and passed it to Kenney. The colonel would find himself on the next plane back to the United States.

With a few days up their sleeves, Harmon arranged a series of tests using a batch of dummy bombs and a locally based B-26 Marauder squadron to 'attack' a series of coral knolls just off the shore. The exercise proved invaluable, driving home to Kenney not only the difficulties in getting low-level bombing right, but the rewards in store if it could be achieved.

'It was quite evident that it was going to take quite a bit of experimental flying to determine the proper height for release of the bomb and how far from the ship it should be released,' Kenney later recalled. From the outset, he realised that the accepted heights were far too high. At 400 and even 300 feet, bombs released simply sank or skipped over the target altogether. Only at the perilously low height of 100 feet – barely skimming the wavetops – could a bomb be released accurately.

The bewildered Marauder pilots of Nadi, accustomed to the luxuries of their relatively soft posting, sat sweating at the controls of their aircraft, nerves jangling, as the instructions came over the radio to fly ever lower and release their bombs ever closer to the 'target'. 'We bounced some bombs right over the targets,' said Kenney. 'Others sank without bouncing, but finally they began to skip along like flat stones.'

The exercise had proven very useful, though one of their main concerns remained the paucity of any forward firepower on their aircraft capable of suppressing a ship's defences at close range. The A-20 had a couple of medium .30-calibre forward shooters, but the B-25 had only one, with a similar arrangement in even the large B-17 Fortress.

In this, however, an ageing, cigar-chomping mechanical genius with the appropriate moniker of 'Gunn' was to come to his aid.

CHAPTER 9
A NEW WEAPON IS BORN

Having been elevated to the unique, albeit vague, title of 'Special Projects Officer', Pappy Gunn was initially given charge of converting all the Douglas A-20 Havoc bombers into strafing machines. The supply of A-20s themselves, however, soon began to run dry. Having converted six, Kenney was informed from high up that all remaining A-20s earmarked for the Pacific were to be reassigned to the European theatre or delivered to the Soviet Union.

Attention should instead be directed towards converting the North American B-25 Mitchells. But before his role in redesigning the aircraft of the Fifth Air Force progressed any further, Gunn needed to unburden himself of an important, long-held secret. While in Brisbane, he approached Kenney's office door and knocked gingerly.

The men greeted each other warmly. After discussing the progress of the conversions, and how the technique would now be applied to the B-25 Mitchell, an uncharacteristically nervous Gunn cleared his throat and announced he needed to make something of a confession. Namely, that having flown for the army over the past year and a half in a variety of situations, including actual combat, he did not in fact possess a licence to do so.

Kenney listened, slack-jawed, for once utterly lost for words. None of this made sense. Had Gunn not spent the past year and a half flying in the Philippines? Conducted transport flights across the Pacific and around Australia, not to mention bombing and reconnaissance sorties *inside enemy territory*? Gunn told him it was all true, but that no one had ever bothered to check to see if he possessed a USAAF pilot's rating, or was in fact a qualified military pilot.

'I guess everyone just assumed I was,' he said.

Unsure whether to laugh or cry, Kenney told Gunn to reveal this to absolutely no one, leave it with him, and under no circumstances to take charge of any military aircraft of any description until this was sorted out. Relieved, Gunn went back to his aircraft.

Firing a request up the chain of command, Kenney was told that his maverick airman could indeed be granted an army pilot's rating, provided he return to the United States and complete a nine-month training course. Infuriated, Kenney wired General Arnold in Washington with a cable marked 'Eyes Only', outlining the exemplary ways Gunn had already served his country, and the importance of his knowledge now being utilised in fighting the Japanese.

Within days Gunn had his rating, backdated to 7 December 1941. He was even invited to collect nearly a year of back pay – in cash. This he did, pinning the large bills to the inside of his shirt pocket. In a cinematic twist, he flew back to Port Moresby on a particularly hot day, removing the shirt and placing it on his lap. Halfway across the Coral Sea, he opened a side cockpit window to allow in some fresh air, and his shirt – cash and all – was sucked out into the void. As Kenney related the tale later, '[Gunn] looked back to see if it had hung up on the tail surfaces. It hadn't.' Reflecting for a moment, Gunn puffed on his cigar and remarked, 'Well, come easy – go easy.' The matter was closed.

While Pappy Gunn's official status as a pilot was being finalised, he continued his work on the ground converting the B-25 Mitchell bombers. Kenney moved him from Charters Towers to the airstrip at Eagle Farm in Brisbane, where in August 1942 he was placed with the 81 Air Depot Group, the supply outfit he had wrenched up from faraway Tocumwal. Here, with staff and facilities, Pappy Gunn went to work.

The B-25 Mitchell medium bomber was by no means a bad aeroplane, but neither was it a particularly remarkable one. From their plant in Inglewood, California, the North American Aviation Company turned out nearly 10 000 of these machines from the time the contract was awarded in 1939, right through until the war's conclusion in 1945.

As a medium-altitude bomber, it did its job well enough, but for Kenney's purposes it was next to useless as it lacked both the range and firepower required to hit Japanese shipping across the great distances of the Pacific. Indeed, the Mitchell's forward firepower consisted of a solitary peashooter .30-calibre machine gun shoved through a hole in the nose. Its performance was impeded by a ludicrously conceived Bendix lower turret protruding from the rear belly firing two .50-calibre machine guns. These had to be aimed by a gunner standing above them inside the fuselage and peering through a periscope. When not making him airsick, this arrangement offered no all-round vision whatsoever. It also produced extra drag, lowering the plane's speed and range and using more fuel.

Pappy Gunn decided the rear turret would be the first thing to go. In its place he would install a large fuel tank to considerably extend the Mitchell's range. More weight would be saved by the removal of the tail gun. In its new role as a low-level attack aircraft, the need for defence from below would be hopefully obviated in any case. To achieve the required precise timing, the bombs would be released by the pilot, hence the bombardier and his position would likewise be removed, and as there would be no room for a navigator, he was out of a job too. Into the new spaces created within the fuselage would now be installed guns – and a good many of them.

Working day and night, Pappy Gunn transformed the modest B-25 Mitchell medium bomber into a low-level juggernaut bristling with weaponry. Four .50-calibre guns were mounted in the now solid nose, then two more on each side of the forward fuselage in specially designed blisters. Still more were added underneath. As if that was not enough, the one remaining top gun turret could be fixed to fire forward, giving the redesigned plane upwards of *ten* forward-firing machine guns.

Gunn's challenges were immense. Each gun needed at least 480 rounds to be effective, and so feed chutes and ammunition boxes had to be incorporated for each of them as well as their respective electrical circuits. Then there was the problem of recoil. In static tests on the shooting range, it was found the B-25 airframes – never built to withstand the pressure of so much firepower – soon popped rivets and developed cracks.

Gunn, a junkyard genius who refused to be beaten by any mechanical problem, strengthened the fuselage with extra steel plates, although this in fact initially made things worse. Felt was then used to cushion the steel from the guns' movement, requiring air force representatives to descend upon Brisbane haberdashers to grab every bolt of it they could get their hands on, the cover story as to its intended use having been lost to history. The felt did the job for a time, but dried to a rock-like hardness after becoming wet. In the end, Gunn settled upon spongy sections of rubber to absorb the impact.

Another task set by Kenney to occupy Gunn's time was the installation of completely new bomb releases in the bellies of the B-25s. The idea was the result of a piece of good fortune that had come Kenney's way in the final days before he left the United States. In their initial meeting in Washington, General Arnold had made no attempt to sugar-coat the job that lay ahead. Despite the Pacific being the theatre which had brought the United States into the war, Kenney was told it was still regarded as a backwater by the government, with the lion's share of resources being directed to Europe and the defeat of Hitler.

Such supplies that would be delivered to Kenney's – and indeed MacArthur's – forces would be done so via a convoluted supply line stretching from the continental United States, transiting through Hawaii, Samoa and Fiji, until finally landing in Brisbane. The Japanese resupply route to New Guinea, by contrast, was both shorter and more direct: just a few days' sailing due south from the factories of Yokohama via secure sea lanes to Rabaul. They also had the advantage of their base of Truk in the Caroline Islands, which they had been building up since taking it from the Germans at the beginning of the last war in 1914.

Aircraft in particular, Kenney was told, would be difficult to obtain, so he was advised to grab any types which were not wanted for Europe, such as the underperforming Bell P-39 Airacobra fighter. Surprisingly, the brilliant P-38 Lightning was initially overlooked for Europe, so Kenney grabbed fifty or so of those before Arnold had time to realise his mistake. He also made sure that a few hand-picked pilots like Richard Bong accompanied them. Just to compound Kenney's problems, the first Lightnings delivered to Australia had faulty wings and, somewhat ironically, leaking leakproof fuel tanks, all problems which had to be rectified before they could be sent into combat.

Weaponry would also be an issue, so in the few days before he left the United States Kenney scoured the stores for anything capable of shooting or exploding. He was then surprised to discover 3000 parachute fragmentation, or 'parafrag', bombs languishing forgotten in an army warehouse outside Los Angeles. Seeing them listed way down on the Army Ordnance Inventory drew from him an ironic guffaw.

Fourteen years earlier, he had invented them.

In 1928, while still a humble captain espousing the advantages of low-level air attack at the Air Corps Tactical School in Virginia, Kenney began experimenting with attaching parachutes to 23-pound fragmentation bombs in order to slow their forward movement once they had been dropped from an aeroplane. The parachutes allowed for both greater accuracy as well as giving the pilot time to escape the explosion. Fitted with a super-sensitive fuse, the bomb would touch the ground, or even a leaf on a tree, detonating upright before breaking into around 1600 steel fragments about the size of a man's little finger, which could cut through just about anything. Even at a range of 100 yards, tests confirmed, a fragment could pass through a two-inch wooden plank. 'A wicked little weapon,' Kenney described it.

Despite his parafrags being initially received with enthusiasm, it would be another eight years before the first order of 5000 was put through, and these were quickly forgotten about, until rediscovered by Kenney himself on a list in July 1942.

'I was speculating about trying them out on some Jap airdrome and wondering if those fragments would tear airplanes apart, as well as Japs, too, if they didn't get out of the way,' he wrote. Before anyone else could get their hands on them, he arranged for the whole lot to be put on the next available ship to Australia. 'I think the Ordnance Department were actually glad to get rid of them.'

Pappy Gunn needed no convincing as to the likelihood of parafrags killing a good many Japanese soldiers, but the aircraft at his disposal lacked sufficient racks to carry them. To this problem too Gunn applied his immense skills, improvising a honeycomb grill arrangement in the B-25's belly to enable up to 100 to be carried, or half that number when mixed with conventional 250- or 500-pound bombs.

In Brisbane on 29 November, Kenney inspected the first of Gunn's modified B-25s, sprouting guns everywhere, and could see at once that this was the weapon he had been seeking to usher in a new era of low-level aerial warfare. He walked around it and noted the wry moniker which had been hand-painted on the nose: *Pappy's Folly*.

Folly or no, the new B-25 took to the air for the first of its trials, engines straining to lift the extra weight off the ground, with Gunn – now finally a qualified pilot with the US Army Air Force – at the controls. After a short flight, he approached the aerodrome in what Kenney noted to be a significantly 'nose down' attitude before thumping heavily onto the runway. Taxiing to a stop, the normally unflappable Gunn was pale and, in Kenney's words, 'sweating like a horse'.

'Er, how does she handle?' Kenney asked cautiously.

'Like a dream,' replied Gunn, barely missing a beat.

Impressed by his bravado, but not convinced for a moment, Kenney's concern shifted to the barely trained young men who lacked Gunn's formidable pilot skills, but who would be required to fly his contraption regardless. Kenney tried to offer practical advice and asked about the aircraft's centre of gravity.

'Centre of gravity?' echoed Gunn. 'Hell, we threw that away to lighten up the ship.'

Several weeks of flight trials now ensued, in which new problems with *Pappy's Folly* presented themselves, such as the nose wheel door suddenly falling off as soon as the guns were fired, and the ongoing problems of needing to squeeze a very large amount of weaponry into a very small space. To remedy the nose-heavy trim, lead weights were placed aft, and three of the side blister guns were moved back towards the tail.

John Arbon flew with the 3rd Attack Group's 13th Bombardment Squadron a.k.a. The Grim Reapers, a nickname which adorned their aircraft alongside the illustration of an appropriately lurid skeleton enthusiastically wielding a scythe from on high. In his somewhat colourful memoir, *The Bismarck Sea Ran Red*, Arbon described flying several test flights with Gunn, as well as participating in many subsequent battles. At their very first meeting, Gunn flouted the strict regulation forbidding smoking by chomping down on one of his ubiquitous cigars even while working on the aircraft. At this point, says Arbon, he correctly sensed that he was dealing with no conventional Army Air Corps officer. By the time they got into the air, his opinion had hardened somewhat, and he was soon convinced he was in fact flying with 'some kind of nut'.

'It would be the roughest flight of my life,' wrote Arbon. 'This Major Gunn was the roughest, wildest, toughest airplane driver in the Pacific. It was clear he had never learned to fly in any US Army Air Corps cadet school ... He made that B-25 fly as a pursuit plane in an acrobatic show.'

At zero feet above the sea, Gunn put his creation through the rigours, flying upside down, straight up and standing on the rudder pedals. Priding himself on being in possession of an iron stomach, Arbon was airsick for the first time in his career. 'We did vertical and horizontal loops, spins, dives and many near-stalls.' He asked Gunn several times if he was trying to kill them both.

'Don't worry, we'll be okay,' came the reply.

When they tested the newly installed ordnance, Arbon could barely believe the effect. 'The recoil of our awesome firepower braked the airplane as if full flaps had just been applied.' Looking forward from the single remaining top turret, he watched as Gunn put the aircraft into a steep dive, then opened the weaponry up on an outcrop of coral on the outer Barrier Reef. Joining in with the two in the turret, Arbon watched as ten forward-firing .50-calibre guns concentrated on the same spot. In a shudder of metal, water and white spray, the coral reef simply 'disappeared'. Arbon was stunned, and went to say something over the intercom but was interrupted.

'Pilot to radio, that's great,' said Gunn. 'Let's try it again.'

Swearing this would be both his first and last flight with Gunn, Arbon decided to stay, soon gaining enormous respect for the 'old man'. Despite his gruff exterior, Gunn was always polite and rarely lost his temper. Arbon soon knew he was in the hands of the most capable of pilots.

Arbon went on to assist Gunn with other teething issues with the new attack aircraft, such as the extra 450-gallon fuel tank which took the place of the redundant rear turret. Though vastly improving the range, once under attack or over the target area, a single Japanese incendiary bullet or piece of shrapnel could quickly turn the tank into a fireball. A system of rails and shackles was thus installed for it to be released in a hurry. But in tests it was found that suction created by the aircraft's airflow held it in place and prevented it from falling free. At one stage Arbon resorted to tying a rope around his waist, securing the other end to the airframe and kicking the tank out. Slowly, after much trial and error, these and other problems with the modified aircraft were solved.

From an adequate but unremarkable bombing platform, Gunn and Kenney had transformed the B-25 Mitchell into the most heavily armed aircraft in the world at the time. The next stage in its development would allow it to accurately place a bomb on a ship.

'If the airplane still flew and the guns would shoot,' said Kenney, 'I figured I'd have a skip-bomber that could overwhelm the deck defenses of a Jap vessel as the plane came in for the kill with its bombs.'

Months later, on one of his visits to the United States, Kenney would urge the Mitchell's manufacturers at North American Aviation to incorporate Gunn's new features at the factory level, to save him the headache of having to convert them one by one in the field. After examining the drawings, Kenney was flatly told in a meeting with the company's engineers in General Arnold's office that what he was proposing was not physically possible, and that any such 'amendments' would render the B-25 both unairworthy and unflyable. After remaining silent for a while, Kenney informed them that he currently had a dozen or more of these 'unflyable' aircraft conducting missions and blasting the Japanese in the South West Pacific.

'Arnold glared at his engineering experts and practically ran them out of the office,' recalled Kenney. Later, Gunn would return to the United States to show them just how to make his 'impossible' improvements to the B-25 a reality. The result would be the B-25 'C1' variant.

Until such time as the factory could begin modifications themselves, though, Kenney ordered Gunn to get working on several dozen more, and gave him the men and the means to do so. From now on, the new bombers were given a name that would eventually become legendary. Kenney and Pappy Gunn's new air weapon was known as the 'commerce destroyer'.

All Kenney needed to do now was train his men to fly it.

CHAPTER 10
GARING GETS TO WORK

Bull Garing was given little time to reacquaint himself with home life after his return from England after his eventful tour with Coastal Command. Returning to Australia in April 1941, he had barely greeted his newborn son and posed for a few publicity shots for his local paper before he found himself standing before the desk of the RAAF's formidable Director of Operations, Air Marshal Frank Bladin, being briefed as to what use the air force intended to now make of him. Beside him was Air Commodore Frank Lukis, a large man with a friendly face and an almost comically large moustache. On Lukis's chest was an assortment of ribbons denoting his service in World War I, as well as the purple and white bars of the Distinguished Flying Cross.

As the air marshal spoke, the two men sensed the weight of responsibility being lowered onto their shoulders.

Sensing that sooner or later the war would reach Australia, the RAAF began – slowly and belatedly – to prepare. Realising the impracticality of trying to run its meagre resources from its headquarters in Melbourne, in early 1941 the RAAF established four separate geographical areas of command, the most vital of which would encompass Queensland, parts of New South Wales, the Northern Territory and, significantly, the Australian territories of Papua and New Guinea, including Port Moresby.

Dubbed Northern Area Command, it would be the crucible of the coming struggle with Japan. Air Marshal Bladin told Lukis and Garing they were to proceed to Townsville to set it up. Lukis would be appointed Northern Area Command's first air officer commanding, while Garing would serve as senior air staff officer. The task, Bladin said, would not be easy. Australia's traditional ally Britain – he reminded them – was tied up in a war of her own on the other side of the world and could no longer be relied upon, while our own forces were drastically unprepared and under-resourced. Not only that, the public was complacent and the local politicians, Bladin correctly predicted, would be less than cooperative with the idea of the military establishing a new headquarters in the middle of Townsville. As the two men left Bladin's office, he wished them luck but added, 'Make sure you win; don't come back if you don't.'

Air Commodore Lukis, although popular and a fine administrator, had the good sense to realise his lack of any operational experience in the current war. Soon after their appointments, he made a pact with Garing.

'Look, Bill,' he said, 'you're highly experienced in this type of modern warfare. You look after the war, I'll look after the people.'

The partnership worked well. Northern Area Command acquired a somewhat grand but vacant three-storey Victorian-era drapers building in Sturt Street to use as their HQ. It was here Garing oversaw the establishment of Australia's first War Operations Room, the template for which he had observed firsthand in England. After completing his tour in Coastal Command, he'd spent several months attached to the RAF learning its procedures, in particular, the functions of its operational control rooms. Presciently believing such facilities would one day be needed back home, Garing went so far as to purloin some original RAF forms and stationery, which he had duly reprinted in Townsville.

Just as Air Marshal Bladin had predicted, the local MP for the seat of Darling Downs was completely opposed to the idea of an HQ in Townsville and did his best to derail it.

Famous for being little more than a man whose ambitions soared stratospherically above his talent, Arthur Fadden was one of Australia's most ineffective leaders, loathed by just about everyone, but no one more so than the parliamentary members of the conservative Country Party, which he happened to lead. Within a few months he would, amazingly and by sheer default, be made prime minister – but only as a stopgap for forty forgettable days before John Curtin assumed the role in October 1941.

In Townsville Fadden saw his chance to decry interference in Queensland's affairs by the power brokers from the southern states, and quietly fomented local resentment towards the RAAF's new HQ. The idea gained some traction until the town was bombed by the Japanese in mid-1942, after which the RAAF was implored upon for protection.

Back in May 1941, despite resistance from a parochial politician, Garing took to his task of establishing Australia's first Combined Defence Headquarters with gusto. Later, when Japan entered the war, he would establish the Operations and Signal Centre to control the movement of ships and aircraft within Australia and beyond. This remarkable facility, cryptically codenamed 'Project 81', was constructed completely underground in total secrecy at the dead end of a suburban street. It replicated closely the RAF Fighter and Bomber Command Operations Rooms Garing had observed in Britain, even – courtesy of his foresight – down to the requisite forms and stationery.

Just as in Britain, the local Australian operators were trained to write essential details in reverse on a glass wall, which would be read by planners and controllers on the other side. In the centre of the room was a large table with a map covering Northern Australia, New Guinea and beyond, giving real-time details of ships as well as squadrons, airfields and their various states of readiness. To disguise it from above, an entire suburban house was constructed, which also served as officers' accommodation with a secret entrance down to the operations room below.

Garing would eventually be called much further afield than Townsville. When Japan entered the war, Australia went almost overnight from peaceful backwater to virtual frontline nation. The military divisions were split further to establish North Eastern and North Western commands and Garing would travel as far as Hawaii to liaise with his new ally, the United States.

In August 1941, while onboard the US carrier *Enterprise* as the guest of Admiral William Halsey, of whom he remembered his 'piercing blue eyes and pleasant voice', Garing was quizzed about every aspect of his operational experience, from tactics to weapons, personalities to politics. '[Halsey] wanted to know who was fighting, what with, and how,' Garing recalled. He was shocked to learn of the deep antipathy that existed between the various branches of the US services, a situation openly propagated by the most senior officers and which permeated down to the lowest ranks. The navy detested the army, which detested the air force, and everybody, it seemed, detested the Marines. In bars, men in one uniform would avoid socialising or even talking to those in another. Garing thought the situation was appalling, not to mention destructive, and vowed to do everything he could to prevent such a culture taking hold among the Australian forces.

•

If General Kenney thought introducing skip bombing to his air force would be an easy task, he was in for a shock, with some of even his most senior officers strongly opposed to the idea. 'General Walker was not for it,' he wrote. 'He was an old bombardment man himself and, as an instructor at the Air Corps Technical School, had written the book on bombardment tactics and was a great believer in high-altitude formation bombing. It was an excellent method for a big target like an aerodrome or a town but not so good against a turning, twisting target like a moving vessel on an open sea.'

Other officers were equally opposed but for different reasons. Colonel Richard Carmichael, commander of the three squadrons of the 19th Bombardment Group, was so worried about the poor morale among his airmen after a dismal and debilitating tour of operations – beginning with defeat and retreat in the Philippines – he feared that 'introducing a new method of attack would break them'.

This was not Kenney's only problem. Simply locating certain elements of his command was proving a task in itself, as some seemed to exist only on paper. 'After two weeks in the job,' he wrote, 'I found out that there was supposed to be another heavy bombardment group in the theatre, the 43rd, but all they had left was the flag and a couple of guys to hold it up.' Having 'run out of airplanes' two months earlier, the 43rd Bombardment Group's personnel had been scattered over Australia performing duties such as watching over supply dumps, manning weather stations, in fact 'everything but what they were trained for'. Kenney would make the rebuilding of the 43rd a priority in the coming months, but expecting them to master a difficult new technique like skip bombing was out of the question.

Kenney also needed to familiarise himself with that other fighting force he would be working alongside in his new role, the Royal Australian Air Force. He knew little of Australia or its people, but appreciated the Australians had been in the war two years longer than the Americans, and that their airmen – though under-resourced, with few decent aircraft of their own to fly – were well trained, and notably superior to US airmen in areas such as air navigation.

Kenney's predecessor, General George Brett, had allowed deep levels of integration between the USAAF and RAAF, and already hundreds of Australian aircrew were flying with American units, sharing experience and engendering great respect between the two organisations. MacArthur, however, hated the practice and used it as one of the reasons to remove Brett and replace him with Kenney. Despite the useful exchange of skills and experience, MacArthur believed American aircraft should be crewed by American airmen only. The proposal to put Australian pilots in charge of American crews was the last straw, and further contributed to Brett's dismissal.

Kenney was not personally averse to the practice but, mindful of MacArthur's paranoiac obsession with disloyalty, had no intention of pushing the policy. Irrespective, many Australian airmen would continue to fly with the USAAF, distinguishing themselves in actions such as the Bismarck Sea and beyond.

•

Landing at the Allied base at Seven Mile Strip in Port Moresby for the first time after his appointment, Kenney wondered how the soldiers were faring following months of Japanese attack in a difficult tropical war zone. If he had expected them to be beaten down or skittish, however, he was quickly corrected.

Riding in a jeep towards the mess tent along the extended runway at Seven Mile Strip after landing, he asked his driver to pull up next to an Australian soldier seated atop a bulldozer in the process of constructing a large circular wall just off the main strip. Observing with curiosity for a while, Kenney asked the bare-chested soldier what he was doing.

'Yeah, we got one of them delay-action bombs down there in the ground and it ain't gone off,' said the soldier, apparently oblivious to Kenney's exalted rank. 'The engineers have dehorned most of the others, but this is a new breed they don't know about, so I'm just putting a bit of dirt around her so she'll fizz straight up when she goes off.' After a moment of stunned silence, Kenney thanked the soldier, and told his driver to proceed to the mess tent, posthaste.

After greeting the man he had put in charge of his air forces in New Guinea, his good friend General Ennis Whitehead, Kenney began to familiarise himself with the problems of fighting in one of the world's most remote battlefronts. For starters, supply was a nightmare, according to an older mechanic sergeant who had served on one of the B-25 squadrons. Five of their aircraft were currently sitting like lame ducks on the runway because they needed new wheel bearings.

'Sergeant,' Kenney said, 'I know about it and there are just no wheel bearings in supply here or in Australia.' The sergeant – whose actual name has sadly been lost to history – simply grinned. 'But General, I know where there are some.'

Kenney was all ears.

It turned out that the previous month a near-new B-25 had gone down near a plateau called Bena Bena in the central highlands. The location wasn't far from a small airstrip onto which a good enough pilot could land a Dakota transport. The sergeant assured Kenney that the B-25 was in good condition and with some rations, a tool kit and 'a couple of Tommy guns', he could salvage the wheel bearings and perhaps some other useful equipment besides. Kenney warmed to the man and gave his permission for the mission, which would need to be conducted perilously close to the Japanese bases at Lae and Salamaua.

The Bena Bena runway had been carved out of the jungle only twelve years earlier by possibly mad gold prospectors. It was close to villages inhabited, according to Kenney, 'by partially reformed cannibals', whose loyalties were undetermined. Although he had some reservations, Whitehead agreed to the mission, and it was decided it should be attempted under the cover of the next raid on Salamaua. Everyone was to pray hard that the Japanese were not patrolling the area at the time.

The mission would be led by a Lieutenant Hampton, a hotshot young sunglasses-wearing troop carrier pilot who said little but who, Kenney was assured, could 'land and take off a DC-3 out of a good-sized well'.

Four days later, the aircraft departed Seven Mile Strip with Hampton, a co-pilot, the sergeant and three of his most reliable 'grease monkeys'. The men were given a sober briefing as to the acute dangers they could well be facing, and were told that they were under no obligation to go.

All were still keen.

After a short, low-level flight over the jungle, Hampton pulled up safely on the Bena Bena runway. The men disembarked then proceeded up a jungle track. Fearing they may be attacked at any time, Hampton and his co-pilot pointed their Tommy guns out the windows and kept the engines warm in readiness for a quick getaway.

The expedition's allotted hour passed, then another with no sign of the soldiers. Perhaps the Japanese had arrived, or perhaps the natives, in Kenney's words, 'had decided the white man had lost the war and joined the Japs. Perhaps there was a meat shortage at Bena Bena ...'

Just as Hampton had decided enough was enough and was getting ready to depart, his sergeant came running out of the jungle.

'Hold everything, Lieutenant!' he cried, 'the gang will be here in a minute.' Hampton and his co-pilot glanced at each other, then the three mechanics appeared, accompanied by what appeared to be a small army of Papuan natives, each laden with aircraft parts of all description.

The sergeant hadn't just found the B-25 and its wheel bearings, he'd also stumbled across a downed P-39 Airacobra in reasonable condition. When approached by some local tribespeople, not only had they shown no particular inclination to devour either him or his men, but had offered to help carry the parts the 5 miles back to the Dakota. With strong arms and smiling faces, the Papuans appeared to have brought back most of both crashed aircraft. On top of shoulders were mounted wheels, landing struts, flight instruments, rudders, ailerons, sheets of cut aluminium for repair work and, of course, the precious wheel bearings.

A few hours later, Hampton and his heavily laden Dakota landed at Seven Mile Strip and disgorged enough salvaged spare parts to put five B-25s and three Airacobras back into commission.

•

After several weeks of invaluable assistance in establishing his command in Australia, Kenney summoned his 'aide', Major Benn, and told the man that he was fired. Benn was delighted to hear these words. Although having proved expert at holding the general's overcoat and laying out his trousers in the morning, Kenney regarded the airman as too valuable an asset for him to monopolise and, true to his promise, posted him to the 63rd Bombardment Squadron as a B-17 Fortress pilot.

Kenney had chosen the unit carefully. The new 63rd had only begun to receive its aircraft in August 1942, and by all indications it wasn't performing well. It had supported Australian ground troops around the battles of Buna and Gona, but its successes against Japanese targets were few, and morale was predictably low. Attacks on the Japanese base at Rabaul were undertaken, but flying at night and at high altitude – as well as operating as single, uncoordinated aircraft – seemed to Benn about as effective as hurling rocks in a fog.

The Japanese had no reason to fear them.

By the beginning of September, possibly due to the influence of his former boss, William Benn was appointed the 63rd's commanding officer.

Immediately he determined to use the squadron in a very new way of bombing.

CHAPTER 11
THE SKIP-BOMBING PIONEERS

Seven months later, a secret report prepared by the Fifth Air Force on skip bombing got straight to the point:

> It is Major William Benn, now missing in action, who can be credited with bringing skip bombing into this area ... he always had maintained that missions were flown to obtain results and that skip bombing would pay big dividends ...
>
> Benn's squadron had experienced many missions wherein they used glide bombing and he was not sold on this method against enemy shipping. Experiments in this new type of attack were approved by the Commanding General of the Fifth Air Force and special fuses were ordered to be made by the Australians.

Tragically, Benn would not live to see the results of his efforts.

On the morning of 18 January 1943, he took off on a reconnaissance mission to the north coast of New Guinea and crashed into one of the thousands of treacherous fog-shrouded peaks of the Owen Stanleys.

•

But back in September 1942, when he took command of the 63rd, Benn determined to transform it into a crack skip-bombing unit. He told his men they were going back to the drawing board as far as flying and bombing were concerned. It would take time, he said to his demoralised airmen, but by the end they would be the best ship-busters in the air force. The problems facing him were enormous, but he was determined to learn and perfect the technique along with his men.

First, he needed to ascertain the ideal altitude and speed for the release of a bomb, and selected a lonely sandbar off a deserted Queensland beach on which to practise. In the bomb bay of his B-17, he arranged for both 100- and 500-pound bombs to be hung. He made his first run at 300 feet, with a small 100-pounder hitting the water about 100 feet from the target. The bomb was observed to 'torpedo into the water and disappear'.

Next, he dropped three more of the smaller bombs at an indicated air speed of 225 mph, at the slightly lower altitude of 250 feet. These hit the water and bounced up into the air about 75 feet, passing harmlessly over the target.

On his third approach, Benn asked his bombardier to select a single 500-pounder, and asked one of his gunners to climb down into the belly ball turret with a stopwatch and measure with as much precision as he could the time between the first and second impacts. 'Three and one quarter seconds … three and three-quarter seconds …' the gunner counted, with the navigator looking through the drift sight in the nose, marking down the notations.

Round and round again flew Benn, each time lowering his airspeed: 225 miles an hour … 220 … 215 … Sometimes a bomb changed its course upon hitting the water, or even tumbled backwards. After emptying his bomb load, he headed back to base, sensing he was on the verge of cracking the secret of a new method of aerial warfare.

William Benn's trials would be one of the last times the B-17 was used for this purpose. As fine an aeroplane as it was, he and Kenney realised that it was simply too slow and unwieldy, and presented far too large a target for any shipborne anti-aircraft defence with enough forward defensive firepower. Thankfully, the Fifth Air Force now possessed not one but two aircraft more suited to the job: Pappy Gunn's heavily modified, gun-bristling A-20 Havocs and B-25 Mitchells. They were faster, and if their manoeuvrability did not put off the Japanese gunners, the immense storm of lead being hurled at them from the aircraft's forward guns surely would.

It was now time to introduce the concept to the men.

•

'I found I had another fireball, in the 3rd Attack Group, named Major Ed Larner,' Kenney writes in his extensive and at times overblown memoir, *General Kenney Reports*. Kenney wasn't exaggerating, however, when it came to Major Edward

L Larner, one of the most courageous and colourful American pilots of the Pacific War. Even before beginning actual combat flying, Larner had acquired a reputation for almost superhuman resilience. While still in training in Louisiana, he was flying an A-20 on a low-level practice mission when his eyes were drawn momentarily away from the windshield. Looking back, he saw a tree right in front of him, which he proceeded to plough straight through.

Another pilot, Jack Taylor, who flew with Larner, recalled the incident. '[Larner] went through that tree ... just cruised right through it ... he was going well over 200 miles an hour and ended up in a sort of semi-clearing full of stumps.'

Larner survived the crash, but his young bombardier in the nose did not. Emerging from the twisted wreckage, Larner was approached by two local Cajuns who had heard the noise. Larner picked up a piece of wood from near a stump, wielding it like a weapon. 'Don't get too close to me or I'll kill you ...' he said, before asking for help. According to Taylor, Larner had 'a broken back, arm, shoulder, ribs, and in about three weeks was out shooting skeet. I mean he must have been put together with steel cables. Toughest man I ever met in my life.'

Whether Kenney met Larner in the United States and arranged for him to be sent out to Australia, or was introduced to him in Queensland via Pappy Gunn, is unclear, but the two mavericks – differences in age and rank notwithstanding – clicked from the start.

'The lad was a bit cocky, bragged some, and swaggered, too,' recalled Kenney, 'but it was all right with me. He had a right to.' According to historian Lex McAulay, Larner 'sometimes dispensed with the usual military methods of justice and punishment, and took wrong-doers out of sight to settle the disagreement with fists'.

True or not, it was indisputable that Ed Larner was tough enough – and possibly mad enough – to assist Gunn in testing his doctored 'commerce destroyer' Mitchells and Havocs, then taking them into action. One of these missions in Buna in late 1942 became part of the (then) Captain Larner legend.

While leading his squadron on a strafing attack against Japanese artillery and machine-gun positions, an anti-aircraft shell burst directly under Larner's tail, tipping the already heavily weighted nose section of the A-20 forward into a line of treetops at the end of his strafing run. Fighting the aircraft's desire to hit the ground, Larner applied full throttle and the aircraft mowed its way through a hundred yards or more of foliage before he managed to gain altitude and bring the plane back to Port Moresby.

With damaged flaps and control surfaces, Larner's landing speed touched on a terrifying 175 miles an hour, but somehow he managed to survive that too. Taxiing up to the dispersal, his ground crew couldn't believe their eyes. The Havoc, like a beaten-up jalopy from a comedy film, limped and spluttered to a stop, losing a few more bits and pieces in the process. Both engine cowlings were full of leaves and branches, and deep grooves ran the length of the underside fuselage. The wings had been bashed in, leaving the ground crew shaking their heads at how the thing managed to fly at all.

Kenney was summoned to inspect the aircraft before it was written off and stripped for what usable parts remained. 'That plane was one of the worst-looking wrecks still flying that I'd ever seen,' he said. 'Ninety-nine out of a hundred pilots would have bailed out before trying to land it.'

Kenney promoted Larner to the rank of Major on the spot and awarded him the Silver Star.

Larner was somewhat more nonchalant about the episode. 'Following this accident I was able to make only two more strafing passes before the plane became so unmanageable that I thought it best to return to base where repairs could be made.'

Kenney was never one to allow rank to impede his admiration of subordinates he considered cast in the same mould as himself, even when the reports of their exploits wandered into the realm of the implausible. 'Larner was at it again,' he wrote. 'He came back from a strafing attack around Buna with his tail bumper all scratched up where he had dragged it through the sand making a "low" pass at a Jap machine-gun position which had a heavy coconut-log overhead covering. Larner said he had to "look in the windows of the bunker to see what to shoot at".'

Exaggeration or not, it was clear that Kenney had found just the man he needed to train his airmen in skip bombing. He gave Larner his own squadron, the 90th, to do so. Further consolidating his faith in the young leader, Kenney arranged the bulk of the nominally 'Dutch' B-25s Gunn had 'acquired' in Melbourne to be converted to super-strafers in Queensland and placed under Larner's command.

'On 29th December Ed Larner flew the B-25 eight-gun job to Port Moresby,' wrote Kenney. 'I made him a Major and put him in command of the 90th Squadron of the 3rd Attack Group, which I had designated to specialize in low-altitude work, including skip bombing. I told Larner I wanted him to sell the airplane and the strafing tactics to his squadron.'

Now all the ship-busting airmen needed was a ship on which to practise.

•

The 4700-ton steamer SS *Pruth* was built strong by the venerable J.L. Thompson and Sons of Sunderland in 1916. But even her sturdy steel hull proved no match for a wet season storm which her captain unwisely attempted to outrun as he left Port Moresby on New Year's Eve in 1923. Just 16 miles from the harbour mouth, the surging tide dragged her up onto a long shallow reef the chart listed as Nateara. Fearing she would break up, the captain pushed her further onto the coral, assisted by the swell. Eventually, with her screws out of the water, she stuck fast and held, and despite the best efforts of tugs over the next fortnight to wrench her free, there she would remain.

In time, people forgot the ship's name, simply referring to her great rusting flanks as the 'Moresby Wreck', a solemn reminder of the perils of sea travel to all those sailing to or from the Papuan capital. In the 1930s, the *Pruth* would feature as a backdrop to a Hollywood movie, then, in 1940, in a supreme irony, she came close to being sold to the Japanese for scrap metal, which would have undoubtedly returned to New Guinea two years later in the form of gun barrels and shrapnel.

Although the deal never went through, the Japanese eventually managed to find some use for the *Pruth*. On

28 February 1942, six Zeros formed a circle over the wreck, then one by one dived towards her, testing their twin guns and cannon on her flanks. Satisfied, they re-formed and swooped low into Port Moresby Harbour. They were watched curiously by the ground crews servicing Catalinas from 11 and 20 squadrons who, having never seen a modern fighter of any description, assumed them to be American. In two deadly strafing attacks, three RAAF personnel were killed, several more were wounded and three irreplaceable Catalinas were set ablaze at their moorings. Both the 11 and 20 squadrons were so decimated, they were withdrawn to Australia.

Nine months later, still largely intact despite twenty years of plundering and target practice, the old *Pruth* would be given one final incarnation: she would be used in teaching young American and Australian airmen the technique of low-level bombing and strafing.

Throughout the final months of 1942, Major Ed Larner and his 90th Squadron repeatedly tormented the poor old *Pruth*. In their nose-heavy B-25 C1 commerce destroyers, they practised hitting the wreck from every angle and every combination of height, speed and distance. This time, however, they were practising with live bombs, and the danger of mistiming a drop and being caught in the explosion was very real.

Back at the base at Port Moresby, endless hours were spent debating the correct fuse timings. Set too soon and it would explode as it hit the water; set too late would see it tear open the belly of the plane which had just dropped it.

After much trial and error, it was accepted that a tail fuse with a four-second delay would provide the minimal distance of 700 feet from the detonation of 100- and 500-pound aerial bombs. As more and more bombs were required for practice, the 3rd Attack Group armaments men complained they were running out of detonators to fit to their M106-type fuses. In the spirit of invention, Kenney rang around to discover that while no more American detonators were currently in the country, Australian detonators worked brilliantly and so were ordered in number.

As Larner and his men honed their low-flying attack skills on what was left of the *Pruth*, two important conclusions were arrived at. First, the skip-bombing method could only ever be as effective as its ability to suppress the anti-aircraft defences of the ship they were attacking. Thus, while the ten guns of a single commerce destroyer certainly packed a punch, twenty guns sounded a good deal better. The pilots would therefore train to deliver a double punch, flying in pairs along a perpendicular angle, the first aircraft strafing the ship from stem to stern moments before the second struck from the beam, releasing the bomb which would skip over the water and – hopefully – destroy it.

The second conclusion was both simpler and far more dangerous. To be absolutely certain of hitting the target almost every time, the airmen believed they would need to fly far lower than the height prescribed by the skip-bombing theory. Whereas a bomb launched from a couple of hundred feet above the water could often go astray, at sea level it was far more likely to hit its target. At just a few yards above the surface, it was often not even necessary to 'skip' it at all, rather fling it horizontally, 'like a bullet', as one airmen said – straight into the superstructure, or beside the hull where the delay fuse would allow it to sink and explode just below the surface.

Yet another new term now entered the South West Pacific air war lexicon – 'mast-high bombing'.

•

In late 1942 and early 1943, Kenney directed his New Guinea commander, General Ennis Whitehead, to oversee a training regime whereby hundreds of airmen of the US Fifth Air Force would throw out all they had learned about bombing and start again from scratch. Instead of steadily cruising at altitudes above 15 000 feet, they would develop the low-level attacks of parafrag, skip and mast-high bombing.

One of those airmen was John Arbon of the 13th 'Grim Reaper' Bombardment Squadron who, having risked his life with Gunn as they demolished several Queensland coral reefs, would now hone his skip-bombing skills on the *Pruth*. In his colourful memoir, Arbon wrote, 'Our speed is well over 300 mph and the ship zooms up to meet us … the hulk momentarily explodes into a cloud of dust and smoke as the bomb in a spin bounces high off the water once, twice, three times …'

Eventually, according to Arbon, the airmen of the 3rd Attack Group would become so confident of their new skills that they boasted once to a group of deeply sceptical ground soldiers that they could hit a target three times out of four – and next time it would be four out of four. The soldiers were assured that this technique would prove a good deal more destructive than any other way of bombing. 'Yeah,' snarled one cynic. 'And a helluva lot more dangerous, too.'

The soldiers' observations were indeed correct, and the many hours of training on the *Pruth* did not come without cost. One of the first fatalities was Flight Lieutenant Vernon Morgan flying an Australian Boston from 22 Squadron. Taking off from Ward's airstrip outside Port Moresby, Morgan was on his first run when, without warning, his aircraft exploded, possibly due to a faulty bomb fuse. Morgan and his two Australian crewmen were killed instantly.

Then, in the first week of February 1943, 2nd Lieutenant Frederick Schierloh of New Jersey made an accurate pass over the *Pruth*, but as he pulled up the tail of his B-25 clipped the old ship's mast, ripping off the entire rear section of the aircraft and sending it spinning at high speed into the sea. Schierloh and his crew of two were also killed.

Second Lieutenant Gordon McCoun was luckier. On 21 February, his B-25 was directly above the *Pruth* when one of his 300-pound bombs exploded prematurely, damaging both of the aircraft's engines. McCoun quickly hit the 'salvo' switch, releasing the rest of the bomb load as one. Suddenly lightened, the B-25 reared upwards and remained airborne for another 25 miles, before McCoun put her down by ditching onto a shallow coral reef. His mixed crew of two RAAF personnel and a civilian passenger were rescued, unharmed, a few hours later.

The undersides of many other aircraft would be peppered with rusting pieces of old iron but the education acquired by the young Australian and American airmen above the *Pruth* was invaluable. In spite of the progress, some of Kenney's colleagues still needed convincing. The commander of his bomber force, Brigadier General Kenneth Walker, was a sceptic to the last. An old advocate of high-altitude strategic bombing, Walker had to be taken out to the wreck of the *Pruth* personally to view the results himself.

One afternoon after witnessing a series of dummy attacks, Kenney and Walker travelled by launch to within a mile of the wreck. They were rowed the rest of the way over the shallows by a corporal. As they approached the still-smoking hulk, Kenney pointed out jagged tears in the metal, just formed by the perfectly placed skip bombing of his pilots.

Impressed, Walker finally relented. 'Okay, you win. I'm convinced,' he admitted to a gloating Kenney. Duly satisfied, Kenney turned to the young NCO holding the oars. 'Corporal, come back here and sit in the stern with me. General Walker is rowing us back to the motorboat.'

Kenney had successfully rebuilt his air force, and convinced some of the naysayers as to the effectiveness of his new techniques.

Now he just needed a Japanese convoy to attack.

CHAPTER 12
THE JAPANESE PREPARE

This will send chills through our conceited enemy. The message sent by Eighth Area Army Commander Lieutenant General Hitoshi Imamura at Rabaul to Tokyo speaks to the renewed confidence felt by the Japanese in the South West Pacific in the first weeks of 1943.

In addition to the success of their January convoy to Lae, the Imperial Japanese Navy had demonstrated its prowess in a brilliant series of destroyer operations which successfully evacuated most of their remaining force at Guadalcanal. Further convoys had landed fresh forces and supplies at the coastal stronghold of Madang, and in December a four-ship convoy had sailed into Wewak to land 2000 troops of the 20th Division completely unopposed. While the battle of Wau had been unsuccessful, the Japanese believed it to have been very much a 'near run thing' in which bad luck – in the form of the courageous stand taken by the scandalously under-recognised

Captain Bill Sherlock and the timely arrival of American transport planes – had played a significant part.

Next time, and with a larger force, they would be luckier.

The Allies were still punch-drunk after the exhausting 1942 campaigns, their equipment worn out and their naval presence pitiful. The slog at Buna had shown how difficult it was for men to capture heavily defended strongholds in the debilitating heat of the tropics, and Japanese planners knew that Western governments were, unlike their own, bound by a social contract which set limits on the number of casualties their people were prepared to accept.

Now, in northern New Guinea, the Japanese proposed to draw thousands more young Allied soldiers into a meat grinder.

Time was of the essence. If the Japanese could move quickly, play to their strengths and reinforce Lae before the Allies were able to recover, they had a good chance of being able to hold it, then restart their conquest of Port Moresby.

In February 1943, another convoy, at least twice the size of that of Operation 18, was proposed, which would once more hand Japan the initiative. In the curious ways of Japanese military nomenclature, it was titled Operation 81.

Breathtaking in its audacity, Operation 81 proposed to transport, in one bold move, five entire battalions – some 6000 fighting soldiers – of Lieutenant General Hidemitsu Nakano's 51st Infantry Division from their base at Rabaul nearly 500 miles by sea to Lae. It was a high-risk strategy, with the strength of Allied air power being well appreciated. Significant losses would be both expected and accepted. But the rewards for the Japanese, with the sudden injection of a massive force such as this to bolster their hopes of conquering New Guinea, were inestimable.

The move would include the division's entire headquarters section, as well as its signals and engineering units, field hospital, artillery and anti-aircraft regiments along with all their equipment.

Another 1000 men of the specialised assault units of the Yokosuka 5th Special Naval Landing Force or SNLF – Japan's so-called 'Marines' – and the Maizuru 2nd SNLF would also be carried, as well as nearly 1500 non-combat personnel including Korean dock workers and debarkation units, army signals units, several shipping engineer regiments, and airfield construction battalions.

The supplies and equipment to be transported would include over 8000 cubic metres of aviation and other types of fuel in 1600 separate drums, and 500 cubic metres each of machine oil, ammunition, aircraft materials, and hundreds of aircraft drop tanks. A small example of the weaponry to be carried included five 150-mm howitzers, three 100-mm cannons, two field guns, three motor cars, two tractors, and no fewer than twenty-three trucks. For the landing operations, the ships' holds and decks would carry thirty-four large Daihatsu motorised landing barges, forty collapsible boats, twenty rowing boats and 1500 floating drums. Add to this several hundred machine guns of various calibre, mortars and thousands of rifles.

No less than eight transport vessels were assembled, ranging from the small coaster *Kembu Maru* at a little over 900 gross tons, to the coal transport *Nojima Maru* at nearly 9000 tons, which had just spent a year under repair after having her bow blown off by an American torpedo in the opening fortnight of the war.

The massive convoy would be split into two divisions, comprising:

No. 1 DIVISION
Shinai Maru (3793 Gross Registered Tons/GT)
Teiyo Maru (6869 GT)
Aiyo Maru (2746 GT)
Kembu Maru (915 GT)

No. 2 DIVISION
Kyokusei Maru (5493 GT)
Oigawa Maru (6493 GT)
Nojima Maru (8750 GT)
Taimei Maru (2883 GT)

With the Guadalcanal campaign now being wound up, the Imperial Japanese Navy was able to spare – albeit grudgingly – an escorting destroyer for each transport. These were:

From the 1923 *Fubuki* Class:
Shikinami (2000 tons)
Shirayuki (2000 tons)
Uranami (2000 tons)

From the 1934 *Asashio* Class:

Asashio (2400 tons)

Arashio (2400 tons)

Asagumo (2400 tons)

From the 1937 *Kagero* Class:

Yukikaze (2500 tons)

Tokitsukaze (2000 tons)

Some of these, particularly from the newer *Kagero* Class, were among the finest destroyers afloat, several powered by twin steam turbines capable of pushing the ships to speeds of up to 35 knots. Each carried a complement of between 200 and 240 officers and ratings, all of whom were veterans of some of the dozens of battles and engagements already fought by the Imperial Japanese Navy over the past two years and more. *Asagumo*, for example, had already fought in the Battle for the Java Sea, where she lost a boiler to British gunfire. After repairs, she was part of the fleet that engaged the US Navy in one of the most daring night attacks of the war at Guadalcanal, in which three American cruisers and four destroyers were sunk. *Uranami* had been credited with sinking two Dutch submarines in December 1941, and *Yukikaze* had sent three US warships to the bottom.

Lessons from past convoys would be learned. At Guadalcanal, one transport laden with food was sunk, resulting in Japanese soldiers starving for much of the campaign. Similarly, in the January convoy, the Okabe Detachment's entire supply of medical equipment went down on the *Nichiryu Maru* when it was struck by Dave Vernon's Catalina off Lae. Other New Guinea convoys had been so poorly organised that upon reaching their destination, the nervous soldiers were so quick to depart the ships to avoid Allied bombing that no one was left onboard to unload the cargo.

Operation 81 would be more carefully planned. There was to be a clear chain of command and a dedicated officer working with Rear Admiral Masatomi Kimura as transport commander in charge of all units for the duration of the voyage. Individual detachments would be broken up and dispersed across the various ships to prevent any single one being wiped out in its entirety if a vessel was lost. The destroyers too would assist in the transport of soldiers with six carrying at least 150 men each, with the remaining two carrying twenty-nine apiece. They would also be required to carry motorised barges and folding landing craft to expedite debarkation.

As his flagship, Kimura chose the *Fubuki* Class destroyer *Shirayuki*. When commissioned in 1928, the *Shirayuki* had been one of the most advanced warships in the world and was still a formidable weapon when the Pacific War erupted in late 1941. Meaning 'white snow', she had been given the considerable honour of being named after – of all things – Emperor Hirohito's pure white stallion, and her crew were hand selected and battle hardened. The *Shirayuki* had seen action in Malaya and Singapore, and had been credited with helping to sink the Australian cruiser *Perth* in the engagement in the Sunda Strait the previous March. It should have been with supreme confidence, therefore, that Rear Admiral Kimura stepped onboard the *Shirayuki* in Simpson Harbour, to the sharp salutes of her officers' company lined up in their crisp white uniforms on the main deck.

But, along with many of his fellow naval officers, the admiral harboured serious misgivings about Operation 81.

General Adachi's orders, which he had developed with his immediate superior, Eighth Area Army Lieutenant General Hitoshi Imamura, and in consultation with the Imperial General Staff in Tokyo, were outlined in his Operational Order A-157 issued on 22 February 1943. The 18th Army forces were to 'establish quickly a strong strategic disposition in the vicinity of Lae, Salamaua and the Markham Valley areas'. As soon as practicable after landing, troops would fan out and join existing Japanese forces, then move up to expand the perimeter along the banks of the Markham River.

General Adachi would be one of the first to arrive onboard the *Kagero* Class *Tokitsukaze*, along with the 51st Division's particularly fanatical commander, Lieutenant General Hidemitsu Nakano, onboard the largest of the destroyers, *Yukikaze*. Nakano's orders were blunt and simple: '… the division will make a vigorous landing in the vicinity of Lae at all costs …' Later in the year, when defending Salamaua against a final Allied advance, Nakano would be on the verge of burning his division's colours and directly ordering his men to die to a man rather than surrender to the Americans. This, even for the Japanese higher command, was too much and he was ordered instead to attempt a strategic withdrawal.

The orders also discussed securing the road between Lae and the secondary Japanese base at Salamaua, 30 or so miles south along the coast. In this aspect of the plan, however, the Japanese strategists would have most certainly been thwarted, as no such road existed, either then or now.

Once the main commanders were ashore, the 51st Division headquarters would be re-established and the fragile outpost of Lae would be consolidated into a new and formidable garrison from which the Japanese conquest of New Guinea would recommence.

A week later, a second, smaller convoy would sail from Rabaul to transport the bulk of the other major component of Adachi's 18th Army, the 20th Infantry Division, depositing them further north along the coast to reinforce another Japanese stronghold at Madang.

As this was to be one of the largest convoys the Japanese planned to put to sea in the South West Pacific, the destroyer escort was to be used to cover a wide variety of contingencies. If attacked by enemy surface vessels or submarines, the escorts were permitted to take either offensive or evasive action in coordination with the escort commander. Under expected enemy air attack, the destroyers were to lay down a smokescreen and direct their firepower against the attacking aircraft. This included dual-purpose 5-inch guns which could be trained upwards to deter high-level bombing attacks, although hampered by a low rate of fire and limits to the movement of the guns' turrets.

Japanese destroyers were also equipped with a number of lighter 25-mm or 13-mm anti-aircraft guns, but again lacked the concentrated punch which could cause serious damage to low-flying attack aircraft. Such deficiencies in their defences were recognised by the Imperial Japanese Navy at the time, but had not been acted upon by early 1943.

The best defence against air attack was still believed to lie with the ships' speed and manoeuvrability. So quick were the responses to the calls for evasive action from the bridge that it was often possible for lookouts to avoid bombs as they fell from above, the ship twisting and turning much like a modern-day speedboat. The destroyer crews were also by now seasoned defenders against exactly this type of aerial attack, having recently endured the cauldron of the many supply runs to Guadalcanal, in which they generally acquitted themselves well.

The merchant vessels were also, to some extent, capable of fighting off aircraft. Half would carry two anti-aircraft guns, a number of quick-firing pom-poms, and all had various numbers of mounted machine guns. To defend against a surface attack, some even carried what were described as 'field guns'. Even so, the sailors who crewed them were well aware of their limitations. Unlike the accompanying warships, the merchant vessels lacked armour plating and watertight doors. As one sailor put it, 'They had no armour-plating, no water-tight bulkheads, but were just small, toy, tinplate ships. If a bomb hit the target they immediately catch on fire.'

The other main aspect of defence for the ships of Operation 81 came from the air. Historical sources vary, but around 100 fighters – primarily Zeros and Oscars – were to be made available to escort the convoy. In the curious division of forces which at times plagued the Japanese ability to execute a coherent war strategy, both the army and the navy had their own air fighting branches, as well as parallel, and often incompatible, training and operational practitioners.

Fierce rivals from the start of the war to the very end, the mistrust between branches spread even to the radio equipment used, with the wireless sets carried by army pilots equipped with radio, being completely incompatible with those of the navy, and no one was capable of communicating effectively with the ships. Nevertheless, the army and navy would split between them the air escort duties required for Operation 81, dividing the job into two separate shifts to give their pilots a chance to rest. From first light at 5 a.m. until midday, navy pilots would provide escort duties, watching out for Allied bombers coming in at high level. With a one-hour overlap period, army pilots would then continue the protection until light failed around 6 p.m. The next morning, the shifts would be alternated. This would be repeated until the convoy reached its destination at Lae.

Japanese bombers would also play their part in suppressing Allied air activity. Attacks by Japanese medium and light bombers were proposed against Allied air bases at Port Moresby, Milne Bay, Dobodura and Wau. Moreover, the convoy's route would be reconnoitred by floatplanes, followed by submarine patrols which would interdict any Allied submarine activity.

Speed being one of the most critical elements of the planning, General Adachi made it clear to both his army commanders as well as those of the navy that he was prepared to go as soon as the convoy could be made ready. With the full contingent of ships yet to arrive from the various points of the empire, he therefore ordered the loading of the first ships to begin on 22 February, the same day he issued his Order A-157.

The heavier weaponry and ammunition were loaded first, followed by general cargo, then more ammunition, food and stores. In the final week of February, more ships gathered in Rabaul Harbour and the soldiers and stevedores went to work on them too. Each vessel was loaded with a variety of equipment to spread the load and prevent total loss of a single particular element, the sole exception being the small *Kembu Maru*, which was loaded entirely with over 1000 barrels of aviation fuel. This, it was reasoned, would be needed quickly by defending Japanese aircraft as the convoy entered its particularly vulnerable unloading phase at Lae.

The last element to be loaded would be the thousands of troops themselves, who would begin to come onboard, it was estimated, on 28 February. Adachi therefore decided the convoy would depart in the first dark hours of the next day, 1 March.

The final consideration on the part of the planners of Operation 81 was the route. Adachi was advised, to his considerable dismay, that the average speed of the convoy would be around 7 knots, meaning a nearly four-day voyage to cover the 500 or so miles to Lae. The successful January convoy had proceeded around the eastern tip of the island then taken the southern route along the coast, where greater protection from Japanese airstrips such as the large field at Gasmata could be relied upon.

This time, however, Adachi wished to cloak his intentions for as long as possible, hopefully deceiving the Allies into believing the convoy's destination was Madang, several hundred miles further along the coast, or the even more distant Wewak. It would be to these destinations, he hoped, that American long-range bombers would be sent, expending their fuel searching fruitlessly for a convoy that was far to the south.

Ideally, Adachi wanted to trick the Allies into thinking the convoy was intending to split in two, half going north, the other half going south. By the time their error had been realised, Adachi would be safely at Lae. Even if his passage along the northern coast of New Britain was discovered, it would force Allied aircraft to overfly the island itself to intercept him, thereby laying themselves open to attack from Japanese airfields situated there.

Only when the Japanese rounded the western end of New Britain and headed south into the stretch of water known as the Vitiaz Strait would the ruse be revealed and the real destination of Lae confirmed. In this, however, Adachi believed the gods to be smiling on him. In the last week of February, meteorological reports continued to predict a stretch of low, cloudy and wet weather all the way across the Bismarck Sea, providing the perfect cloak for a mixed convoy of sixteen merchantmen and warships.

The navy, however, found themselves decidedly unable to partake in the army's enthusiasm for the plan. Although having performed well in the recent and gruelling Guadalcanal campaign, they were under no illusions that the expanding American might they had witnessed there would not continue to grow, particularly in the air. And although the recent January convoy had rebuffed the bulk of Allied air attacks, the efforts of the American and Australian pilots had been both numerous and valiant. Eventually, the pilots would find a way to break through, and the Japanese naval commanders dreaded what the results would be when they did.

They also knew that their ships carried serious design flaws. The famous speed and agility of the destroyer fleet had been engineered as a trade-off against conventional shipbuilding defensive measures like thicker armour and integrated fire-fighting equipment, as was to be found on most comparable Allied warships. However, in the Japanese military code – which refused to countenance either failure or defeat – such defensive measures were looked upon as weaknesses, and the training of crews in measures which could very well save a ship were a low priority. Now, the Japanese naval commanders felt themselves slipping behind. The war at sea was evolving fast, and their increasingly antiquated doctrine was forcing an ever-widening gap between their own abilities and those of their enemies.

Of primary concern to the navy was the destination itself. Naval staff pointed out to Adachi that Lae was well within range of the bulk of Allied air power located at Port Moresby, and which would then inevitably be concentrated on the ships in their final leg. Yes, it had worked back in January, but with a smaller and faster convoy than this.

Alternatively, they had proposed the convoy's destination as Madang, a far more challenging target which would stretch the range of all but the larger US aircraft. But the army commanders baulked at this. Madang would necessitate their soldiers travelling overland across many hundreds of miles of rough and exhausting jungle tracks. The army would stick to its original plan of making a direct approach to Lae. It was expected the navy would supply all requisite assets to protect it.

The Japanese naval commanders at Rabaul shrugged their shoulders, bowed and complied.

•

In the early evening of 28 February 1943, the young Japanese soldiers of the six battalions of the 51st Infantry Division filed onboard the transports and destroyers. Several days had passed since their arrival, with many hours spent waiting in the heat of the tropical summer, and partaking in drills designed to master the difficult art of scrambling down the side of a ship into a bobbing landing craft in full kit, via a rope mesh ladder. Upon their arrival in Lae, they were expected to leave the ship quickly.

Finally, in darkness, the ships of the Lae Reinforcement Convoy, Operation 81, received the departure signal, weighed anchor, and sailed down the elongated hook of Rabaul's Simpson Harbour, then to port past the 700-foot sentinel of Mount Tavurvur, Rabaul's perilously active volcano which only six years earlier had erupted, killing over 500 people. The sickly odour of sulphur could be smelled by the men on the ships' upper decks, and many were happy to be departing its disconcerting presence.

Immediately outside the harbour on the stroke of midnight, 1 March, the convoy assembled in rough sailing order, with the destroyers *Shikinami* and *Uranami* out in front like sentinels. At first light, the daytime sailing formation would be adopted, the convoy's two divisions of cargo ships lining up in three pairs, some 900 yards apart. Not much more than a mile away at any time were the escorting destroyers, screening for enemy shipping, submarines and aircraft.

As the men grew accustomed to the steady throb of reverberating engines, they settled in, ate some of their rations, and tried to find a corner of the ship in which to steal a few hours' sleep.

CHAPTER 13

THE CONVOY SAILS

For his seminal work on the war in the South West Pacific and Battle of Kokoda, *Blood and Iron*, historian Lex McAulay was given permission to examine some of the Australian Army's wartime Allied Translator and Interpreter Section transcripts of prisoner of war interviews, bringing to light just a few of the individual Japanese soldiers and sailors who sailed from Rabaul on that fateful first day of March. Each gives a fascinating insight into how the Japanese themselves viewed the battle.

Onboard the *Teiyo Maru*, which at 6869 tons was one of the larger ships in the convoy, 24-year-old Superior Private Mikio Omiya sat on the floor of a crowded gangway wondering why the writing embedded into the ship's internal layout was in German, not Japanese. No one was able to inform him that the *Teiyo Maru* began life in 1924 as the *Saarland*, built in Hamburg and only recently purchased by a Tokyo shipping company. She was a large ship, but her crew of just over sixty deckhands and engine room attendants were vastly outnumbered by the nearly 2000 men of the 51st Division. Having been in the army for nearly three years, Omiya had seen fighting in China, but this was his first trip to the tropics. After two and a half months of waiting at the tedious outpost of Rabaul, he was glad to be finally leaving.

Also onboard the *Teiyo Maru* was a warrant officer from the 115th Regiment, Shichi-Hei Matsushima, who at thirty-nine was one of the oldest fighting soldiers in the division. Matsushima had thought his time soldiering was done, having also fought in the seemingly endless China war in the thirties. He then spent several peaceful years with the Nissan Motor Company, only to be recalled five months before the Pearl Harbor attack. Those days of peace now seemed far away indeed.

Having spent several years in the merchant fleet, Maduda Reiji was drafted into the navy and given the lowest possible officer rank, sub-lieutenant. His ship, the destroyer *Asashio*, was at least powerful, the first of ten almost identical *Asashio* Class vessels. None of this endeared Reiji to the ways of the navy, though. At the great Pacific naval base at Truk, he witnessed Japanese class divisions firsthand, with the old-school naval officers being given permanent stations onboard the great battleships like the *Yamato* and *Musashi* which never went to war, while lowly former merchantmen like Reiji were constantly being sent into the furnace of battle.

'People like us,' he wrote, 'graduates of the merchant marine school, were shipped off to the most forward positions, while those bastards from the Imperial Naval Academy sat around on their asses in the *Yamato* and *Musashi* "hotels".'

But the *Asashio*, Reiji knew, was a survivor. She had already fought in the Battle of Badung Strait, then the Philippines, then later Midway, where an American 500-pound bomb killed twenty-two crewmen. Reiji sailed with her into Guadalcanal and she survived that ordeal too. His optimism for the convoy and its outcome for Japan's prospects in New Guinea was high. 'If we could just get those troops and their heavy weapons there, they could turn back the Allies,' he wrote.

Onboard the almost brand new merchant ship the 2746-ton *Aiyo Maru*, 22-year-old Private Akio Fujiwara was already a veteran. Called up from Korea, where he was working on a fishing boat, he was deposited on a beach in January 1942 and fought his way down the Malayan Peninsula, eventually taking part in the capture of Singapore, a feat neither he nor any of his fellow soldiers could quite believe they had achieved.

More victories followed in the Philippines, but in early February Fujiwara's unit was detailed to sail to Rabaul. With only 250 or so soldiers with him onboard the *Aiyo Maru*, he had more room than most of the men on the accompanying ships, but such luxury was negated by the unsettling smell of aviation fuel which permeated everything. In fact, the ship was crammed with over 500 cubic metres of fuel in more than 350 drums, along with a similar amount of ammunition. As the cargo was intended to be used immediately after landing, it was stored, noted Fujiwara, high up in the ship. As well thought out as this was, Fujiwara dreaded to think what might happen should the *Aiyo Maru* come under enemy torpedo or air attack.

Morale among the more than 6500 soldiers onboard the convoy was good. This can be partly explained by the true state of Imperial Japan's recent losses and setbacks having been deliberately withheld from the common soldier. They were instead regaled with ebullient propaganda trumpeting the still-fresh victories of Malaya, Singapore and the Philippines, and promises of many more to come. Instead of the defeats of Midway and Buna, the Japanese soldier was told of the absurd number – dozens and dozens – of American and British cruisers, battleships and aircraft carriers which had been sent to the bottom. They also believed that Wau had already been taken, that Port Moresby had been wiped out by Japanese bombing and all Australian air power annihilated. Their own air force, they were assured, now controlled the skies above New Guinea.

It wasn't until they reached the front line that they would discover why New Guinea – which would eventually devour over 200 000 Japanese soldiers, sailors and airmen – had been dubbed 'the island from which no one returned alive'.

That was, however, all to come. As the convoy steamed away from Rabaul, optimism was high and a stirring speech was delivered by the commander of the 115th Infantry Regiment, Colonel Torahei Endo, run off on the ship's mimeograph and distributed among his men:

Our regiment is about to enter the decisive battle area of the Great East Asia War. From the first, this has been the inspiring deed for all officers and men. There is no greater feat than this. It has been observed that this task is extremely serious and at the same time important. It is our objective to bring the Great East Asia War to a close by suppressing New Guinea and then subjugating Australia, which is our appointed task, thus sealing the fate of our enemy. One cannot refrain from saying that the result of this decisive battle will decide the destiny of the Great East Asia War. Therefore, all officers and men, advance vigorously, fight bravely, and plunge into the jaws of death. Exalt the brilliancy of our regimental colors. Display the traditional spirit of Joshu boys. You must be determined to accomplish this important task.

As the convoy made its stately progress along New Britain's northern coast, even more luck seemed to be falling the Japanese commander's way. The weather, which had been predicted to be a cloaking cover of low grey cloud, was deteriorating into a full-blown tropical storm. As dawn broke on 1 March the weather closed in completely, with squalls whipping the sea into whitecaps which blew a foamy spume across the decks of the pitching ships.

Onboard his flagship, the *Shirayuki*, Admiral Kimura could not have been more delighted. No Allied aircraft would dare come anywhere near the convoy in weather like this, and even if they did, the chances of finding them were virtually nil. Over on the *Yukikaze*, the 51st Division commander, Lieutenant General Nakano, felt exactly the same, as did the overall commander of the 18th Army, Lieutenant General Adachi, onboard the *Tokitsukaze*.

As the rain set in, each man settled into the rhythm of the ship's throbbing engines drawing them on to New Guinea. Not one of them suspected that the Americans and Australians had been watching them for weeks, and knew they were coming.

CHAPTER 14
THE CODEBREAKERS

After the successful Australian defence of Wau, the annihilation of the Japanese at Buna, and the withdrawal from Guadalcanal, the question asked by many among the Allies was, 'How much fight could the Japanese possibly have left in them?' The answer would come as a shock, as would the complacency which nearly led the Allies to miss Japan's next move altogether.

For all their inter-service rivalries, the Imperial Japanese Army and Navy nevertheless employed a single and largely integrated approach to fighting the Allies. On the other hand, the complex American system of command in the Pacific gave rise to a far more disjointed force, with the US Army and US Navy at times often appearing to be fighting separate wars against a common enemy.

As with the Japanese forces, this stemmed from a fundamental mistrust between the services, a situation personified by the respective senior officers. Douglas MacArthur was by nature a deeply paranoid man, but the supremo of the US Navy, Admiral Ernest King, was perhaps an even more impossible figure. Notoriously explosive, King detested absolutely everybody, but none more so than his own subordinates, politicians, the British, and anyone from any service other than his own.

With leaders like these, interservice cooperation was not always guaranteed. Indeed, the schism was clearly reflected in the US Pacific command structure, which was effectively split between MacArthur's South West Pacific Area (SWPA) and Admiral Halsey's almost overlapping South Pacific Area (SOPAC). Although fighting the same war, the two commands often developed strategies and fought campaigns independent of one another, particularly prior to the middle of 1943, when more streamlined strategies were developed for the great American 'island-hopping' campaigns which would eventually end the war.

As the Japanese began their month-long withdrawal from Guadalcanal in mid-January, Admiral Halsey's exhausted and battle-weary SOPAC forces paused, observing the enemy, but ever wary of another full-scale offensive.

SOPAC air operations were scaled back to regroup. In the lull, the destroyers and merchant vessels which would make up Operation 81 proceeded unhindered towards Rabaul. There, for a crucial fortnight, they remained undetected by the Allies.

The first inkling of Japanese plans came on 7 February, when a naval floatplane usually employed in anti-submarine patrols was sighted near Gasmata on New Britain's southern shore. Japanese submarines were soon reported by coastwatchers around Lae, then more aircraft typically used in forward deployment for convoys were observed the following week apparently patrolling the sea lanes between New Britain and New Guinea.

When aerial reconnaissance recommenced, significant enemy activity was observed on the runways and aircraft revetments of the Gasmata airstrip. But the real shock came when intelligence officers began examining photographs from Rabaul. Always a hub of Japanese activity, Rabaul was both regularly observed and attacked by Allied aircraft, who could always expect a vigorous reception from its extensive defences.

From mid-December 1942 to mid-January 1943, an average of sixty-five vessels were observed in Rabaul's vast harbour, representing roughly 170 000 tons of shipping. In the last week of January, as the evacuation of Guadalcanal was underway, this number dipped to less than forty-five. Complacency thus crept into Allied thinking, as the evidence of a reduction of Japanese power in the region seemed irrefutable. This, timed as it was with the scaling back of SOPAC operations, as well as extensive training being undertaken by the skip bombers and strafers of Kenney's Fifth Air Force, led to attention being diverted from Rabaul for the fortnight before Operation 81 set sail.

It was not until 12 February that a US photo-reconnaissance mission revealed a dramatic spike of around eighty ships – or 250 000 tons – suddenly cramming Rabaul's Simpson Harbour. In the third week of the month, this figure climbed even higher.

With a jolt, the Allies realised that far from being punch-drunk with defeat, the Japanese were in fact preparing their counterstrike, the planning for which they had carried out in plain sight, right under the Allies' noses. A convoy, it could be seen, was gathering, but its strength, destination and date of departure were as yet unknown.

Luckily, the Australians and Americans had an ace up their sleeve in the form of a group of dedicated men and women in faraway Townsville and Melbourne, working in absolute secrecy to provide signals intelligence, or 'SIGINT'. This vital information detailed Japanese strengths, deployments and intentions. The story of how it was discovered and used remains to this day one of the great untold stories of the war. Indeed, it parallels the intelligence saga of the European theatre, 'ULTRA'. In the Pacific, the Allies chose another name for the information gathered on their enemy: 'MAGIC'.

While a detailed account of the remarkable American and Australian Pacific intelligence partnership remains outside the scope of this account, it is difficult to envisage any other single weapon – save perhaps for the atomic bombs – that yielded such demonstrably palpable results in defeating the Japanese in the Pacific. Signals intelligence resulted in Japanese defeats in the battles of the Coral Sea, Midway, Milne Bay and the Solomons, but also enabled smaller operations, such as the assassination of Admiral Isoroku Yamamoto.

What is particularly under-appreciated, even eighty years after the events, is the role Australian operators played in the checkmating of Japanese intelligence almost from the beginning of the Pacific War. For this, the nation has to thank Theodore Eric Nave, a young Royal Australian Navy (RAN) officer, as brilliant as he was enigmatic. Depending on which of the admittedly scant biographical details one might choose to believe, Nave was either 'a gregarious and charming man who had many friends' or 'a very secretive and mysterious person'.

Hailing from Adelaide, Nave joined the RAN and served in the Pacific in the latter stages of World War I. As a young midshipman, he noted he'd be paid more if he learned a foreign language. In the case of French or German this meant an extra shilling or so a week, but *five times* that amount if he studied an Asian language. As fate would have it, Nave chose Japanese, which he mastered so quickly that in 1921 he was given an attachment to the British Embassy in Tokyo. Here, he so impressed British intelligence officers that they requested the RAN 'lend' him for use in the Far East to translate intercepted Japanese diplomatic cables. Here, Nave's genius truly came to the fore, and in a few years he had managed to break four separate Japanese military and diplomatic codes. Along the way, he became a master not only of English-based Morse Code but the difficult *katakana* variety used by the Japanese.

When war came to the Pacific, Nave's usefulness to Allied intelligence was so paramount, he was put in charge of the Fleet Radio Unit Melbourne (FRUMEL), which operated in secrecy from a newly requisitioned apartment block at 17 Queens Road, South Melbourne. One of several clandestine intelligence services at work across Australia, FRUMEL was a joint Australian–American unit which received, decoded and translated Japanese diplomatic and military traffic of the highest level.

FRUMEL, as well as the innocuously titled Number 1 Wireless Unit (1WU), which operated from a purpose-built concrete bunker complex on the outskirts of Townsville, recruited – also in complete secrecy – only the most brilliant of minds capable of carrying out its complex and taxing work. A large proportion of those minds belonged to women and it is estimated that for much of its wartime life, 1WU was staffed by a 90 per cent female workforce.

Security checked, sworn to secrecy, and threatened with dire legal consequences should they disobey, SIGINT operatives were forbidden to discuss their work with anyone, even their own families, from whom most of them were purposely separated, even spending leave with fellow members of the unit. Diaries and notes on calendars were forbidden, as was any kind of official acknowledgement or recognition. At the end of the war, the US government sought to award a special citation of recognition for the work to members of FRUMEL and 1WU, a gesture the Australian government overruled without even telling them.

•

In early 1943, the long-range listening aerials of 1WU, cleverly intertwined with the tall gum trees beside the bunker complex (which, even from 20 feet away looked like an innocent farmhouse), began to pick up a steady increase in Japanese military traffic.

On 19 February, a transmission cryptically mentioning the assembly of ships was detected, followed by another emanating from the Imperial Japanese Navy's 11 Air Fleet headquarters. While only captured in part, the recipient of this salient piece of information was none other than the Japanese Combined Fleet and Naval General Staff.

This in itself indicated that whatever was being discussed was of considerable import.

Two days later, more messages were sent regarding a transfer on 6 March of the 51st Infantry Division to 'DZM', the Japanese code for Lae. This would be followed on 12 March by the 20th Division, which would be sent to Madang. Another fragment mentioned six vessels, and the capacity and availability of the Army Air Force to cover their passage. Seventeen hours later, more ships were mentioned, particularly destroyer escorts. A further, far clearer, message discussed a convoy bound for Wewak transporting the 41st Division.

With communications received in Townsville and pieced together in Melbourne, the US and Australian cryptanalysts had hit the jackpot.

The information was marked 'Most Secret', compiled into CinCPAC – (Commander-in-Chief Pacific) bulletin #347, and forwarded to generals MacArthur and Kenney. The intelligence was then integrated with what had been recently observed via aerial reconnaissance at Rabaul.

As remarkable a windfall as this had been, for the dedicated men and women of SIGINT – toiling away in secret inside their windowless rooms, bending their powerful intellects to solve complex challenges of cryptography, and under the immense pressure of knowing their efforts were of national importance and carried, literally, the weight of life or death – it was all in a day's work.

For the Allies, a picture of Japanese intentions had emerged. They could now confidently predict that the long-awaited reinforcement convoy to Lae was imminent. Thanks to

SIGINT's tireless work, the Allied generals had the rough details of the convoy's strength, make-up and date of departure. It was now up to them to plan the response, and for that there was precious little time.

CHAPTER 15

THE ENEMY SHOWS HIS HAND

There was still one missing piece of the puzzle being assembled in the final week of February by General Kenney and his commander in New Guinea, General Ennis Whitehead. The intended route of the Japanese convoy – possibly convoys – was a question which, they knew, could well decide the battle. There would be little point in sending out Kenney's recently retrained airmen to attack empty ocean, so in locked conference rooms in Townsville and Brisbane three scenarios were played out.

'Whitehead and I went over all the information at hand and tried to guess how we would run the convoy if we were Japs,' Kenney wrote. The generals believed they were being presented with a trio of possible scenarios: a) a direct route to Lae along either the north or south coast of New Britain; b) splitting the formation in two to reinforce both Lae and Madang and/or Wewak; c) the entire force being sent up the New Guinea coastline towards Madang or Wewak.

Kenney's main problem was the range of his aircraft. If Madang or Wewak was the intended destination, only his heavy B-17s and B-24s would be capable of reaching them, and with reduced fighter cover. His medium bombers would in this case be reserved for attacks on Japanese airstrips. If the convoy headed for Lae, however, every one of his aircraft would be able to be deployed, including the squadrons of the RAAF.

The north–south question was also vital.

If the Japanese followed the pattern of January's Operation 18, it would turn right out of Rabaul and proceed around the tip of New Britain then along its long southern shore, indicating that its destination was Lae. Should the shorter and more direct northern route be taken, it would not be known for some days if the Japanese intended to split north to Madang/Wewak, or head south to Lae. The question, believed Kenney, lay in the weather, and for the next week the meteorological reports would be studied with particular intensity.

From whichever direction, and in whatever strength the Japanese convoy eventually presented itself, Kenney and Whitehead, with their new and brilliantly conceived weapons and tactics, were confident of being able to meet them and stop them.

However, one man who had already had a good deal to do with deploying aircraft against ships failed to share their enthusiasm. In fact, the deputy commander of the seven squadrons of the RAAF's 9 Operational Group, Group Captain William 'Bull' Garing, believed the Americans could be facing a disaster. Despite the Americans' confidence, the Japanese convoy had every chance of making it unscathed to Lae.

Bull Garing's 1942 had been eventful. Having helped establish the control rooms of the RAAF's Northern Area Command just in time for the sleepy backwater of Townsville to be transformed into the front-line city of a nation at war, his hopelessly inadequate air force withered in the face of the experienced and ruthless Japanese in Malaya, Singapore and Rabaul. By March, stunned into virtual stupefaction, Australia could only watch as Japan's blitz descended towards them from the north.

New Guinea was the last line of defence.

During April and May of 1942, Garing had witnessed the heroic stand of the green pilots of 75 Squadron, holding off the Japanese over Port Moresby. In September, Garing was given the important operational command of the newly formed 9 Operational Group, a mixed bag of seven squadrons of varying strength and quality – Kittyhawks, Bostons, Hudsons, even a pathetic handful of Wirraways – all tasked with defending New Guinea from their bases at Port Moresby and Milne Bay.

His first day on the job was perhaps his most perilous, flying into Milne Bay on 1 September in – of all things – a Tiger Moth biplane. Here, on No 1 airstrip, at the tipping point of the battle with the advancing Japanese just a couple of miles to the east, he told his nervous pilots that retreat was unthinkable, and to go out and win. His instructions were followed assiduously, and a few days later at the hands of the army, in close cooperation with the RAAF, the Japanese suffered their first land defeat of the war.

Towards the end of the year, Garing's role afforded him a closer appreciation of his American allies and he became convinced that if it weren't for their assistance Australia would have fallen. As he said years later, 'Australia couldn't fight its way out of a paper bag at that stage and without the Americans we would have lost the war anyway ... I know that many people will hate my guts for saying it but if the war had been left to Australian admirals, generals and air marshals of the time, we would have lost.'

Garing also developed close relationships with both Kenney and his New Guinea commander, Ennis Whitehead. He shared their enthusiasm for killing as many Japanese as possible, and believed close, low-level attacks by aircraft on ships were an excellent way to do it.

However, as grateful an admirer of America and Americans as he was, Garing nevertheless harboured considerable reservations regarding aspects of USAAF training and tactics and was not shy in saying so. What astounded him in particular was what he considered to be many if not most of the American airmen's lack of navigation skills. '[They] couldn't find their way to the other side of the street on a shiny day,' he said.

As harsh as it sounds, he made a good point.

Many US pilots were trained in the 'follow the leader' method, whereby the formation leader would essentially be the only one who knew where they were at any given time. This also applied to bombing, when the same lead aircraft would drop its load over the target, providing the only visual cue for the others to do the same. Results could, therefore, be wildly inaccurate, especially if a formation was spread out, as many US attacks tended to be.

This, however, did little to dampen American enthusiasm for reporting what Garing believed to be wildly exaggerated successes. American gunners frequently reported dozens of attacking Zeros and Oscars as definite kills, even though the numbers claimed exceeded the number of aircraft the Japanese were actually sending into the sky.

Simply firing at a Japanese aircraft, in the eyes of many US airmen, constituted its undoubted destruction. If several gunners in different aircraft fired at the same Zero or Oscar, the claim was often repeated, amplified and accepted, without the two-stage verification required for similar claims in the RAAF.

Successes against shipping were also exaggerated, with vessels frequently reported as sunk, only to reappear again, apparently unharmed, or at least only slightly so. Particularly irksome to Garing was the fact that these statistics were forwarded daily up the chain of command to General MacArthur, who famously and enthusiastically forwarded them to his masters in Washington. There, it was taken as gospel that the US forces in New Guinea were achieving astonishing successes.

Garing's scepticism won him some favour with that other famous straight talker, General Kenney. Failing to be at all impressed by Garing's former boss in Townsville, Air Commodore Frank Lukis, Kenney and Garing seemed to have clicked from the beginning, with Kenney later describing his first meeting with RAAF officers in the following terms:

The only one in Townsville who had the answers to very many of my questions was an Australian RAAF officer named Group Captain Garing. They called him 'Bull', but he was active, intelligent, knew the theater, and had ideas about how to fight the Japs … I decided to keep my eye on him for future reference.

Not every American commander appreciated Garing's candour, though, particularly when it ran counter to their own beliefs. Even after his rowing adventure to see firsthand the damage to the *Pruth*, bombing leader General Walker remained a diehard advocate of high-level strategic bombing. As commander of the Australian squadrons of 9 Operational Group, Garing was always ready to try to convince him otherwise, and less than subtly made known his scepticism. He repeatedly raised doubts about the Americans' claims of Japanese ships being blasted out of the water thanks to the supposed pinpoint accuracy of Walker's B-17s and B-24s from tens of thousands of feet above.

By luck, a series of photographs have survived, taken on the occasion of a welcome reception given to General Kenneth Walker in Townsville by a group of RAAF officers in late 1942. Among the Australians can be seen Garing's boss, Air Commodore Frank Lukis, as well as North East Area Commander and Great War flying hero Harry Cobby, and of course Garing himself. In all three images, however, General Walker stands out, not only as the only one wearing a tie in his distinctive olive uniform, but as by far the most uncomfortable man in the room. His body language is awkward, his eyes are fixed downwards on the table in front of him, and his disposition speaks of a man desperate to find himself anywhere but in this room among these people. One can well imagine his reaction to a man like William Garing.

Senior RAAF officers, many of whom were bewitched by the prestige and glamour of their far more powerful American counterparts, were never happier than when asked – even obliquely – to serve the whim of an American general, particularly one involving a prickly and less-than-diplomatic serving Australian commander.

Hence, in early February 1943, after several months of an indisputably successful command at the head of 9 Operational Group, and despite being one of only seventeen Australians seen fit by the Americans to be awarded their Distinguished Service Cross for 'extraordinary courage, marked efficiency and precise execution of operations during the Papuan Campaign', Garing was replaced by an HQ staff officer by the name of Air Commodore Joe Hewitt, a man with no operational command experience of any kind. Hewitt had only recently become South West Pacific Director of Intelligence, a position to which he would be quietly returned when it became apparent that he was out of his depth in this, the RAAF's most important operational command. In fact, he appears to have had the good sense to realise this himself, as upon ascending to the position he deferred many operational matters to his former commander, now his deputy, Group Captain Garing.

Thus it was as the recently *demoted* 9 Operational Group commander that possibly Group Captain Garing's most important conversation of the Bismarck Sea battle took place late one February morning in 1943, as he stood on the sand outside an operations tent in Port Moresby. Garing did most of the talking and General Kenneth B Hobson, General Walker's successor, listened. Unlike his predecessor, however, Hobson needed no convincing as to the merits of low-level attack bombing, and was more than willing to take some tough advice from this experienced and plain-speaking Australian airman.

Although impressed by the Americans' newly adapted commerce destroyer B-25s and the tactics they had developed around skip and mast-high bombing, weapons alone, insisted Garing, would not be enough to win a battle. Nor would the standard American approach of sending individual units – sometimes even individual aircraft – to attack a target independently. Such a piecemeal strategy would simply rob the bombers of the vital elements of concentration and surprise. To have any chance of success against the large and well-defended Japanese convoy now approaching from Rabaul, a plan was needed, and from what he could see the Americans had nothing.

Garing determined to give them one.

•

While Kenney's task of reforming and rebuilding the Fifth Air Force had well and truly begun, it still had a long way to go. Only a single squadron of his four B-25 Mitchell units – the 90th under Major Larner – had so far been converted and trained for skip bombing, and its pilots had yet to test their mounts in combat, despite several weeks' practice on the *Pruth*. An armed and fast-moving convoy would be a very

different prospect from an undefended old wreck, the men
would find, and over recent weeks several sorties had been
undertaken to locate and attack Japanese shipping, but none
had been found.

As for the rest of Kenney's Fifth Air Force, by late February
the rigours of flying and fighting in the South West Pacific had,
despite his efforts to improve supply chains and morale, taken
their toll. His heavy, light and medium bombardment groups
were still understrength, and even his 3rd Attack Group could
only muster seventeen B-25s and fifteen A-20 Havocs between
them. Another group, the 22nd, had been so badly shot up
that Whitehead had sent its four combat squadrons of B-26
Marauders back to Australia for rest and recuperation.

Garing was as aware of the situation as the Americans, and
knew they would need to muster everything they could get
into the air. Every single aircraft that could carry a bomb or a
belt of ammunition would be used in the coming battle.

The key was timing. Using pieces of driftwood and sticks,
Garing laid out his scheme in the sand like the workings of an
intricate watch.

The attack against the convoy must be a coordinated, three-
phase approach timed to the second.

The strafers, he said, must go in first. With cannon and
machine gun, they would rake the decks of the Japanese
vessels from stem to stern, killing the gunners and, as he put
it, 'removing the ships' brains and teeth'.

Then the skip bombers would arrive, hurling their
500-pounders against the undefended flanks, or placing them
below the waterline to cause the most damage.

Standing behind the cockpit of an RAAF Beaufighter, war photographer Damien Parer captures Squadron Leader Ron 'Torchy' Uren taking a swig from his canteen as the battle rages below. *The Australian War Memorial 127968*

A US B-25 Mitchell from the 405th Bombardment Squadron stalks a Japanese vessel in the Bismarck Sea just before the attack. Note bursts of anti-aircraft fire exploding above. *Courtesy Rob Garing*

The magnificent Bristol Beaufighter. In the hands of Australian 30 Squadron pilots, their devastating strafing firepower tore open the bridges of the Japanese ships, allowing the US skip bombers to come in and finish the job. *Wikimedia Commons*

Convoy sighted! A US reconnaissance photo shows some of the Japanese ships dispersing prior to the attack. It would do them no good, and all eight transports – along with four escorting destroyers – would be sent to the bottom. *Courtesy Rob Garing*

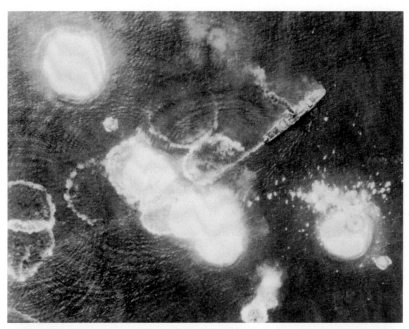

Japanese destroyer *Arashio* under attack from B-25s of the US 90th Squadron, 3rd Attack Group. The ship's bow would be blown off, causing her to career out of control into the merchant vessel *Nojima Maru*, sinking them both. *The Australian War Memorial AWM128159*

Close quarters. A doomed enemy merchant vessel flashes by under the cockpit of an attacking Australian Beaufighter. *State Library of Victoria, Argus newspaper collection of war photographs H98.104/3641*

Death on the water. Some of the ships of Convoy 81 burn, denoting a disaster for the Japanese from which they would not recover. *State Library of Victoria, Argus newspaper collection of war photographs H98.104/3753*

Damien Parer, Australia's greatest war photographer, flew with the Beaufighters of 30 Squadron, capturing unforgettable images of the battle. *The Australian War Memorial AWM2889.001*

With its distinctive painted bow wave, the merchant vessel *Taimei Maru* under attack from US Havocs of the 89th Attack Squadron. Three bombs would strike home, sinking the ship and taking 200 Japanese soldiers and sailors with her. *Courtesy Rob Garing*

Carrying 500 cubic metres of aviation fuel, *Kembu Maru*, the smallest ship in the convoy, quickly becomes an inferno. *The Australian War Memorial AWM141996*

From his A-20 Havoc bomber, Captain William J Beck of the US 89th Attack Squadron swoops in low, barely clearing his target, the Japanese destroyer *Uranami*. His bomb-release mechanism would fail, however, and the ship would survive to fight another day. *Courtesy Rob Garing*

Architects of the Bismarck Sea victory: Australia's Group Captain William 'Bull' Garing (left), and General George C Kenney, commander of the US Fifth Air Force. *Courtesy Rob Garing*

High above, the B-17s and medium bombers would have a go. Hopefully, they would be attacking sitting targets, dead in the water. American fighters would also patrol constantly, guarding against the inevitable Japanese fighter cover and keeping them from the bombers if they broke through.

Garing mapped out his blueprint of the destructive force that would form in the sky over the Japanese convoy. Garing's biographer, historian Jim Turner, reconstructed much of the conversation based on interviews with Garing in his final years. 'This is the Jap convoy with their destroyer protection around them. Their air cover will be high, probably at twelve or more thousand feet,' Garing told Hobson.

Intelligence indicated that Japanese air defence would be 'solid'. Garing estimated this meant twenty to thirty Zeros and Oscars over the convoy at any one time. As such, it would be essential that the American P-38 Lightning pilots kept them away from the bombers as they made their run. 'We can't afford any disruption of the bombing plan. Our higher-level bombers could have a lot of success if their aim is not put off by the attacking Zeros,' he stressed. 'We'll need all the fighters we can get above them.'

Hobson said nothing, but listened intently as Garing continued.

Up top, the fighter umbrella, then at 20 000 feet, the B-17s and B-24s. Below them, say at about 5000 feet, the mediums like the Mitchells. Then the skip bombers can come in low, and from different directions; but only after strafing runs, again from different directions, to suppress the Japs' anti-aircraft fire. The gun crews and the bridge crews would both be the prime targets so we can essentially leave the ship decapitated.

Garing and Hobson then went over various technical details, but the essential elements were there. Garing laid them out again. 'A multi-level bombing strike … with fighter protection … and the dedicated suppression of ship anti-aircraft defences.'

Hobson wanted to put the plan before Whitehead and Kenney immediately but Garing demurred, as if girding himself for what needed to be said next. 'Before we do,' he said, 'I've first got to say something absolutely vital. None of this is going to work if we don't get it all together at the precise place and at the precise time. Unless this attack is coordinated with complete precision, with people arriving exactly where they should and exactly when they should. We might well fail. Worse, we might have heavy losses for very little gain.'

After a pause, Garing went on. 'I say this with the greatest respect, but some of your aircrew don't always display the sort of navigation skills needed for a precision operation of this nature. It's not their fault just inexperience.'

'I won't argue with that,' replied Hobson quietly. 'But what do you propose we do about it?'

'Simple,' said Garing. 'We have a rehearsal.'

•

'A rehearsal?' questioned a flummoxed General Whitehead later that day. 'What on earth do you mean?'

There were no sticks or driftwood with which to illustrate his vision in Whitehead's Port Moresby office, but with Hobson beside him, Garing managed to convey its essence nonetheless.

'If you're going to fight a naval force the first thing you must know is how they behave and what they think,' he explained.

> There are two things the navy can't take – to have their position, course, speed and composition reported in plain language – which we did in the Coral Sea battle – and the other is concentration – being attacked by [a] vast number of aircraft and not being able to tell which is the strongest part of the enemy.

Whitehead agreed, and knew that Kenney would also, but the notion of a rehearsal seemed odd.

Taking his time, Garing explained that at Milne Bay he had seen firsthand what the Japanese soldier was capable of – visions he would be haunted by for the rest of his life. He knew also that the Allied ground forces, having endured the hellish tropical campaigns of Kokoda, Buna and Gona, were worn to the bone. A fresh injection of Japanese soldiers into New Guinea at this juncture of the war could change the dynamic dramatically, and for the worse. The consequences of prolonging this bitter struggle would, he knew, be measured in thousands of young Australian and American lives.

The convoy which had arrived virtually intact in January was a disaster which must not be repeated. This one, he told Whitehead and Hobson, had to be stopped. There would be one chance to do it, and everything had to work perfectly. It would not be easy. He reminded them that for the first day or so the convoy would be out of range to all but the heavy bombers. For it to come within range of the medium bombers, it would need to be located and attacked perilously close to its destination. The window of opportunity to destroy it, therefore, would be a narrow one, and everything would have to go right. Garing then once again broached the subject of the Fifth Air Force's pilots' navigational skills, or lack thereof.

Whitehead agreed and scheduled a rehearsal for the morning of 28 February, two days hence.

Garing thanked the officers and reminded them that at the rehearsal – as well as at the attack itself – they would be joined by another group of airmen, a group whose skill was unquestionable, whose navigational prowess was superb, and who needed no hastily reconfigured bombers to take the war to the Japanese. They would instead wield one of the most devastating air weapons in the sky: the magnificent Bristol Beaufighter.

These men, he explained, were the crews of 30 Squadron, Royal Australian Air Force.

CHAPTER 16

THE REHEARSAL

One can well imagine the bemusement felt by the Australians at the efforts being made by American engineers like Pappy Gunn to convert their B-25 Mitchell medium bombers into gun-studded ground attackers. After all, they'd been flying just such an aircraft for months and nobody had had to convert anything.

Formed at the Richmond RAAF base in New South Wales in March 1942, 30 Squadron had arrived at Port Moresby's Ward's airstrip (which, though sealed, noted one airman, looked alarmingly short) in September and immediately went to work blasting anything Japanese they could find. Bridges, barges, airstrips and personnel were all targets for 30 Squadron as they headed out over the Owen Stanleys then slithered low up the jungle valleys to emerge on top of the Japanese, spitting cannon and machine-gun fire.

The first of the five RAAF squadrons that would eventually operate the British-built (from 1944 Australian-built) dual-engine heavy fighter, the Bristol Beaufighter, 30 Squadron quickly established a reputation as a lethal outfit of hunters, prowling the far corners of New Guinea for Japanese prey. Most of its combat involved ground attacks, for which few World War II aircraft were better suited.

So low were the heights at which they flew and fought that many 30 Squadron aircrew had dispensed with parachutes altogether.

Conceived in haste at the beginning of the war to fill the urgent gap in British night-fighter protection, the Beaufighter was thrown together using many of the readily available components of its stable mate, the Beaufort. From the prototype onwards, it proved itself a vastly superior aircraft, going on to become one of the truly great machines of the war.

Throughout its many roles across many theatres of conflict, in none was it more suited than in the hands of Australian pilots, attacking Japanese ground positions and shipping in the South West Pacific. Highly manoeuvrable at both low altitude and low speed, and married to its relatively quiet Hercules sleeve-valve engines, the first the Japanese would often know of a 'Whispering Death' Beaufighter attack was the sight of one bursting out of a long, winding valley, a few hundred feet above the ground in its jungle-green livery, and opening up with its devastating firepower. At this stage of the war, the Beaufighter was the most powerfully armed purpose-built fighter in the world, wielding an extraordinary four Hispano 20-mm cannons in the nose as well as six Browning .303-calibre machine guns in the wings.

So effective was the Beaufighter in RAAF service that the fledgling Australian aircraft construction industry would eventually start building them under licence from their factory in Melbourne. The process required photographing 55 000 technical drawings which were transferred to microfilm and sent to Australia in the utmost secrecy. Eventually, 373 Australian Beaufighters would be built, but for the time being, 30 Squadron's 'Beaus' were all British-made.

In its almost daily incursions into Japanese ground and maritime facilities, 30 Squadron was led by one of the most colourful of air force personalities, Group Captain Brian 'Blackjack' Walker. From South Australia, Walker had joined up in 1935, and by the time the Pacific War had begun he was one of the RAAF's most gifted and experienced pilots. Another maverick, his outward lack of deference in regard to some of the more arcane aspects of military discipline had already seen him endure one court martial as well as a number of air crashes, all of which he survived. Not the sort of officer the RAAF were prepared to unleash upon more delicate British sensibilities, Walker was a perfect fit for the crisis engulfing his own country in the Pacific, and was given command of the brand new 30 Squadron, which he led brilliantly into battle.

Although not enamoured of paperwork and in favour of lax uniform standards (at one stage he even allowed his airmen to grow beards before Garing put a stop to the practice), Blackjack nonetheless detested, in no particular order, waste, poor flying and casualties, and did his best to eliminate all three. To raise the flying standards of his airmen, he pulled strings and managed to fill his ranks with some of the instructors currently trapped in flying training schools around the country, who were desperate to be given a chance to fly with an operational squadron.

He was also a famous purloiner, and somehow managed to get his hands on a genuine Harley-Davidson motorcycle from the Americans at Durand, as well as some of their excellent throat microphones for his pilots, which were far less cumbersome than the British-made rubber oxygen mask with the microphone attached. Flying so low, oxygen was rarely needed anyway.

One of the many famous anecdotes of Blackjack's reign over the squadron involved his exasperation at his pilots' habit of damaging their Beaufighters' wing tips by hitting tree trunks during sloppy taxiing. According to 30 Squadron navigator, Fred Cassidy, Blackjack became so exasperated:

> ... he threatened that the next pilot to smash a wingtip would be sent south immediately. Not long afterwards, Bob Cummins had the misfortune to do just this to his starboard wingtip, and of course he had to front up to the CO. 'Cummins,' said Blackjack, 'I'm not going to send you south for what you did, I'm going to shoot you.' At which point he picked up from the table the German Luger pistol he had acquired from somewhere and ostentatiously carried as his service revolver, and pointed it straight at Cummins's head. So Bob pulled out his own revolver and said, 'Sir, my bullets aren't as big as yours, but I can pull the trigger just as fast as you.' There was a pause, the CO put down his gun, and sent Cummins about his business.

Once, when a brand new Beaufighter arrived from Australia at the officially 'dry' base laden with a modest quantity of alcohol, Blackjack held a closed-door conference with his aircrews, asking them if they'd prefer a limited daily ration for a couple of weeks, or a full-on party right now.

All voted for the party.

Even before Garing had revealed his plan of attack to Hobson and Whitehead, he held a special council with Blackjack at his headquarters at the rapidly growing complex at Ward's airstrip outside Port Moresby. The convoy believed to be currently making its way towards New Guinea, Garing told him, had to be stopped, and 30 Squadron would help stop it. He then outlined the details of his plan, informing Blackjack that it would be the largest and most critical air engagement of the war thus far, primarily an American effort, and the prospect of failure was unthinkable.

Blackjack told Garing he and his men were up to the task and thanked him for the confidence he had shown in allowing 30 Squadron to participate.

'Participate?' echoed Garing, looking at Blackjack squarely. 'You're going to *lead* it.'

•

Just over 100 miles east along the coast from Port Moresby, the small peninsula of Cape Rodney juts out into the ocean, a patch of jungle and rubber plantation a little less than halfway between the capital and the island's easternmost tip at Milne Bay. This was the unremarkable feature chosen by

Kenney, Whitehead and Garing for their airmen to practise the techniques they would need to bring to the coming battle to have any chance of preventing Operation 81 reaching Lae.

Every available aircraft in Whitehead's New Guinea arsenal was alerted, as were bombardment squadrons based to the south in Australia, and the RAAF crews of Garing's erstwhile command, 9 Operational Group. The instructions were specific, though the airmen's eventual target was not revealed. Aircrew were instructed to rendezvous at predetermined heights, form up, then travel as one to Port Moresby, where an attack was to be mounted against the wreck of what was left of the *Pruth*, which by now had been reduced to little more than some rusting steel plates, though its two great boilers still stood as defiant sentinels high up on the reef where the ship had come to ground nearly twenty years earlier.

Garing already had confidence in the airmen's ability to deliver a bomb accurately onto a target. As far as he was concerned, the purpose of the exercise was timing. To succeed, the attack must be carried out with the utmost precision. Whitehead and Kenney having been convinced of the need for such a rehearsal, they now embraced the idea and watched it from the vantage point of a hill not far from the wreck inside the harbour. Little did they know that even as they prepared for the show their airmen would soon be providing, the Operation 81 convoy was preparing to steam out of Rabaul Harbour.

From Gurney and Turnbull airstrips at Milne Bay; from Jackson, Durand, Schwimmer (or '14 Mile', as some of the older hands still called it) and the many other hastily constructed wartime aerodromes which ringed Port Moresby, and from faraway Mareeba in Queensland, young airmen lifted off runways and flew towards the anonymous spot on the New Guinea coastline marked on their maps.

From there, they would coalesce at predetermined heights – the briefing notes were still being studied by the pilots and navigators as they flew – and fly to Cape Rodney. Then they would proceed to Port Moresby and from various heights take turns in attacking the remains of the *Pruth* with bombs and machine guns. The P-38 Lightning fighters would fly at the top of this box, maintaining combat air patrols against a squadron of Airacobras posing as Japanese Zeros. Still, the pilots knew nothing about the actual convoy itself, or the coming battle. As one P-38 pilot remarked, 'We thought it very strange at the time. We were just told what to do, and not given a reason.'

As the morning wore on, Garing, Whitehead and Kenney anxiously trained their binoculars to the east. A deep drone indicated the arrival of a flight of B-17s, but as they watched it became apparent they were on their own. The Beaufighters of 30 Squadron then arrived, followed by some of the American mediums, but nowhere near the designated quota. Some bombs were dropped wide from high above the wreck, then a flight of Major Ed Larner's 90 Squadron commerce destroyer Mitchells arrived, circled for a while – something they could never afford to do in a real combat situation – and came in for strafing runs.

It all looked very haphazard.

If Garing was agitated, Kenney and Whitehead were furious. 'Where in hell is everyone?' they asked in exasperation. After an interminable twenty minutes, other units appeared but by then it was clear the exercise had been a failure. Some squadrons got lost and others failed to show up entirely.

Flying Officer Bob Brazenor from 30 Squadron recalled, 'The timing was for us to be there at ten o'clock but unfortunately it didn't work out that way. Nothing seemed to click at all. It was just a shemozzle'. After circling aimlessly for a while, 30 Squadron simply turned around and went home.

If this was repeated in earnest against the Japanese, Garing – and now Kenney and Whitehead – knew, the battle would be lost.

In the skies above New Guinea, the following forty-eight hours were a period of intense activity for the Australian and American air forces, particularly their commanders. No one was happy with the rehearsal, but it did uncover crucial deficiencies in the airmen's navigation and timing, deficiencies Kenney, Whitehead and Garing were determined to fix. Whitehead had been particularly embarrassed by his airmen in the presence of his boss and, according to Garing, '... tore a most unholy strip off them for their navigation and their timing'.

No sooner had the aircraft landed than they were ordered to refuel, take off and do it all again. The next day, even as the Japanese convoy was underway, Kenney toured all the American airfields he could reach, speaking to the men, haranguing and imploring them as required.

'This must be a coordinated attack, or it will fail,' he urged. Timings were critical, accuracy was imperative. 'Every one of you has been given a designated role, position and altitude in the overall formation – so damn well stick to it! Now, get up there and try it again.'

Garing briefed his Australian pilots. He was also unimpressed by the rehearsal. Even his 30 Squadron Beaufighter crews had let him down, arriving independently of the American formations, attacking the wreck with scant regard for accuracy, and failing to coordinate with larger aircraft bombing from higher altitudes. Such a performance on the day – he emphasised with the urgency of a man whose pride was at stake – would not be good enough.

In postwar interviews, Garing alluded to a second rehearsal having taken place in Port Moresby Harbour, but there are no records of such an event. The passage of time may have conflated memories, but what is not in dispute is the urgency with which the Allied airmen reviewed the errors of 28 February 1943, went back over the plans and reconsidered the specific parts they were to play. The lessons learned in that vital 24 hours proved to be invaluable, and not a moment too soon as, over 300 miles to the north, the great Battle of the Bismarck Sea was about to commence.

PART TWO

CHAPTER 17

THE CONVOY FOUND – AND LOST

By 4 p.m. on 1 March 1943, after several tedious hours bashing through some of the filthiest weather he had ever encountered, Lieutenant Walter E Higgins had had enough. Flying reconnaissance missions over the sea lanes of northern New Guinea was an enervating job at the best of times, but today had been especially draining. The weather, hardly ever clear and certainly never reliable, had started bad, and gotten worse as they approached the southern coast of New Britain.

Higgins watched through the windshield of his B-24 Liberator, the four engines humming monotonously in his ears, as chunks of white and grey cloud appeared to approach slowly, then sweep past in a flash. This at least gave him something to look at. Those other clouds, however – looming towers of sinister-looking cumulus – were to be avoided. The updrafts inside those monsters could tear the wings off an aeroplane – even a Liberator – as if it were a butterfly.

For a couple of hours now, neither Higgins nor his crew had been able to catch so much as a glimpse of the ocean they were supposed to be scouring, let alone any Japanese ships they might find sailing upon it. Something, they knew, was up – there usually was when they were told to scout such a specific location – but the details had been scant. At the briefing, Higgins had sensed his CO knew far more than he was letting on.

His orders had been to make his way, alone, from the 321st Bombardment Squadron base at Jackson Airfield, Port Moresby, over the hump of the Owen Stanleys to fly up and down New Britain's roughly 400-mile-long southern coast. What they were supposed to see in all this was anyone's guess, particularly as Higgins's plane had not been fitted with radar.

It would normally be a quick trip of a few hours, but the weather today had forced them to battle every mile of it. As monotonous as it was, the job required everyone to stay alert. It was a significant flight – the first in nearly two months since the disastrous attack on the January convoy which had made it all the way to Lae. On that occasion – again in bad weather – they had managed to find the enemy, but were immediately bounced by escorting Zeros. One of his gunners had managed a couple of hits on their attackers, but then a line of bullets raked the length of the fuselage, followed by another across the wings. One engine burst into flames and they began a slow descent, eventually ditching in the sea and swimming for their lives to a small island in the Trobriands.

Seven of Higgins's crew made it ashore, but engineer Neil Gaudet drowned in the plane, while Gunner Henry Satterfield later died of his bullet wounds. The rest of the crew buried him there on that lonely island. Luckily, they'd been spotted by a passing Beaufighter and the next day were picked up by an Australian Catalina piloted by an Aussie also named Higgins.

Today, though, the weather was worse, and the absence of their two crewmates was weighing heavily on their minds. Nevertheless, it was good to be back in the cockpit. The nose of his new aircraft sported the moniker *Miss Deeds* and bore the 90th Bombardment Group's distinctive black-and-white skull and crossbones on the vertical tail fins.

Reaching Jacquinot Bay, the weather worsened and visibility dropped to almost nil. Blinded, Higgins was on the verge of turning back, but asked his navigator, George Sellmer, what he thought about crossing the island to try their luck on the northern side. If they found nothing there, they could simply continue on their westerly route home. Replying cautiously, Sellmer said it wasn't a bad idea, as long as they watched out for the Japanese airstrip at Gasmata.

Swinging to starboard, Higgins took only a few minutes to traverse the sixty-mile-wide island before turning to port to resume the patrol far to the west of his intended search zone. To his surprise, occasional patches of blue now appeared and the ocean could be seen in squally, whitecapped snatches below. Here, to the north, the cloud cover was thinner, so Higgins decided to risk dropping below it. Emerging barely above the slate-grey water, he became momentarily mesmerised by the patterns of the currents.

'Convoy!' erupted Sellmer's voice in his headphones.

Turning, Higgins saw his navigator frantically pointing from his vantage point in the Liberator's plexiglass nose. Banking hard, Higgins now saw the ships too, skulking under cover of the storm. Luck, pure luck, he knew, had brought them to this spot. If he had continued south as intended, or crossed the island at even a slightly different spot, they would not have seen them.

'Count 'em, quick!' he yelled, all traces of his torpor swept away in a rush of adrenaline.

'Fourteen! Jesus Christ – fourteen ships!' said Sellmer. They counted again and Higgins agreed, even though both had in fact missed two of the sixteen-vessel fleet. Higgins banked once again, now expecting anti-aircraft fire to erupt around him. In line astern, he could see two lines of cargo ships and destroyers. Even in this weather, it was clear one ship was packed with troops.

'Zeros, Skipper!' called one of his gunners. 'Three in front, three behind!' With a sickening rush of déjà vu, Higgins pulled back up into the cover of the clouds, immediately ordering radio operator Ralph Wolf to transmit a message:

FOURTEEN SHIP CONVOY AT 0455 SOUTH 150.45 EAST HEADING COURSE 260 DEGREES STOP ZEROS IN VICINITY STOP AT LEAST FOUR DESTROYERS

The message was acknowledged, and Higgins, to his relief, was spared from being ordered to attack. In fact, after the January debacle, single-aircraft attacks on multiple shipping targets had been officially – though quietly – set aside. Pointing his nose towards the clouds, he headed for home, thankful beyond words that, this time, no escorting Zeros had seen him.

When he reached Jackson Airfield, he was given a debriefing like no other he had ever experienced. Every detail of what he had seen was reiterated several times to an unusually large number of intelligence officers, some of whom he'd never met before and all of whom took notes.

Something, he thought, was definitely up.

•

The men at Port Moresby were not the only ones to pick up Higgins's signal. Far below, in the radio room of the destroyer *Tokitsukaze*, the wireless operator had heard it as well, and also the speedy acknowledgement. Scribbling on a notepad, he handed the paper to his superior, who then handed it to the destroyer's captain, Commander Masayoshi Motokura, who read it without expression.

Operation 81's sixteen-hour run of luck was over.

The news was swiftly relayed to Rabaul, then back to the convoy commander, Admiral Kimura. Army leader General Adachi, also onboard *Tokitsukaze*, was likewise informed, but appeared strangely unconcerned. This, he indicated, was all part of the plan. The Allies were always going to find them, but an attack in this weather was unlikely. If it stayed this way all the way to Lae, the mission would be a success. But no harm would be had in making the men aware of the situation, just to keep them on their toes.

One of the soldiers later recalled that after the news went around, the atmosphere grew solemn. 'Security and black-out orders were more rigid,' he said. 'All individuals arranged their belongings in order.'

•

Higgins's signal was relayed to Kenney and Whitehead, who then informed MacArthur in Brisbane. On the great map of New Guinea and the South West Pacific in the Port Moresby operations room, the convoy position was plotted. Higgins and Sellmer had found the Japanese roughly 100 miles west of Rabaul, 60 miles off the coast near Cape Hollman. This posed as many questions as it answered. Where were they headed? More patience, the Allies knew, was needed until the Japanese showed their hand by either turning north, splitting the convoy in two, or staying together and turning south. Their window to do so, however, was fast closing.

Senior navigation officers began plotting ships' courses, working out relative speeds, assessing tides, and trying to provide answers to the questions the commanders needed to know. Where would the ships be at dusk? At what point would they need to turn for Wewak, and where would they be at first light tomorrow? The most important question of all was when would they get in range of General Kenney's bombers and commerce destroyers?

Even as Higgins turned for New Guinea, more aircraft were dispatched to continue the search during the night. At 8.40 p.m., another 321st Squadron Liberator – this time fitted with radar – managed to find the convoy but only because the pilot, a Lieutenant George Shaffer, noticed anti-aircraft shells bursting around him in the darkness. Dropping to 1500 feet he tried to get a look, or even a radar reading of the ships, but saw nothing. Frustrated, and after flying as long as he dared, Shaffer figured he may as well drop his 500-pound bombs anyway. No result was observed. Turning back to base, he signalled that the weather, once more, was closing in.

An hour later, eight B-17 Flying Fortresses from the 63rd Bombardment Squadron at Port Moresby appeared at the point of Shaffer's sighting, having just delivered a bomb load onto the Japanese base at Gasmata, again without confirmed results. Now they found themselves flying headlong through the middle of a full monsoonal storm. A dozen flares were dropped but these illuminated nothing except banks of thick cloud, as did the incessant shimmers of sheet lightning. Heading for home, a message was sent to Bomber Command in Port Moresby:

SEARCHING TO 151.00. NIL SHIPPING SIGHTED. TWELVE FLARES RELEASED

The Fortresses headed back to base, the recently discovered convoy once again lost. In fact, they were much closer to it than they realised, as Japanese soldiers onboard the *Kyokusei Maru* later recalled the sound of aircraft engines, and flares falling from the clouds, illuminating the mist and empty ocean to their starboard. This time, however, their anti-aircraft gunnery officers had the sense to hold their fire and keep themselves hidden.

For a further six hours, the convoy steamed west along the New Britain coast under the protective blanket of weather, which appeared not to have lifted as the first grey streaks of light climbed into the eastern sky. At dawn on 2 March, six RAAF A-20 Boston bombers of 22 Squadron took off from Ward's airstrip to attack the Japanese airstrip at Lae, their report later claiming their bombs fell accurately, many scoring hits on the runway, and a strafing run reportedly damaged a number of parked aircraft. Although the Japanese were adept at speedy airstrip repairs, Lae would nevertheless be out of action for any Japanese fighters seeking to protect the convoy.

Other RAAF units were likewise readied. At Milne Bay, 75 and 77 squadrons would several times throughout the day scramble their Kittyhawks, but no contact with the enemy would be reported.

As 22 Squadron returned to Ward's airstrip after a job well done, yet another B-17 was sent aloft to find the Japanese ships, but again they were unsuccessful. At the airstrips around Port Moresby, word had started to get out that 'a do was on', and a big one at that.

In his memoir of the battle, *None Shall Survive*, Burton Graham, an intelligence officer working in the RAAF Fighter Sector, recounts the many rumours that instantly sped around the camp. 'I've got the absolute good guts,' one airman confided, offering assurance that 'sixty-two ships are on their way to Buna'. Another told him that forty-four Japanese vessels were currently heading to Salamaua, while one wild-eyed American breathlessly took him aside with an urgent, 'Listen, Bud, I'm telling you – there's one hundred and twenty-three ships spread out all the ways down from Rabaul! I ain't a-kiddin'!'

The atmosphere among the Lightning pilots of the 9th Squadron at Schwimmer was more sombre. Here, the pilots and ground crews, having been told what to expect, knew that they would be the first to encounter any escorting Zeros, and there'd likely be a lot of them.

However, more than twelve hours after Lieutenant Walter Higgins tapped in his initial report, the convoy had still not been found. At 7.30 a.m., another B-17 from the 65th Squadron, 43rd Bombardment Group arrived at Higgins's last coordinates, but the ships were nowhere to be seen. The monsoon continued to conspire with the Japanese to camouflage their presence, and yet another B-17 turned for home.

The next group to report in were the American Lightning pilots of the 39th Fighter Squadron. They were sent to rendezvous with a strike group of twenty-six B-17s, but had no more luck finding the Japanese ships than the earlier sorties. They did notice three Japanese Oscars patrolling over the ocean, apparently oblivious to their presence. Diving and firing, Lieutenant Wilmot Marlatt scored hits on one aircraft which spun smoking away, prompting the others to turn and fight. Lieutenant Charles King fired on another, hitting it too, and a third was claimed to have been damaged. This brief encounter marked the first aerial engagement of the battle.

Finally, at 8.15 a.m., another lone aircraft – this time a Liberator from the 90th Group's 320th Squadron – reported the dramatic news that they had just observed a formation consisting of 'a light cruiser, five destroyers and eight transports'. The 'cruiser' was in fact one of the larger *Asashio* Class destroyers. Approximately 30 miles north of Cape Gloucester, the westernmost point of New Britain, the convoy had again been found. Significantly, the pilot also reported that it appeared to be making for the Vitiaz Strait between New Britain and New Guinea.

The Liberator was ordered to stay where it was, circle, hide in cloud if necessary, but under no circumstances lose the convoy, at least not until another formation of eight B-17s from the 63rd Squadron arrived. These were led by Major Edward W Scott from Mississippi, a rising USAAF star who would eventually attain the rank of brigadier and command a bombardment group of four squadrons. This morning, Scott had been ordered to leave Jackson Airfield and fly north, avoiding Lae, then swing around Rooke Island, lying directly between New Britain and the New Guinea coastline to pick up the convoy from the circling 320th Squadron Liberator.

At 9.50 a.m., they arrived and immediately confirmed the ships' presence. Passing west over the convoy, they reported seven vessels – two destroyers and five transports – which were now visible through the slowly improving weather.

In his aircraft named *Talisman*, Scott descended through the rain with two other aircraft piloted by lieutenants Denault and Staley, while the others split off to pursue attacks on other ships in the formation. As they began their run, escorting Japanese fighters descended from above, trying to break up the trio. Ignoring them, and the anti-aircraft fire now being thrown up from below, Scott swung around to cross a line of ships, then ordered his bombardier to hit the release. The two other Fortresses followed suit and a cascade of bombs hurtled towards the convoy. Bombs from both Staley's and Denault's aircraft crashed onto one of the transports, straddling it along the bow and base of the funnel. It was difficult to see how many bombs had actually struck, but some counted five blasts. A cloud of smoke and spray flew up, then the entire ship seemed to vanish in a series of explosions.

The first blows in the Bismarck Sea battle had been struck against one of the larger merchant ships in the Operation 81 convoy. The 5493-ton *Kyokusei Maru* was loaded with 1200 troops and 2000 cubic metres of ammunition, which most likely accounted for the secondary explosions. Historian Lex McAulay relates a vivid account of the attack as recalled by a diarist with the 3rd Battalion's 115 Infantry Regiment:

Two bombs hit No. 1 hold and two other bombs scored a direct hit on No. 2 hold, thus starting large fires. While we were engaged in extinguishing the fires and saving the wounded, the ammunition and gasoline caught fire and exploded. We were then forced to stop work. The fire was getting worse and worse, and finally spread to the bridge. At 0830 the transport commander ordered all personnel to abandon ship. Through the cooperation of the ship's crew and men of other units, the wounded of Headquarters No. 9 Company were taken out of the ship. Their position had received such a direct hit, that almost all of them were badly wounded. They were unable to get out of the fire and only a few were saved. The rest, who were either unconscious or unable to walk could not get to the deck.

Finally, after all the survivors had abandoned ship, the flaming vessel exploded and sank at 0922 (Tokyo time).

A handful of rafts and lifeboats were launched, but in the driving rain, the escorting destroyers *Asagumo* and *Tokitsukaze*, with General Nakano onboard, swiftly appeared and gathered some 800 survivors, an astonishing figure given the foul weather and an exploding, burning ship. Somehow, even the parts of two large-calibre 75-mm field guns were salvaged and reportedly still worked when they were later reassembled. From Rabaul, Admiral Kimura ordered the two destroyers to proceed at high speed to Lae and disembark the survivors, as the ships would be too overloaded to engage the enemy if required.

At 9.30 a.m., the *Kyokusei Maru* sank, taking 480 soldiers and sailors with her.

Relieved at being able to finally open up their engines to something near their top speeds of over 30 knots, the *Asagumo* and *Tokitsukaze* bolted ahead of the convoy into the night and turned south through the Vitiaz Strait. By 11 p.m. they would arrive safely at Lae to offload their human cargoes, then immediately turn around to rejoin the convoy before daybreak.

Meanwhile, the rest of Scott's formation of B-17s headed off to find quarry of their own. They would be followed throughout the day by a succession of air strikes by American heavy bombers from many different units, beginning one of the most confusing aspects of the entire battle, as a tangle of false, duplicated and contradictory reports of sinkings, burnings and heavily damaged Japanese ships clogged the planners' ability to keep abreast of what was actually occurring in the ocean off New Britain.

One of Scott's pilots, Lieutenant Jim Murphy, flew into the rain and attempted to attack a destroyer which deftly manoeuvred around his bombs while retaliating with accurate anti-aircraft fire of its own. Murphy switched his attack to one of the transports with a single bomb which, he claimed, fell accurately, blowing out the side of the ship, snapping the vessel clean in two.

Captain Sogaard reported similar success, claiming two direct hits on one of the smaller ships, claiming that flames were seen to shoot dramatically from its hold.

Bombardier Lieutenant Fred Blair dropped his entire load of eight 500-pounders on a cargo ship, all of which missed, but Blair nonetheless reported severe hull damage to the vessel. In that instant, his aircraft was attacked by Zeros, causing his pilot, Jim Dieffenderger, to dive hard away. From the nose, Blair had a terrifying view of the ocean rushing up to meet him, and recalled seeing large sharks.

The attacks continued throughout the morning.

One squadron of B-17s, the 403rd, who'd flown up from Mareeba in Queensland, claimed two direct hits on a '6000-ton' ship, as well as two near misses on another and two more near the stern of yet another vessel, this one '5000 tons', which reportedly lifted the stern clean out of the water.

With aircraft flying at between 4500 and 7500 feet, the men onboard some of the transports could observe them clearly as they made their runs. Flying with the 64th Squadron, Captain Ray E Holsey from Oklahoma dropped his bombs relatively close to the *Oigawa Maru* but inflicted no damage. Under attack from several Zeros, his B-17 received a direct hit in the open bomb bay, rupturing the hydraulics and starting a significant fire. In bravery fuelled by desperation, crew members Lieutenant Peeves and Sergeant Young doused flying suits in firefighting retardant and fought the flames – smothering them when they had to – and, despite burns, gradually got the fire under control.

Holsey called up his squadron commander, Captain Charles Giddings, who was observing the proceedings from another bomber up above. Holsey told the boss he would most likely have to ditch on a nearby island. The sangfroid of Giddings's calm reply, 'Hold on, Ray, I'll be right down,' immediately passed into squadron folklore.

At one stage, a Japanese voice broke in on Holsey's frequency, taunting him in excellent English. Holsey's response was too colourful even for the official 64th Squadron history to record.

Giddings swooped and drew off the fighters while Holsey managed to put out the fire and return to Port Moresby, where the ground crews were astonished to see whole sections of the aluminium skin burned away, exposing the bare spars underneath.

A lull in the battle lasting several hours developed in the middle of the day, during which some of the fighters and reconnaissance flights reported seeing survivors of the *Kyokusei Maru* rescued by the two destroyers, and their subsequent departure at speed.

Later in the afternoon it was the turn of a small formation of Liberators from the 321st Squadron to engage the convoy, but – far from claiming any direct hits – their report later stated that the bomb loads of all their aircraft fell harmlessly into the sea.

Another B-17 squadron, the 65th, then appeared on the scene and began its run, claiming three definite hits on a transport, as well as a near miss on another 'cruiser'. As the formations left the area in the failing light, they reported seeing 'two ships of 5–8000 tons' burning.

As the usually circumspect official history of the RAAF noted:

> These US crews returned to report, with understandable excitement, that they had left one transport 'burning and exploding', another 'burning amidships'. A third was 'seen to explode' and a fourth was 'in a sinking condition'. Probably there was some exaggeration in these claims …

It transpired that not one of these reports was accurate.

The only verified bombing success on 2 March was the sinking of the *Kyokusei Maru* by the formation led by Major Scott. Even claims of damage to some of the transports seem doubtful, as after the attacks the formation managed to re-form and stay together for the next twelve hours.

With operations and intelligence staff at Port Moresby being presented with more than twenty-two reports containing multiple references to hits, fires, near misses, sinkings, capsizings and similar descriptions, they might have been forgiven for believing much of the convoy on that first day of the battle had been wiped out. But as returning crews began to submit duplicate or contradictory information – while others openly stated their bombs had hit nothing at all – serious doubts about the engagement emerged.

In subsequent interrogations, surviving Japanese soldiers would indeed report many attacks by the American bombers that evening of 2 March, as well as a cascade of bombs aimed in their direction, but almost every one of them fell wide. In the cold light of analysis, no damage of any sort can be confidently stated to have been inflicted on any vessel besides the *Kyokusei Maru*.

Just on dusk, around 6.45 p.m., the last reported sighting of the convoy steaming off into the night was radioed in by a reconnaissance aircraft which tapped out the signal before turning around and heading back to Port Moresby. It would be up to some other crew to locate them again.

With just a single transport having been destroyed, and at least some of its soldiers saved, the Japanese commanders looked forward to the night ahead, convinced they had already won the battle. Having seen off multiple Allied challenges, they would, with a little luck, reach Lae while still under cover of darkness.

At the outset the Japanese had been willing to accept losses of up to 50 per cent, so were now pleased to find themselves in exactly the same position as with the successful January convoy. They had no reason to yet believe the Allied air forces had learned anything from their January experience, nor were they capable of seriously challenging Japanese domination of the waters of the South West Pacific.

This convoy, like the last one, would make it through largely unscathed.

As the light faded and the ships prepared to swing south into the Vitiaz Strait, the soldiers and sailors of Operation 81 looked up and gave thanks to the solid screen of grey which had protected them thus far, and would no doubt continue to do so for the final leg of the journey.

Of course, they still had to make it through the night.

Unbeknown to them, Wednesday, 3 March 1943 would be a very different day.

CHAPTER 18
NIGHT CAT ENCOUNTER

The most dramatic night in Flight Lieutenant Terry Duigan's war began with a leisurely waterfront taxi ride. Between Kerwin and Minnie streets along the elegant Cairns Esplanade, the new base of 11 and 20 squadrons had been recently completed, an unremarkable row of three-ply gable-roof huts housing the orderly and ops rooms as well as the medical block and some of the barracks for the airmen and crews. Duigan, luckily, had no use for those as, being a married man, he and his wife, Gwynne, were able to live off the base in a charming former doctor's residence in nearby Maranoa Street.

Married the day Duigan received his wings, Gwynne decided the role of the patiently waiting airman's bride was not for her. When 11 Squadron's Catalinas were relocated to Cairns, she took the air force's offer of paid-for married quarters and the couple made the move up from Melbourne.

A qualified architect and cartoonist whose work appeared regularly in the *Bulletin* and *Digger* magazines, flying also ran in Duigan's veins. In 1910 his father, Reg, and uncle, John, built and flew the first aircraft to take to the air in Australia. They were what you'd call true aviation royalty.

Relieved at not being sent to Europe as a newlywed, Duigan's life as a nocturnal 'Black Cat' Catalina pilot was somewhat surreal. When on duty, he would kiss his wife goodbye at the front door before heading off to work in the government-paid-for cab. He'd then edge his entirely black-painted aircraft off the water in Cairns and turn north to begin night operations bombing Japanese shipping, laying mines, conducting reconnaissance, and generally making a nuisance of himself to the enemy.

The squadron labelled all such missions 'milk runs'. These milk runs in the slow but reliable Catalinas were long and arduous, not helped by the noise of the aircraft with its twin engines placed directly above the fuselage. 'Cats were so noisy inside,' said Duigan, 'that most of the crews were more or less stupefied most of the time.'

By late 1942, Duigan was already an experienced pilot, having chalked up more than 1800 flying hours in his logbook, most of those as skipper, and over 400 at night.

Tonight's trip would be his thirty-first with 11 Squadron.

The briefing had been somewhat unusual. As Duigan later put it, 'I don't recall ever being sent to search north of the Vitiaz Strait on a milk run.' On such a long flight, a refuelling stop would be required at Milne Bay before proceeding north.

Beginning earlier than usual, Duigan took off from the still waters of Cairns' Trinity Bay for the nearly five-hour flight to Milne Bay. Upon arrival, with time to kill until the mission proper began at dusk, he looked around the jungle camp and airstrip, so recently the sight of a ferocious week-long battle, and quietly thanked his stars not to be stationed there. At one stage while using the toilet, he encountered an American pilot who, seeing his wings, asked who was in charge of the big black 'Cat' parked just off the waterfront. Duigan replied that it was he. The American introduced himself as Lieutenant Walter Higgins, the man who had first located the convoy the day before. The two compared notes.

Whether Higgins's advice to Duigan was of use will never be known, but at around 10.40 p.m. that evening, Duigan and his crew succeeded where many others had failed over the previous forty-eight hours.

In a lively account written years after, describing this eventful night, Duigan talks of a 'sky as black as the inside of a cow'. To illuminate the gloom, armourer Bill Clough placed one of the large flares inside the release chute. Waiting on the skipper's word to release it, however, Clough felt a hard click as the inner mechanism of the flare begin to prematurely stir. In a moment of masterfully quick thinking, he yanked it back out of the chute and hurled it through one of the aircraft's thankfully open blister hatches into the night sky, where it erupted instantaneously in a blinding magnesium flash.

Illuminating more of his own aircraft than the enemy, Duigan waited for his eyes to adjust and followed the flare's path down towards the ocean.

There, directly below him, was the unmistakeable white line of a ship's wake, travelling southeast.

Turning onto it, Duigan was 'charmed to see half a dozen substantial ships, with hints of more beyond the illumination, all quickly adopting a disturbed ants' nest configuration'.

Clough's prompt actions in all likelihood saved the aircraft, as the flare's white-hot compound could easily ignite the aluminium interior or burn through it like paper. Several aircraft, in fact – including that of the squadron's former CO – had been recently lost, with the words 'on fire' being transmitted prior to a terrible silence. Duigan later suspected that faulty flares such as these were the cause.

The signal Duigan now sent to Port Moresby prompted one of the most important pieces of the Bismarck Sea puzzle to fall into place. The convoy, in its entirety, observed to be travelling southeast below the Vitiaz Strait, could only be heading for Lae.

Now that they'd found the Japanese, they would not lose them again.

Duigan was ordered to maintain contact or, as he put it later, to 'stick around and pester the enemy' until dawn. Having no desire to be anywhere near the Japanese as the sun rose, he took this to mean 'well before dawn'.

For the next hour or so, like a harassing bird, Duigan made runs over the convoy at 2000 feet, dropping the occasional – and carefully released – flare. In the tropical fug, visibility for both hunter and hunted was equally dismal, and Duigan could make out only 'black blobs against white wakes'. After several dummy runs in which no bombs were dropped, the Japanese ships were lulled back into maintaining course and speed. For Duigan's finale, however, something special was planned. Choosing a destroyer (like many, he believed them to be cruisers), he dropped a flare in its wake, then threw the cumbersome flying boat into the tightest turn he could manage to approach the ship from behind. This time he was ready with a stick of four 250-pound bombs which he intended to drop at almost point-blank range.

As Bob Burne, the navigator and bomb aimer, worked the sight in the nose, his voice issued the standard set of instructions: '… left … left … steady …' Finally, 'bombs gone' was the call and the stick fell away, exploding in a perfect – but perfectly harmless – line, 'marching up the ship's wake'.

Surprised, Burne checked the bombsight and groaned. In his haste, or possibly fatigue, he had adjusted the settings as if to attack a stationary target. 'If he'd set 20 knots for it,' reflected Duigan, 'we'd have split it in half.'

Bombs and flares spent, and with dawn threatening the horizon, Duigan relayed the Japanese position once again back to base, then headed for home, but not before receiving a most curious signal from Port Moresby, instructing him to remain shadowing the convoy in order to guide a 'flight of RAAF Beaufort torpedo bombers to their targets'. Although indeed part of the plan, to have it thus broadcast, in plain speech, referring specifically to 'torpedo bombers', was so contrary to the rules that Duigan chose to ignore the signal altogether.

This, as it turned out, was the perfect reaction, as the message was intended not for Duigan's ears, but the Japanese. The Allied intelligence officers back at base were certain the enemy was listening. Their assumption was correct, and the false transmission a stroke of genius which would later bear significant rewards.

Duigan then handed over to the Australian Beauforts, noticing their navigation lights pass beneath him as he left the area.

Hours later, little did an exhausted Flight Lieutenant Duigan know, as he climbed into his government cab outside the 11 Squadron base in Cairns, that he had just won the Distinguished Flying Cross. In truth, he would probably have been too tired to care, as eighteen hours had elapsed since taking off the previous afternoon. The cab driver asked whether the night's mission had been a long one.

Duigan smiled and assured him it had.

CHAPTER 19
THE BEAUFORTS STRIKE

Flying Officer Lew Hall nearly missed his big moment altogether, for no other reason than someone forgot to wake him. This would be just another in a series of remarkable timings – and mistimings – which marked his career as a pilot with the RAAF. A clerk from Perth, in late 1941 Hall was initially earmarked to fly with Bomber Command in Europe. Just in the nick of time, he was grabbed off the boat as it prepared to pull away from Circular Quay. 'It seems that some clever person thought there might be a chance of a war with Japan,' he recalled of the incident years later.

A few weeks later, Hall arrived at his first posting on the island of Ambon in Indonesia, just in time to be evacuated back to Darwin ahead of the advancing Japanese. In February 1942, he flew into Timor ahead of another imminent Japanese invasion. He was tasked with evacuating RAAF ground staff whom he packed so tightly into the interior of his Hudson that, 'there was literally no chance of them falling over'.

After being congratulated for having saved a couple of dozen valuable RAAF personnel from almost certain death, Hall was told to go home and get some well-deserved rest. This took the form of a long and leisurely bath. Soon, he was interrupted by the sound of aircraft engines low overhead accompanied by booming explosions. Racing outside, he stood slack-jawed on his back lawn, dripping wet, in nothing but a towel and witnessed the 19 February Japanese attack on Darwin.

A year later, having retrained at Nowra on the New South Wales south coast in the art of dropping a torpedo from an aeroplane with the Beauforts of 100 Squadron, Hall was stationed at Milne Bay where he impatiently awaited his chance to repay the Japanese. On the night of 2 March, the squadron was informed they would be setting off before dawn to rendezvous with a Catalina which had been shadowing a Japanese convoy during the night.

On his canvas stretcher bed, Hall slept soundly. Too soundly, it transpired, as an orderly failed to notice his slumbering form until passing his tent a second time. 'Get up! Get up!' he said, frantically shaking the young pilot awake. Aghast, Hall was still pulling on his boots as the first of the squadron took to the air. Racing outside and muttering expletives, he pledged to deal with the orderly when he got back, warning him it would most likely involve a noose.

At 5 a.m., a full fifteen minutes after the rest of 100 Squadron's eight aircraft had departed, Hall opened up the throttles of his Beaufort and hurtled along the mud-soaked metal mesh runway. Onboard, he had an American-built torpedo so large that it had to be slung under the Beaufort's fuselage. Through a shower of mud and muck, the outline of palm trees sped towards him, and for a moment he doubted his chances of clearing them. Slowly though, the aircraft lifted into the dark tropical sky and headed out on a course northwest. 'I honestly didn't think we were going to get off at all, then it was rain and cloud nearly all the way,' he said in a postwar interview.

Having been directed to proceed 'somewhere between the western tip of New Britain and the Vitiaz Strait', Hall suspected the mission would be pointless, but he pushed on nonetheless, flying solely on his instruments. Two of the squadron had already turned back, having run into a wall of weather along New Guinea's eastern coast. Somehow Hall managed to get through it, and by the time he reached the target area, he found conditions on the other side of the front were abating, though still far from ideal.

With no idea where the rest of the squadron might be, Hall kept his eyes out for the flares his CO, Squadron Leader John Smibert, had arranged to drop to sea level for crews to come down and take a closer look. For another half-hour, Hall followed a grid above the ocean. Then, some way off to the north, the white glow of a parachute flare was visible in the gloom. Wheeling around, Hall pointed his Beaufort's nose towards the light, which sputtered out after a few minutes, before another was sighted, this one coloured green, signalling the end of the mission, and for all aircraft to return to base.

Hall cursed.

Having arrived at the party late, he was in no mood to go home so soon. 'Let's go down for a look anyway,' he said to his crew over the aircraft radio.

Levelling out just above the water, Hall was surprised to find the sea almost dead calm. Heading towards the first pink blush of dawn, he began scouring the horizon. In the distance, a dark shape – formless at first – began to grow in his windscreen, barely contrasting against the leaden, slowly lightening sky. 'Jesus!' he blurted to his crew, realising what it was. 'A ship!' More vessels appeared, and Hall realised he was looking at an entire convoy. 'I could see every one of them, in three neat lines, all spread out and stationary.'

As Hall would later discover, only he and one other of the eight Beauforts sent out managed to locate the Japanese convoy. Even Squadron Leader Smibert, despite dropping several flares almost on top of the flotilla, failed to see it.

Earlier, Pilot Officer Ken Waters, one of the original 100 Squadron members, had attacked with his sole torpedo but, despite a perfect drop close to a Japanese ship, he observed no result whatsoever and took it to be a dud.

Now it was Lew Hall's turn.

'I thought all my birthdays had come at once,' he recalled. Swinging around, he had to pull up over one vessel to avoid hitting its mast, then lined up on the largest cargo ship he could find, later estimating it to be around 8000 tons. 'I aimed to put the torpedo right under the bridge of the ship and break it in half,' he said.

Suddenly, the eerie morning tranquillity was shattered as seemingly every gunner on every ship began shooting at him with long lines of red and orange tracer. Ignoring them, Hall kept one eye on the ship and the other on his airspeed indicator, which needed to read a steady but torturously slow 150 knots at an altitude of just 100 feet.

On the 1000-yard run in to the ship, Hall knew he was presenting himself as the easiest target in the world.

Finally, with the hull now filling his windscreen, he hit an electric switch on his control column and heard the whirring of the torpedo release mechanism come to life.

Then, nothing.

Instead of the sudden jolt upwards at the release of the heavy weapon, the Beaufort lumbered on. Hall frantically tried to work the manual release lever, but it was stuck fast. Cursing, he banked around and directed his gunner to open up with the front machine gun on another ship, which, according to the later testament of rescued sailors, turned out to be the *Shinai Maru*. But their twin Brownings were akin to swatting the ship with a broom compared to the potential death blow of the torpedo.

Hall's rear gunner called in a disbelieving tone. 'They're trying to get a shell over us!' One of the destroyer's big guns had begun firing shells into the water ahead of the Beaufort, throwing up great white screens of water to bring it down or at least put the gunner off his aim. Hitting one of those, Hall knew, would be like running into a brick wall.

It was time, he realised, to go.

Back at Milne Bay, Hall reported his near miss in fatalistic terms to a sympathetic intelligence officer who mumbled something about 'next time', and how Hall had most likely come close to winning a Distinguished Flying Medal, but not quite. Deep down he sensed – correctly as it happened – that such an opportunity would never present itself again.

The armourers, as disappointed as Hall, examined the stubborn torpedo, still clinging to the underside of the Beaufort. A tiny securing pin had become slightly bent, blocking the release mechanism. Positioning the loading cradle directly underneath the aircraft, one of the armourers barely had to tap the pin with his little finger for the torpedo to release and fall straight into it. 'It was a perfect opportunity, but nothing came of it,' Hall would reflect, still bewitched by the 'what if' years later.

As dramatic as Lew Hall's near miss might have been, of far greater significance were his reports of the convoy's location, confirmed later by US reconnaissance flights. For a time, they had the intelligence officers scratching their heads. The Japanese simply weren't moving fast enough. If the convoy's previously observed direction had been maintained, it would by now be much further into the Vitiaz Strait.

The Allies were perplexed.

Had the aerial attacks inflicted more damage than previously thought?

Were the Japanese being joined by more vessels from Rabaul, or Lae, or somewhere else?

The intelligence officers at Port Moresby and Brisbane had no way of knowing the convoy's commander, Rear Admiral Masatomi Kimura, was in the process of making one of the most catastrophic blunders of the entire Pacific War.

Perhaps the admiral's memories of the Battle of Midway were still fresh when, as captain of the *Suzuya* the previous June, he had rescued survivors from another cruiser, the *Mikuma*, sunk by US dive bombers and taking 650 sailors with her. Perhaps he doubted being able to reach Lae by sunrise and wished to make certain of having air cover at first light, which would then escort him all the way to his destination.

The logic behind his actions remains flawed, but at some stage during the early hours of 3 March 1943, Kimura ordered the ships of his convoy to mark time and circle in the dark, wasting at least two precious hours of the cover of night.

The consequences of his miscalculation were soon to become tragically apparent.

If, at sunrise, he had expected to look up and see Japanese aircraft, he was to be sorely disappointed. The sky would indeed be filled with planes, but they would not be Japanese. Nor would he be afforded the continued cover of inclement weather. No less startling than Hall's positioning of the convoy was his report that, contrary to all expectations, the new day was dawning clear and brilliant, with barely a cloud to be seen.

Wednesday, 3 March 1943 marked 'Hinamatsuri', the ancient Japanese festival that celebrates little girls. Traditionally, the festival features dolls, red carpets and sugary treats. Onboard the ships of the convoy, in possibly the most surreal moment of the battle, sweets were handed out to the soldiers and sailors, some still barely out of childhood themselves. Talk was of home. Having survived the night with their destination close at hand, morale was high. Those who could do so ventured up on deck to greet the unexpectedly cloudless tropical sky.

Many took it to be the finest of omens.

CHAPTER 20
THE SQUADRONS DEPART

A short time earlier, from Port Moresby to faraway Queensland, teleprinter machines inside airfield operations huts shattered the early morning calm and clattered into life.

From his headquarters in Brisbane, General Kenney issued the orders for Mission 61. Here, in one and a half succinct and closely typed foolscap pages, the blueprint for the destruction of the Japanese convoy was outlined. The recipients were all Fifth Air Force bombardment and fighter groups under his command, as well as those of the RAAF.

Months in preparation across Kenney's Australian air bases, crystallised by Bull Garing in the sand outside a tent in Port Moresby, and finally practised on a wreck inside the harbour, it was only now the final, essential element of the plan could be put in place. Thanks to the observations of RAAF Catalinas and Beauforts, as well as USAAF reconnaissance Fortresses, it was now clear that the Japanese convoy was destined for Lae.

Kenney's order began:

MISSION NO. 61 GENERAL

1A1 ENEMY CONVOY CONSISTING OF ONE CRUISER, SIX DESTROYERS, TWO TRANSPORTS, FOUR CARGO APPROACHING NEW GUINEA; PROBABLE DESTINATION LAE LAST REPORTED POSITION LATITUDE 0654S LONGITUDE 14805E, COURSE 270 SPEED 10 TIME 0615/L

1A2 CONVOY PROTECTED BY ENEMY FIGHTERS DURING DAYLIGHT HOURS ...

1B2 V BOMBER COMMAND WITH MAXIMUM STRIKING FORCE OF MEDIUM, HEAVY, AND LIGHT BOMBARDMENT SUPPORTED BY P-38s WILL ATTACK ENEMY CONVOY WHEN IN RANGE OF LIGHT BOMBARDMENT. THE ATTACK WILL BE MADE BY ONE SQUADRON B-17s (12 AIRPLANES) FOUR SQUADRONS B-25s, ONE SQUADRON BEAUFIGHTERS, ONE SQUADRON A-20s ESCORTED BY TWO SQUADRONS P-38s

Following the summary, every bombardment group was addressed separately and allotted their roles in the great production: altitude, bomb load, make-up and even the fuse settings to be used:

3.2 THE 43RD BOMBARDMENT GROUP WILL PROVIDE ONE SQUADRON B-17s (16 AIRPLANES) AS LEAD ELEMENT; ASSEMBLE ON COMMAND; RENDEZVOUS 9000 FEET OVER CAPE WARD HUNT; ALTITUDE OF ATTACK 7000 TO 10,000

FEET. BOMB LOADING; FULL LOAD 1000 POUNDS DEMOLITION, INSTANTANEOUS FUSES.

THE 38TH BOMBARDMENT GROUP WILL PROVIDE ONE SQUADRON B-25s AS FIFTH ELEMENT; ASSEMBLE ON COMMAND; RENDEZVOUS AT 5500 FEET. ATTACK CO-ORDINATED TO UTILIZE SUPPORT OF BEAUFIGHTERS; ALTITUDE OF ATTACK MINIMUM ALTITUDE (MAST HEAD) BOMB LOADING; FULL LOAD 500 POUND DEMOLITION BOMBS, FIVE SECOND DELAY FUSES.

THE 3RD BOMBARDMENT GROUP WILL PROVIDE ONE SQUADRON B-25s AS FIFTH ELEMENT; ASSEMBLE ON COMMAND; RENDEZVOUS AT 5500 FEET OVER CAPE WARD HUNT. ALTITUDE OF ATTACK: MINIMUM ALTITUDE (MAST HEAD). BOMB LOADING; MAXIMUM LOAD DEMOLITION BOMBS, FIVE SECOND DELAY FUSES.

Then it was the Australians turn to be addressed, and the vital part which would be played by the Beaufighters of 30 Squadron was revealed.

THE 9TH OPERATIONAL (RAAF) GROUP WILL PROVIDE ONE SQUADRON BEAUFIGHTERS AS FOURTH ELEMENT CO-ORDINATED IN SUPPORT OF FIFTH ELEMENT; ASSEMBLE ON COMMAND; RENDEZVOUS AT 6000 FEET OVER CAPE WARD HUNT.

Kenney's order was succinct and to the point. His men were trained and enthusiastic, but much would depend on luck. No rehearsal could prepare them completely for what was to come, and the unknowables were beyond counting. Like every American aviation commander, Kenney was haunted by the recent fate of VT8, the navy squadron of fifteen obsolete Devastator torpedo bombers. The previous June, the squadron had taken off from the deck of the USS *Hornet* to attack Imperial Japanese aircraft carriers at Midway. All fifteen were shot into the sea, with forty-five of its forty-eight airmen lost.

Now, Kenney was ordering his men to carry out a similar strike using aircraft and tactics never before employed in battle. For today's action to be a success, all the myriad elements of the vast apparatus he had constructed must work together seamlessly, and not a single one could fail.

Many of Kenney's airmen had sensed for days that something big was brewing, and that their many hours of practice were soon to be tested in earnest. Competition to be included on the combat list for what the eager young airmen believed would be the South West Pacific's biggest show yet was fierce. The log of the 90th Bombardment Squadron summed up the mood:

> News at night of a 14 ship convoy coming down from Rabaul ... off the coast of New Britain ... all of Port Moresby alerted for this shipping ... the 90th working feverishly ... guns loaded ... bombs aboard ... crews listed ... silently but efficiently, the 90th were at their jobs.

Before dawn, hundreds of airmen were roused, given breakfast and sent to early morning briefings. At 7.30 a.m. at Durand airstrip, formerly known as 17 Mile, Major Ed Larner, the man hand-picked by Kenney for his courage and aggression to train and lead the men who would fly his newly converted B-25 Mitchells, entered the aircrew briefing tent and addressed his men solemnly. The purpose of their many hours of perilously low flying, he told them – not to mention having to relearn the basics of combat flying in completely redesigned aircraft – was about to become evident.

Today they would form part of a combined and meticulously coordinated effort to deal a devastating blow against the enemy. The squadron must understand its role in the overall effort; every aircraft must understand its role within the squadron; and every man on every plane must in turn understand their own individual job within their crew.

Remember what you've learned over the past months of training, Larner said, as well as the rehearsal in Moresby Harbour on the *Pruth*. Some things had gone wrong that day, but those mistakes can not, and must not be repeated today. Timing, he stressed again, will be absolutely critical. Remember there's going to be a lot of airplanes in the sky, so stick to the designated altitude at the rendezvous point: 5500 feet. Time your arrival at Cape Ward Hunt to the minute, and don't go stooging around. We'll be at the same height as the boys from the 38th Group and maybe a whole bunch of others, so anyone who's got a pair of eyes, use 'em. Listen to your radio for the signals. When we head out to attack the convoy, we'll be leaving as one in the biggest single formation you're ever likely to be a part of. When we reach the convoy, remember the schedule: the heavies – B-17s and B-24s – will attack first from up top, then the Aussies go in with their Beaufighters to strafe the ships to knock out their defences.

Then it's our turn.

There'll be conventional bombing from more B-25s courtesy of the 38th Bombardment Group, too, so look out for those guys. There'll also be the A-20 Havocs from the 89th led by Captain Clark, who we all know and respect. And above all of this, the P-38 Lightning boys will be looking after the Zeros. But don't be surprised to see a few of those too. It'll be quite a party.

You've read the orders: when we go in, we go down low, way low, to mast height. Choose your target carefully; and make sure some other guy isn't choosing the same target at the same time. Make the approach just like you've done in training.

Remember, get in low, and skip bomb the bastards to hell.

At 8.40 a.m. the take-off order came through. As he made his way to his B-25, Larner called out, 'To Cape Ward Hunt – let's go!'

Afterwards, American airmen who'd participated in the battle were asked how they rated their chances of survival as they prepared to fly out that morning.

Most answered that it was somewhere around 50 per cent.

•

Over at Ward's airstrip, the teleprinter had not yet been hooked up. The orders for 30 Squadron therefore had to be taken down by hand over the telephone. In fact, the Beaufighter crews didn't receive the finer details of their orders until after they'd taken off. Group Captain Brian 'Blackjack' Walker, however, the Squadron CO, needed no official instructions to brief his men on the impending battle. In the big tent, the two-man crews of the twelve aircraft slated to participate in the coming action crowded in and listened to his words.

'The Americans,' Blackjack announced with his characteristic directness, 'are new to this strafing game, but we are not. It is us therefore, who have been given the job of attacking the Japanese ships first, and hard – strafe from stem to stern; suppress the anti-aircraft defences; knock out the bridges; kill the captain and the officers, leaving the ship decapitated.

'This will create a window of precious seconds for Ed Larner and his boys to come in from the side with their skip bombers. Watch out for them, because they'll be watching out for us. Then, it'll be the big bombers dropping their loads from high above. If we miss anything, the A-20s will come in behind us and strafe the ships a second time. Hopefully they'll be sinking by then.'

Blackjack also pointed out that unlike almost all their previous operations where the enemy was invisible in bunkers or canopies of green jungle, the Japanese today would be *extremely* visible. He reminded them of the miseries the blokes in the army had already gone through at Kokoda, Milne Bay, Buna and Gona. He told them what they had suffered at the hands of the Japanese, and the unspeakable horrors inflicted on those poor bastards who had been captured. 'Today would be a chance to avenge them,' he said, 'give the enemy a blow from which he would not recover, and see to it that a few more blokes make it home to their wives and girlfriends.

'Oh,' he added, 'it's also a chance to show the Yanks just how bloody good the pilots and crews of the RAAF really are!'

At this, the tent erupted into a sustained cheer.

Ironically, it was not Blackjack, but another officer, who would be leading the attack this morning – Squadron Leader Ross Little, a senior flight commander from Sydney. Blackjack's observer had been rated by the medical officer as unfit, rendering the boss's crew incomplete and himself relegated to the 'spare pilot' list, a situation which pleased him not one little bit.

Deferring to protocol, Blackjack handed over the briefing to Little. 'We will attack today,' Little began, 'in line abreast – two flights of six aircraft: "A" Flight will be lead by me, and Torchy will be in charge of "B" Flight.' Despite being without Blackjack, the men knew they were in good hands. Ron 'Torchy' Uren was one of the squadron's finest and most experienced officers. 'Blackjack has already spoken of the importance of what we are about to do,' Little went on. 'Now it's up to us.' According to radio operator Bruce Robertson, Little's final words to the pilots and observers were, 'Make your attack from 500 feet, pick your targets and go, go, go!'

At 8 a.m. the Beaufighters roared into life and began taxiing through the trees along the metal mesh and dirt lanes from their dispersal bays to their take-off position on the runway. On the ground, with their two engines sited slightly forward of the nose and cockpit, the great green-liveried Beaufighters looked strangely awkward, even comical. Their exhaust stubs threw up great spirals of dust and with their air brakes emitting an odd beeping sound, they jostled and jolted into position 'like racehorses straining at the barrier ... the air throbbing and packed with sound', as the RAAF intelligence officer Burton Graham noted.

Lined up along the runway, the ground crews, joined by staff personnel and some of the Americans from adjacent fields, offered encouraging 'thumbs up' to the observers who sat grinning in their open plexiglass hatches.

'You bloody beauts!' some called out, and, 'Give 'em one from me!' Some of the native Papuans had arrived as well, calling out *'Ba Maui!'*, or 'God be with you!'

At precisely 8.30 a.m., the take-off signal was given and the pilot of the first Beaufighter opened the throttle, the aircraft seeming to leap a little before heading off down the runway. As soon as the wheels were off the ground, they were drawn smoothly into the wings, and the Beaufighters lost all semblance of their earth-bound awkwardness, one of them coming back and performing a perfect 'split-S' around some B-25s which had just taken off from an adjoining airstrip.

Pilot George Drury later recalled his feelings as the squadron departed. 'As we took off on the coordinated air attack on the Jap convoy, it was expected that a lot of us would "get the chop", although you didn't adopt that attitude. In those days you were coming back, you knew you were coming back; of course you were coming back.'

Now, the whole sky above Port Moresby seemed filled with aircraft, as the American Mitchells and Havocs came together and flew off to join the heavy Fortress and Liberator squadrons of the 43rd and 90th Bombardment Groups. The throbbing of more and more aircraft engines was overwhelming.

In the surrounding hills, Australian soldiers in observation posts and anti-aircraft gun emplacements lent their own voices of encouragement, then stood in silent awe at the sight – and the thundering sound – of the largest group of aircraft they had ever seen.

Torchy Uren was soon airborne and forming up, keeping an eye on his charges who would be following him into battle. In fact, Torchy was flying with an extra passenger on this trip – and a celebrity at that: Australia's most famous war photographer, Damien Parer.

Although officially employed by the Department of Information, Parer was determined to film the war from the point of view of the ordinary soldier. In his quest to bring pictures of what it was *really* like for the men on the front line, he continually displayed indifference to his own personal safety. Quietly spoken, with intense dark eyes, Parer's fame had recently been sealed with his vivid account of the Kokoda Campaign in his lauded films *Kokoda Front Line!* and *Assault on Salamaua.*

Now his mission was to capture the work of Australian airmen, and he had been living with 30 Squadron for a couple of weeks, flying with different crews, often returning from one sortie to leap straight into the next aircraft about to take off. 'Parer was the most incredible person,' according to Drury, who knew him. 'With the greatest respect, he simply had to get killed. Bravest man I ever met. No one could do the things he did and expect to live out the war.'

Standing behind Torchy in the Beaufighter's small one-man cockpit, feet straddling the aircraft's belly hatch pit and filming through the windscreen, Parer would record the most startling and vivid moving images of the battle to come.

The only man observing the take-off with something less than ebullience was Blackjack Walker, who sensed he was on the verge of missing out on the most famous day in the squadron's history. Not one used to having his will thwarted, he devised a plan. 'I saw these twelve aeroplanes take off and it was more than I could stand,' he later said. 'I thought, "I can't let those characters go out alone."'

With the last of the squadron having taken off, their engines still reverberating, Blackjack, like a man possessed, set off through the camp.

Standing beside his tent, Sergeant William Clark, a quiet Englishman who had not long been on the squadron, watched mesmerised as the display gathered overhead. Suddenly, the wild visage of the CO was in front of him. Clark had barely spoken to Blackjack and was terrified of him, and now here the CO was, piercing him with his dark eyes.

Wondering what misdemeanour he may have unintentionally committed, Clark went to say something but the words had barely left his mouth. 'You! Get into that aeroplane!' Blackjack yelled, pointing towards Beaufighter A19-3, one of the few machines still on the ground. Without waiting for the order to be repeated, a stunned Clark gathered up his flying gear and headed towards the aircraft as Blackjack yelled at ground crew to prepare her for flight.

Minutes later they were airborne, but with the rest of the squadron already way out in front, Blackjack formed up instead with the American Lightnings of the 39th Fighter Squadron who had just taken off from *Schwimmer*, as they had named it after one of their fallen airmen, killed over Moresby flying a P-39 Airacobra. With the Americans not known for their adherence to radio silence ('They'd never heard of it!', Blackjack would later say), they delighted at being joined by the familiar and popular Australian officer. But they sounded a warning. 'Listen, Blackjack, you better get that Beaufighter out of the way, it'll be no damn good in a dogfight!' And they were right. As fine an aeroplane as the Beaufighter was, it was no match one-on-one for a nimble Zero.

Today, Blackjack would have to content himself with tagging along as an observer.

And what a sight awaited him that morning over the Bismarck Sea.

He later reflected on his unlikely crewman. 'He was some poor little green observer bloke who had just come up from down south and I don't think he'd ever flown a mission.'

The young man's first trip – with the boss, no less – would be a memorable one, to say the least.

•

RAAF Radio Station 315 was still a month away from becoming operational, but 150 feet up on the impossibly steep knoll of Cape Ward Hunt, Sergeant Charlie Wilkinson was busy. With its commanding views north to the Huon Gulf, east into the heart of the Bismarck Sea, and beyond to distant New Britain and Rabaul, this lonely outpost – it had been solemnly and repeatedly impressed upon him by his superiors – would be one of the most important links in a vital chain of stations providing early warning for Port Moresby and other Allied bases in New Guinea of incoming Japanese air attacks.

As far as Wilkinson was concerned, therefore, the newly installed Mk II AW radar set could not be switched on fast enough. Until then, he was to make sure the Civil Construction Corps workers under his instruction did their job. While this was a relatively straightforward proposition when it came to regular army personnel, civilian workers were entirely different.

For more than a week now, a series of dismal tropical storms had meant work had been at a standstill. In these conditions a cotton shirt left on the ground – for even a day – would begin to rot. But this morning, 3 March, the sun finally reappeared and work could resume apace.

At the sound of aircraft engines approaching from the south, Sergeant Wilkinson paused in the complex task of running cables up from the generator. His first instinct – always – was to determine if the planes were Japanese, but on this occasion the soft throb of the Beaufighters' twin motors assured him they were friendly. Aircraft of all types were spotted regularly at Cape Ward Hunt, but usually distant, and always on their way to somewhere else.

Today was different.

On the site overlooking the water, the men downed tools and shielded their eyes from the bright sunshine as the first of the Beaufighters appeared. Instead of passing overhead, however, they executed a tight turn at 6000 feet and began to circle in the clear morning air: six RAAF aircraft, flying smoothly as one, their spacing perfect as if connected by an invisible rod. Then another group of six arrived and lined up behind them. A minute later, a different engine throb was heard and a formation of American Mitchell bombers appeared, flying a few thousand feet higher. They too began circling.

'Will ya have a look at this!' was all Wilkinson could say as the sound built to a deafening crescendo.

In a few minutes, the sky was filled with aircraft.

Higher up, the pale undersides of B-17 Fortresses and a few Liberators could now be seen, then above them the unmistakeable twin boom of a score of P-38 Lightning fighters. In the distance, in a great stream, the shapes of more aircraft – dozens and dozens – were sighted pouring through The Gap, one of the most formidable of the high passes of the Owen Stanleys, usually concealed in cloud.

'The Beaufighters were there first and we just gently circled round and round,' recalled pilot George Drury. 'I think our position was 6000 feet, from memory. There was not a cloud in the sky and the squadrons of B-25s, A-20s, and B-17 bombers would arrive at their allocated position and then circle and circle and circle.'

Awestruck, the men on the ground watched as a mighty tower of aeroplanes formed above their heads.

The sight was no less spectacular in the air, and the 30 Squadron pilots gaped as the components of this fleet came together into a single apparatus. 'Look! More 25s! They're still coming up through The Gap!' one pilot exclaimed over the intercom. Instead of climbing above them, however, this group slipped underneath and began to assemble below. Further down on the lowest tier, twelve Havocs from the 89th Squadron – the first of Pappy Gunn's aircraft to be converted into commerce destroyers – took their place just above the water.

Nothing like this in the Pacific War had ever been witnessed: the aircraft of sixteen Allied squadrons converging on one small piece of sky. 'The most impressive single spectacle I have ever seen,' recounted Drury. Sergeant Dave Beasley, his observer, had the finest of views from his position in the perspex astrodome along the Beaufighter's back. 'Looking up, I saw a circular staircase of planes. It was impossible to count them,' he said.

It was incredible.

Damien Parer, in Torchy Uren's plane, described it as 'the greatest show I'd ever seen. I had a tight feeling in the pit of my stomach looking at it.'

From the grandstand at the top of the staircase, the P-38 Lightning pilots looked down into the vortex of this panorama of power, and shared their feelings about the occasion in excited wisecracks to their compatriots in the bombers as they weaved in and out among them.

'All right you so-and-sos, what are you waiting for?'

'Come on, fellas, quit your stooging!'

'Jeez, look at those 25s!'

'Go on in there, give it to those yellow bastards!'

Some were far more ribald, and by contrast an Australian airman distinctly recalled an American impersonating Ella

Fitzgerald, crooning the words of 'What's your story, Morning Glory ...' in a surprisingly fine voice.

Captain WS Royalty, flying as a navigator in a Mitchell with the 71st Squadron, was equally impressed:

> As we made our first circle, we could see, coming over the mountains, an almost unbelievable number of planes. Eight B-17s were getting into formation slightly above us. Below us three separate flights of B-25s were already in formation and beginning to circle. Below that were a great number of Beaufighters, A-20s and P-40s [in this, Royalty was mistaken as no P-40s took part in the battle this day], all in formation, more or less. It was the most concentrated flight of aircraft any of us had ever seen.

At the very top of the pile, a Lightning pilot circled in the still air, mesmerised by the 'beautifully clear day', with the distant coast of New Britain just visible as a green wall, made hazy by the slightest of sea mists.

Whatever doubts or misapprehensions the men might have harboured prior to the mission began to melt away. In their Havocs, the men of the 89th Squadron had not even had the chance to properly practise mast-high bombing, and despite being led by the greatly respected Captain Glen Clark, rated their chances of returning at even money at best. 'The thought of attacking warships at mast height did not thrill the hell out of us,' admitted one of them. The sight of the irresistible force of which they were a part, however, went some way in assuaging their apprehensions.

Skip-bombing B-25 pilot Lieutenant Walter Lee, from the 90th Squadron, recalled, '... the mass of airplanes was an exceptional sight by itself. The sky seemed almost black with them. Everywhere I looked I could see at least one flight of some type of airplane ... We kept circling in one huge circle until it was certain that everyone who was coming was there.'

In each of the Fortresses were ten men; in the Mitchells, up to five; three in the Havocs; two in the Beaufighters and a single pilot providing top cover in each of the Lightnings. In all, nearly 500 highly trained young airmen, carrying between them over 120 tons of bombs and 200 000 rounds of ammunition.

As the pilots concentrated harder on maintaining their altitude and avoiding the considerable risk of collision, a hush came over the airwaves as the gravity of the spectacle took hold. Upon these men, this army of youth, a dread responsibility had descended: to strike a blow never before attempted against an implacable enemy who neither gave nor expected any quarter, and who fought with a brutality beyond their reach.

On this bright March morning in 1943, the entire force of the great air weapon to which they belonged would be unleashed in one almighty spasm of aggression with nothing held in reserve.

It was a gamble for which there were no precedents and few certainties.

Failure was unthinkable.

Finally, at 9.30 a.m., the signal was received: *Advance on target*.

PART THREE

CHAPTER 21

'LAST NIGHT, I DREAMED I SAW A DRAGON RISING OUT OF THE SEA'

Setting their compasses to 035 degrees, thirteen of the heavy B-17s of the 43rd Bombardment Group were the first to peel off to the north. Assembling above them, around thirty 39th Squadron Lightnings would provide top cover. The pilots were told that contact with an enemy combat air patrol was imminent – prepare to engage. Weaving in and out of the bomber formation, the Lightnings washed off their speed a little so as not to get too far ahead.

Like in a handicap race, the big bombers straightened out of the whirling circus of aircraft, before uncoiling towards the enemy. Two flights of three B-17s led the way, pulling out to about a quarter of a minute ahead, the navigators in the lead 'ships' (as the Americans called their big aircraft), following the latest indicated coordinates of the convoy's position. From their perspex observation posts in the noses of the Flying

Fortresses, eyes scoured the sea below as pilots executed long shallow dives down to 7000 feet.

As Captain Royalty noted, '... the B-17s headed out to meet the convoy and the circle we were in straightened out. Much the same as you would see if you took the loose end of a coil of rope and started pulling. This is undoubtedly the largest Allied air offensive ever put into the air at one time here in the South West Pacific. It must have affected everyone the same as it did me.'

The faster B-25s then pulled out and moved into position behind the Fortresses, but held speed with them as they glided gently down in the clear, still air to their allotted slot 4000 feet above sea level.

Captain Garrett Middlebrook, who would go on to become a sixty-five-mission veteran and earn a Distinguished Flying Cross, was flying his one and only sortie as co-pilot this morning with the 405th Bomb Squadron. 'I thought I was fortunate,' he would later write. 'The pilot was doing all the work and I was a witness to history being made – we knew this was a big show that would live in the history books for 100 years.'

As the air above the Beaufighters of 30 Squadron cleared, Squadron Leader Ross Little indicated his pilots to move off in their two flights, flying line abreast. They fanned out as if carried in a stream, following the long river of aircraft stretching to the north in front of them, using zero boost at 2000 revs, gently dropping to their attack height of just 500 feet.

Behind them more B-25s followed, both the several squadrons of mid-range bombers, as well as the first of Ed Larner's commerce destroyers. At the rear came the fast-moving Havocs with their distinctive high tail fins.

Pilot George Drury, in Beaufighter A19-11 with Dave Beasley in the rear, remembered that, 'right at the appointed minute, this air armada started going along the north coast of New Guinea and towards the Japanese convoy. Our instructions were to get the transports.' Looking up, Beasley counted thirty-two Lightnings high above.

One among their number, however, made him look twice.

'What the bloody hell?' Beasley uttered over the radio to Drury.

'What's up?'

'There's a single-boom fighter up there among the 38s.'

'Where?'

'Way behind and up high to hell above us ... it's a Beaufighter!'

Then, 'It's Blackjack!' burst from them both.

Blackjack Walker was never going to miss his ticket – even if only as an observer – to the greatest aerial spectacle he was ever likely to see.

•

Some twenty minutes later, less than 100 miles from Cape Ward Hunt, the Allied armada found its target.

'The word went out among the formation that one of the lead Fortresses had sighted a faint dark outline of a ship several miles ahead,' recalled Bob Guthrie, one of the many highly valued Australian navigators attached to the Americans. Guthrie was flying with the 90th Squadron in a modified B-25. 'Then the excited call went out over the radio: the convoy was in sight, and the game was on.'

The Japanese ships were spotted as they rounded the Huon Peninsula, turning west into their final run for Lae, now just over 100 miles away. Had they not thrown away those valuable hours of night cover to circle in the Vitiaz Strait, they might well now be unloading at their destination.

Instead, the moment the Allies had waited for was upon them.

George Drury recalled the rush of adrenaline. 'We couldn't imagine in our wildest dreams that anything like this could happen. I just kept repeating to myself our instructions: get the transports, get the transports ...'

In Beaufighter A19-5, piloted by Torchy Uren, Damien Parer was doing his best to set up his camera with one hand and to hang onto something – anything – with the other. Being unstrapped and standing in a small floor well right behind Torchy's cramped one-man cockpit, this was no easy task. Occasionally, Torchy would turn around to the famous war photographer and apologise for the Beaufighter's distinct lack of comforts when it came to catering for passengers. Parer didn't seem to mind and found the best place to steady the camera was on Torchy's head. The pilot reportedly took the imposition with good grace.

Eager to spot the ships, Parer peered through the front windshield at the ocean and, in a light sea mist, began to make them out. Afterwards, he would say it was not what he expected. This was no tight and orderly formation, proceeding martially across the seas. Rather, they were surprisingly spread out, stretching haphazardly back for what seemed like miles. What he took for two 'cruisers' – in fact the two larger *Kagero*

Class destroyers, *Yukikaze* and *Tokitsukaze*, a mistake made by many during the battle – seemed to lead the parade with four smaller warships on the south side travelling southwest in loose single file. To the north, three more destroyers could be seen, but in between, a hotchpotch of different-sized merchant vessels seemed almost comical in comparison.

Squadron Leader Little flicked away out in front, indicating his pilots to form up line astern, then led his men downwards into a shallow, powerful dive. Parer gripped a spar in the aircraft, bracing against the dropping sensation in his legs as Torchy inched open the throttle. Every second, the ships below grew clearer and larger. Pinpricks of orange light then seemed to flutter across their decks amid grey clouds of smoke, as their anti-aircraft guns opened fire, both the lower-altitude pom-poms and the large 5-inch guns, firing in sharp flashes, not at them but at the B-17s who were now approaching the convoy from 10 000 feet.

This would be one of the Japanese defenders' most costly mistakes.

In a flash, the Australian pilots were at a mere 500 feet above sea level and every detail of the ships was now visible. A long, curving swoop across the convoy was made. Observer Fred Cassidy in A19-15 noticed a hatch at the rear of one merchant ship painted white with a large red cross. He was not fooled. 'Hospital ship, my arse,' he muttered to his pilot, Bob Brazenor.

Completing a wide circle, the line of Beaufighters levelled out, then A Flight suddenly spread out line abreast and, without warning, moved across the path of the following flight. The pilots adjusted accordingly but not without a startled 'Jeez, boss ...!' Careful to avoid the chaos of multiple aircraft closing in on the same ship, the pilots spread out wider as they approached the fleet from the south, preparing to manoeuvre into the ideal attack position of a head-on approach.

Anti-aircraft fire continued to fly up towards them from below. The highly trained Japanese anti-aircraft gunners were excellent shots, with explosions erupting barely 100 feet forward of the Beaufighters, even from distances of up to 10 miles.

Radio silence was strictly maintained. The pilots relied on a shared sixth sense – well honed over dozens of missions flown in close-combat formation – each man anticipating the movement of his neighbour, sensing his smallest action.

Then, from above, in the corners of the pilots' eyes, they saw a cascade of spinning and twisting, followed by splashes as the Beaufighters began their run. The first thought was that they were bombs being dropped by the 'heavies' above. In the rear of the aircraft, the observers looked upwards. 'Drop tanks, Skip! They're just drop tanks!' they called. Up top, the Lightnings had spotted the enemy. But their Lightnings being no certainty over a nimble, skilfully piloted Zero, they had discarded their external fuel loads and were climbing, stripped for action.

Relieved as they were not to be flying through a shower of actual explosives, the Australians knew the damage a falling auxiliary fuel drop tank could inflict on a plane. Thankfully, luck was with them as the flurry fell close, then wide. One observer later said he thought the falling drop tanks resembled 'heavy, dew-covered gum leaves'.

With the merchant vessels being the first priority, the Beaufighters ignored the protective outer rim of destroyers, flying so close to the water the ships' larger guns were unable to depress low enough to fire on them. Like a swarm of green, snub-nosed bats, they flashed by, the warships' guns violently swinging to follow them.

The pilots could see the merchant vessels clearly now. Most had been applied with grey and green camouflage, one ship – the *Taimei Maru* – had been adorned with a painted bow wave, another had the number '967' clearly marked under the bridge. The top deck of one of the larger ships, a four-master of about 6000 tons, was crowded with stores and crates and machinery, strapped down for the voyage. Many carried large motorised barges, destined to be lowered away and filled with men on their arrival. On many of the other ships, men in the olive drab of Japanese army uniforms could be seen crowding every open space.

Pulling up from mast height to attack altitude, the Beaufighters advanced, spread out, as one observer noted, 'like a cavalry charge of old'. Then, unexpectedly, when the bombers were around 1000 yards away, the ships suddenly turned as one, like a herd in unison, swinging their bows towards their attackers.

The pilots – astonished – now witnessed one of the great ruses of the Allied battle plan to deliver its deadly reward.

Admiral Kimura, having been earlier fed the information about approaching 'torpedo bombers' – which had so astonished Catalina pilot Terry Duigan he chose not to respond – followed by the abortive dawn attack by the Beauforts of 100 Squadron, had taken the bait. Through his binoculars, he spotted the twelve approaching Beaufighters, and could well have been forgiven for believing them to be another squadron of Beauforts.

The two aircraft shared, after all, many of the same components: wings, parts of the tail assembly, and virtually identical profiles. Once again, Kimura thought he had outsmarted the Allies, and ordered his ships to turn and face his enemy, presenting the narrowest possible profile for a moving torpedo.

For an attack by strafing Beaufighters, however, it was the *perfect* position.

Kimura's ships turned quickly, obeying his command within seconds.

The 30 Squadron pilots pressed their firing buttons. Each round of their six .303 machine guns could tear up wooden decking, puncture metal plate and shred rubber. But this paled in comparison to the devastation wrought by the exploding shells of their four 20-mm Hispano cannons.

In combination, each plane let loose a ferocious stream which flayed everything it touched, creating a river of fire and destruction running the length of the ships. From stem to stern, a parade of exploding shells caused instant chaos: crates of cargo disintegrated, drums of fuel erupted, gun emplacements were wiped out, and railings and bulkheads collapsed.

Nowhere was the horror more savage, however, than inside the ships' bridges.

Firing close to the horizontal, the Beaufighters' guns ripped open the ships' thick armoured windows as if they were made of cellophane. Barely had the captain and officers had time to register the approaching attack when they were cut down: men decapitated, bodies sliced in half, limbs ripped off and hurled in every direction. Witnesses cowering on the deck below looked up and saw the bridge – one moment crowded with officers – vanish in clouds of red.

Some of the ships stopped dead in the water. Without their bridges, they were devoid of order and command. Others began to turn wildly as if panic and hysteria had engulfed the very ship itself.

Describing the action later, observer Fred Cassidy recalled:

It was our goal to put the bridge out of order. You would begin the approach sideways, maybe three-quarter speed, perhaps 220 knots, and about 4 miles off. Then we'd run parallel. We'd make a big wide turn, get into line astern, usually a flight of maybe three. We'd start at the back of the ship and make a big sweeping turn and come in from the front and begin the dive from about 500 feet. The ship would be about 600 yards in front. You'd let go with your cannon at maybe 100 yards from the ship, aim straight at the bridge, and turn straight off. You'd pull up over the mast. In the Bismarck Sea battle we strafed from the front. The ships were careening in all directions.

In a flash, the initial pass of the Beaufighters had left the first of the ships shattered and ablaze. Concentrating on the heavy bombers high above, one Japanese three-man ack-ack crew remained totally unaware of the low-level Beaufighters until the moment they appeared, practically on top of them. One gunner was observed by a pilot to point frantically, grabbing the attention of his comrade when, a split second later, both vanished in a wall of steel and flame.

Fred Cassidy then watched the ship 'kind of disintegrate'.

Bob Crawford described it as 'an energetic exercise. You'd hit one ship, whip around, then do another, then come up underneath another Beaufighter going the other way ... we ended up strafing one destroyer and three transports.'

George Drury managed to line his Beaufighter up on the *Taimei Maru*. The ship's crew were so oblivious to the impending danger that their change-of-watch ceremony was still underway on the bridge as his aircraft loomed in, unseen, from over the waves. Drury recalled 'pressing that firing button with gay abandon' as his guns tore across the ship and devastated the bridge. Mesmerised by the level of destruction he was creating, he admitted he 'left the pull-out a bit late and had to bank to go through the masts'.

'We went in so low that the Japs firing at us were possibly firing at their own ships.' He then found three more ships 'beautifully lined up' and so decided to attack the first of these. But the tremendous vibration of his guns blew the bulb in his illuminated gunsight, robbing him of his automatic deflection. Undeterred, he aimed his tracer fire at the waterline then 'just eased the nose up so our guns were striking the bridge. I could see fires starting as I passed overhead.'

Above, an audience of American pilots watched on, awestruck. Even from several thousand feet away, the impact of the Beaufighters swooping on the ships – like terrible birds of prey – could be clearly seen as bridges collapsed and deck cargoes exploded in sheets of flame. The Australian pilots, whose training banned unnecessary radio chitchat, were surprised yet grateful hearing the Americans' excitement and encouragement in their headphones.

'Get in there, boy! Get into them! Go! Go!'

'Shoot 'em up, you bomber bastards!'

'Jesus, will you look at that! Give 'em da works!'

'Boy-oh-boy-oh-baby! Will you take a look at those Beaufighter sons of bitches!'

'Go you Aussies! Give it to those yellow bastards, for the sake of dear old Brooklyn!'

Drury recalled that 'it was always the Australians' strict procedure to keep radio silence. You wouldn't say a word unless it was a dire emergency. But as soon as we got in sight, the Yanks came out on their wireless systems and they were really yelling. It really did build up the excitement and the adrenaline was pumping'.

This was only the beginning. Coming around for another attack, the Japanese anti-aircraft defences erupted. Barrages of fire followed the Australian airmen, with some shells bursting as low as 50 feet. Then, as the Beaufighters began their second sweep, great splashes of water erupted in spouts around them. Having earlier contended with falling drop tanks, now bombs – *actual bombs* – were falling from above.

Sergeant Cassidy recalled that '… the Liberators and B-17s were dropping [bombs] from 6000 to 10000 feet and they'd make huge splashes when we were about 20 feet off the sea. These splashes were 30 to 50 feet across and followed by a tremendous spout of water. We had to fly through those.'

In the confusion of whirling and firing aircraft, the delicate timetable of the triple-wave attack began to unravel. The heavy bombers were supposed to wait until the aircraft at the lower levels had finished their job, but no one had apparently told the Fortress and Mitchell pilots that the Beaufighters would be making a second run.

Flying Officer Bob Brazenor remembered those first moments well. 'We attacked, we went in low, and bombs were, well, to be honest with you, bombs were coming from everywhere. Coming from B25s, Fortresses … the ships more or less opened up their bridge to us, so it was a pretty effective attack.'

George Drury was philosophical. 'It worked well. I don't think we made any mistakes. Probably some of the bombers were a bit ahead of their schedule and bombs were falling around the Beaufighters.'

In Beaufighter A19-87, Flying Officer Dick Roe and observer Flight Sergeant Peter Fiskin were on the verge of pulling up from their strafing run when a 500-pound bomb, dropped from a Mitchell above, exploded directly underneath them. The force of the blast tossed them 300 feet into the air like a toy flung by a child. At the top of the apex the aircraft stalled, flipped nose down, but somehow managed to pick up enough speed for the wings to grip the air. Roe regained control, levelling out just above the water. It was an extraordinary feat of airmanship, and except for a large dent in the belly, the two men were later to discover the aircraft was completely undamaged. 'It gave us a hell of a shock,' Fiskin said afterwards.

Nor did the falling bombs seem to deter the next player on the scene of destruction, the B-25 commerce destroyers of Major Ed Larner's 90th Squadron.

Having held off the eleven aircraft of his squadron five minutes from the target while the Beaufighters did their work, Larner emerged from some puffy cumulus cloud and ordered his men into a V echelon, then went into a fast descent.

Finally, thought Larner, these bizarre new aircraft – after months of modifying and rebuilding, training up the crews in new tactics, the endless back-and-forth consultations between himself, General Kenney and Pappy Gunn – would be put to the test. Larner opened fire and the massed arrays of .5-inch guns made the aircraft shudder, the deafening noise overwhelming even the sound of the engines.

The ammunition of the American attackers had been belted in the sequence: one tracer, two armour piercing, two incendiary. At close range, this cocktail created even more mayhem than the Beaufighters' solid .303 shot and cannon. So stunned were the Japanese by the array of muzzle flames erupting from the Mitchells' noses, they took the aircraft to be on fire and cheered their anti-aircraft gunners on.

For many, it was to be the last action of their lives.

Squeezing the firing buttons on their control columns, the Allied pilots watched the deadly mixture tear up the ships like a gigantic claw. As the 90th Squadron combat report put it:

From then on for half an hour, chaos reigned for the Sons of Nippon … a panorama of bursting shells, diving planes, exploding bombs, planes dog-fighting, and occasional burning planes falling into the ocean an [sic] veritable hell broke loose.

John Arbon, flying alongside Ed Larner, recalled the tense atmosphere.

The hot breath of the inside of the airplane is unbearable. It was just like climbing into an oven. We wear nothing but a pair of shorts, Aussie flying boots, a shoulder holster filled with a loaded .45 automatic, a knife, and a Mae West [life jacket] in case we have to swim.

Now, amid this macabre choreography of multiple and simultaneously attacking aircraft, the skip bombing commenced. Larner was not supposed to enter the fray until the Australian Beaufighters had finished their runs, but now found himself attacking alongside them.

The first Australian observer Sergeant Fred Cassidy knew of the Americans' arrival was looking out his hatch and seeing a 500-pound bomb travelling along beside him. Calling up his pilot, Sergeant Moss Morgan, the phlegmatic Cassidy quietly suggested the Skipper 'shift a little to the right' as bounce by bounce, the bomb seemed intent on 'coming over to say hello'.

Ed Larner had made a pledge to General Kenney when he inspected the squadron at Port Moresby just two days earlier. In no uncertain terms, he said that when it came to skip bombing, his men 'wouldn't miss'. Kenney, smiling, had replied that he had a feeling 'the Japs were going to get the surprise of their lives'. Larner did not want to let the boss down, and as squadron commander carefully guided and cajoled his men into the attack over the radio, insisting they adhere to the details of the plan.

Pulling up from sea level to avoid more splashes from the fighters' drop tanks, Larner spotted another group of ships, including some of the destroyers and headed towards them. Singling out one to attack, he noticed others from his flight following close behind. Concerned about the danger of collision, he switched on his radio. 'Dammit, get the hell off my wing and find your own boat!'

They quickly banked away.

Larner continued in a wide circle, then went in towards the ship's bow. At 1500 yards he straightened out and pressed long and hard on his firing button, 'butterflying' with his rudders to spread his fire and avoid a little of the barrages of anti-aircraft fire coming up to meet him.

The defences went quiet.

Larner dropped down again to mast height, and pulled a secondary switch on his control column, releasing two 500-pound bombs.

'Men were running on the decks of the ships in disbelief, bewildered, terrified,' recalled John Ambon. 'They showed the awful destruction of our machine guns, cannons and bombs. Hundreds were lying on the decks in their own blood.'

In the melee that was the Bismarck Sea engagement, it is difficult to now state with certainty which aircraft struck which vessel at which particular instant. Some pilots indeed flew low enough to read and record the names of the ships they were attacking, but with multiple strikes on multiple vessels, the details of the battle cannot realistically be determined.

Compiled soon after the battle, the 90th Squadron combat reports capture the frenetic, even chaotic nature of the attack.

> Captain Henebry picked a 5000–8000 ton transport and dropped a 500-pound five second delay bomb on its water line ... on a second run he had a miss of 15 feet ... the ship was burning violently as he came in and strafed it ... Lieutenant McKee scored two direct hits on a 5000 ton transport ... one in bow and one in the gun position in the stern ... it seemed to blow up, then stopped its forward movement ... Lieutenant Chatt scored two direct hits and two near misses on a large destroyer or small cruiser ... Superstructure entirely blown away ... ship made 90 degree turn and stopped immediately ... Lieutenant McCoun peeled off onto a [sic] 8000 ton transport gutted with full-laden soldiers on [sic] jungle equipment ... he laid one hit at the waterline and another in the middle of the ship ... Lieutenant Moore scored two direct hits on a 5000 ton transport ... left it rocking violently ...

From the enemy's point of view, much was later gleaned from interrogations of small numbers of Japanese prisoners of war. In his 1991 study of the battle, historian Lex McAulay painstakingly pieced together evidence taken from such interrogations, as well as interviews conducted postwar.

Japanese witnesses stated that Admiral Kimura's flagship, the *Shirayuki*, was struck early on in the engagement by a Beaufighter in a strafing attack which wiped out or wounded many of the officers on the bridge. This was closely followed by two bombs dropped by a Mitchell, most likely flown by Larner himself, as his own report of the destruction closely matches the Japanese recollections. His first bomb hit the deck next to the aft .5-inch gun, but Larner cursed as his second missed, exploding in the water beside the hull. The ship rolled onto its side, then quickly righted itself again like a child's toy in a bath. But the damage was done.

The combination of the two bombs wielded almost perfect destructive power. While the near miss cracked and buckled the ship's external plates, Larner's initial bomb penetrated the ammunition handling room directly underneath the aft gun. A fire ignited the ammunition which, in a huge explosion, ripped the stern clean off, allowing water to flood the ship's internal compartments. It was a testament to the vessel's construction, however, that it did not immediately begin to sink. Watching from above, Dave Beasley yelled out to George Drury that an American bomber just 'blew the arse right off a destroyer', with 'iron hurled in every direction'.

One of the survivors of the carnage on the bridge was, incredibly, Admiral Kimura himself, who received bullet wounds to his left thigh, right shoulder and stomach. He was fortunate to have been hit with the Australian .303 calibre as wounds from the larger American .5-inch rounds would not have been survivable. So certain were his subordinates of his death, however, signal flags were hoisted communicating news of his demise to the fleet.

But to their amazement, after a short time, Kimura simply got up, 'walked it off and continued to command'.

Close at hand, the *Shikinami* was quick to help the admiral's flagship, which accounts for the relatively low loss of life onboard the *Shirayuki* despite its catastrophic damage and eventual sinking. Of her company of 219, just thirty-two sailors went down with her; the rest, including Admiral Kimura, were spirited onboard the *Shikinami* and whisked away to the safety of Lae.

Perhaps not without some symbolism, the warship named after the divine Emperor's magnificent white stallion was the first of many to be sent to the bottom.

Ed Larner was not finished. After striking the *Shirayuki*, he proceeded to the far side of the convoy, swung around, and strafed a transport vessel which instantly caught fire. He then dropped the third of his four bombs amidships. Banking away, he used his last 500-pounder on another destroyer but missed with no visible damage observed.

Fellow 90th Squadron pilot Walter Lee recalled:

As we were coming in the Jap battlewagons started swinging broadside so they could use all their guns on us … The first flight attacked the destroyers and cruisers, each selecting one in the order in which they flew. A destroyer is the most vicious thing to attack because they have so many pom-poms and multiple machine guns. It wasn't a pleasant sensation to see the whole side of one of those things suddenly burst with flame from one end to the other and watch those red tomatoes come out at you. They never did hit any of us though. Their range was slightly short ...

The two mid-level Mitchell squadrons of the 38th Bombardment Group – the 71st and 405th – were also in action above Larner.

Garrett Middlebrook, 405th Squadron co-pilot, would never forget what he saw that day:

We circled out there waiting our turn to go in, a good mile away ... then the strafers of 30th Bomb Group arrived. They went in and hit this troop ship. What I saw looked like little sticks, maybe a foot long or something like that, or splinters flying up off the deck of the ship; they'd fly all around and twist crazily in the air and fall out in the water. I thought, 'What could that be? They must have some peculiar cargo on that vessel.' Then I realized what I was watching were human beings.

Three minutes after the first bomb was dropped, the A-20 Havocs of the 89th Squadron arrived, but many could see that it was already a rout. Led by the experienced and popular Captain Glen Clark, the six aircraft flew in three elements of two. In one element, Second Lieutenant Jack Taylor flew wingman to Captain 'Dixie' Dunbar, and both men initially aimed for what appeared to be the largest freighter in the convoy. They were forced to break off the attack several times at the last instant to avoid hitting other bombers intent on doing the same thing. 'Otherwise,' wrote

Taylor years later, 'we would have been shooting at our own people.'

Taylor in fact found every ship he tried to attack already spoken for by a number of aircraft coming in from a variety of angles. 'Every time we found a destroyer that looked pretty good, someone came in on it and was right in our way.'

Finally, having been thwarted in attacking the largest ship, they came upon what appeared to be the smallest. 'It was all by itself and no one was bothering it,' wrote Taylor, 'probably because it was so small.' It was in fact the 915-ton coaster *Kembu Maru*, indeed the most diminutive of the convoy's freighters, currently weighed down with a cargo of over 1600 drums of aviation fuel and other assorted oil.

Both pilots came down low for a beam-on attack, Taylor flying slightly behind and to the left of Dunbar, the flight leader. 'We must have been going about 275 miles an hour by the time we got down to our attack level and homed in on this dude,' wrote Taylor.

Dunbar dropped first, letting go two 500-pounders which both missed their mark. Immediately behind him, Taylor only intended to release one of his two bombs on the small and difficult target but, in his words, he 'got a little excited' and released them both. 'On the switch release, up was one, and down was the other and I just went "flip-flop" and released both of them inadvertently.' He cursed, sensing that he too had blown his chance.

Dunbar pulled up hard, a manoeuvre Taylor reluctantly followed, exposing as it did the plane's vulnerable underbelly. But then Taylor felt a double shudder as the five-second delay fuses detonated. Glancing back, he was stunned to see the *Kembu Maru* seemingly jump out of the water then fall back, minus her stern. 'It immediately started to take water and by the time we had moved away, it was obviously sinking.'

Captain Ed Chuboda came zooming in a couple of hundred feet above the water towards a ship surrounded by white splashes from the bombs of the B-17s above. 'I couldn't see any Fortresses,' he said, 'but I could see where they'd been.' The ship had already been damaged, but he roared towards it anyway, beam-on, and released two bombs which skipped perfectly along the water. After having performed this very manoeuvre countless times in practice sessions against reefs and wrecks, it felt almost surreal to be doing it in action against a real target. He might have been slightly mesmerised by the sensation, as a loud 'clunk' reverberated throughout the aircraft as he whipped over the ship. Surveying from the rear, Chuboda's observer reported that he had just collided with the ship's radio antenna. The two bombs, meanwhile, hit and detonated within a split second, and the already damaged hull of the ship was awash in flame.

Lieutenant Walter Lee had a similar close encounter:

We approached [the target] at about twenty feet, strafing and dropping two bombs. As we crossed the boat our left wing tip narrowly missed the mast. After we crossed, we got down on the water again and flew out always looking for our next target. On a turn to our left we observed the results of our bombing. Our first bomb hit the waterline and the second was a near miss, which is almost as disastrous.

The ship had burst in flames; the bulk of it a great orange tower 75 to 100 feet high. It was an exhilarating sensation to know that we could sink one with such devastating results.

Also observing from above was a highly experienced pilot who nevertheless had no official role to play in the morning's attack. Having dropped height to avoid the Japanese Zeros which were now doing their best to tear up the American Fortresses, Blackjack Walker looked on, slack-jawed at the spectacle below. In the rear of the aircraft, Sergeant William Clark, who had anticipated a day spent safely on the ground, said very little.

'I was observing it from the side and all these ships – honestly, I've never seen anything like it,' Blackjack later recalled. 'Dozens of planes all going in at zero feet. In fact, I could see a Beaufighter and a B-25 both going in at the same target and I thought, "Get out, one of you!"'

The ship Blackjack saw was most likely the *Kembu Maru*, and he was relieved when both aircraft scored hits and managed to avoid each other. Then, following an explosion, a large smoke ring formed above the vessel, as if puffed from a gigantic cigarette, and hung like a grey halo in the sky. His attention drawn away for a brief moment, when he glanced back, the ship was gone. 'It had simply disappeared,' he said. '… a complete ship … it must have just blown up.'

Confirmed by several other airmen and dubbed 'Tojo's halo', the ghostly smoke ring lingered in the air above the doomed ship for some time.

In his book *Whispering Death* author Mark Johnston writes that:

The spectacle of Japanese ships burning, smoking, exploding, firing and sinking amidst aircraft flying, bombing and firing in all directions was unforgettable, even exhilarating to those who participated, though no one person could see it all at once or even sit still to contemplate it.

Flight Sergeant Fred Anderson, an observer and navigator in Beaufighter A19-15, spent much of the battle replenishing the 20-mm cannon magazines. This difficult process involved lifting the full, 60-round-capacity canisters off a rack along the inside of the fuselage, freeing the spent one, pulling back the heavy, spring-loaded breech and fitting the full magazine. Only then would it be ready for pilot Flying Officer Bob Brazenor to begin firing, all while being thrown around the sky as the skipper twisted, turned and dived on multiple targets. Anderson's job wasn't helped either by the choking cordite fumes which filled the aircraft's interior.

Conversation between the two crew was necessarily brief. 'I didn't like to bother him,' said Anderson, 'as he was a little bit busy.' Brazenor would keep Anderson informed in short updates such as, 'I've just attacked a 7000-ton freighter', or 'bit of stuff coming up at us from this ship here, Fred ...' Only in snatched moments could Anderson look out and see the battle for himself.

Those images would never be forgotten.

As he later recalled:

It was like a pack of sharks in a frenzy, or wild dogs, perhaps. Smoke, ships on fire, some listing, bows underwater; people in the sea everywhere. People on rafts and barges and little boats they'd managed to find somehow. Flaming aircraft, falling out of the sky. I heard Bob just say under his breath, 'bloody hell', and looked out and saw a wing – just a wing – flutter down, spinning like a leaf falling from a tree, still on fire from the fuel tank inside it. No idea what sort of plane it was from. And planes just coming in at all angles at those ships, even after they were already ablaze. I looked out and saw what looked like a whole destroyer over on its side with smoke above it. Never seen anything like it. Not before or since.

Far below onboard those Japanese ships that were still afloat, claxons and bugles rang out signalling an air attack, and men sprang into well-rehearsed drills. Strikes by Allied aircraft were nothing new, and veteran anti-aircraft gunners, adept in repulsing attacks from altitudes high and low, manned their stations with confidence.

But no one, in over a year of constant warfare, had seen anything like this.

It was as if the ships had steered into a typhoon of explosives. As historian Lex McAulay writes, 'The Japanese were swamped by attacks from all angles and heights, making defence of the entire convoy impossible; each ship was on its own, whether destroyer or transport.'

From every angle, Allied aircraft swarmed over their heads, and no one knew which way to aim. Concentrated fire on any one aircraft, usually a reliable defence, was impossible to coordinate. 'Together they numbered fifty planes,' one

Japanese survivor later recounted. 'Everyone had a feeling of helplessness. There were none of our planes.'

This last observation was not strictly true. Something in the order of fifty Zero fighters had been assembled to protect the passage of the convoy from Rabaul to Lae, comprising a dozen or so each from two army Air Groups, and eighteen from the light carrier *Zuiho*. But a series of timed attacks on Japanese airfields at Lae, Salamaua and New Britain, carried out by US bombers and Australian Havocs of 22 Squadron, had done their work in suppressing much of the convoy's protection. One can only imagine the shock of the Zero pilots when, with Lae only a few sailing hours away, the great Allied aerial fleet came into view from the south.

Flying at high altitude and without radios, it's also possible many Japanese pilots were unaware of the low-level attacks underway far below. This may have led them to initially concentrate on the high-level heavy bombers, whose attacks on the convoy were largely ineffectual. Although one Fortress was shot down, and several damaged, the real danger was being wreaked by the Beaufighters and Mitchells.

Eventually, a group of Zeros swooped down to attack. Having hit one ship, and preparing to dive on another, observer Dave Beasley urgently yelled to his pilot, George Drury, 'Zeros! And the bastards are firing at us!' Drury instinctively put the Beaufighter's nose down and threw open the throttles. 'A little speech like that from one's observer only means one thing,' he recalled. 'All taps open! I put the nose at the water and simply urged the old lady to her last knot. We clocked 263 knots straight and level and the Zeros couldn't stay with us.'

Although unable to mix with a Zero in combat, a Beaufighter could confidently outrun one in straight and level flight.

Mutual support between the Americans and Australians abounded. It was something of a minor miracle that no midair collisions – or even friendly fire – scarred the Allied victory. Second Lieutenant Robert McKee, at the controls of one of Ed Larner's 90th Squadron Mitchells, took care to break away several times as Beaufighters came in on a ship he himself was preparing to attack, then pulled away while they completed their deadly runs. The Beaufighters, he later said, did a 'superb job'. The prime reason for the battle's success lay in the spirit of cooperation between the forces, as well as the fighter cover provided by the Lightnings.

Ross Little, 30 Squadron's leader, returned some of the goodwill by noticing a B-25 under attack from a Zero and swinging hard left to challenge it. This was a dangerous activity at the best of times as the Beaufighter was no match for the Zero's breathtaking manoeuvrability.

Though well beyond range at 600 yards, Little opened fire, his ten guns making an impressive sight for anyone facing them. True to form, the Zero broke away, but executed a feather-like high-speed stall turn to drop perfectly down behind Little's tail, redirecting his attack with a burst of cannon fire. Little's observer, Flying Officer Alec Spooner, had had the foresight to install a rear-facing machine-gun mounting in this usually undefended position and promptly returned fire with a tracer-laden burst of .303.

This was enough to spook the Japanese pilot, who promptly left them alone.

In Beaufighter A19-24, pilot Len Vial was also chased by a Zero, but without the luxury of Spooner's hastily installed weapon, all his observer Alf Nelson could wield was his Aldis lamp, which he managed to flash so quickly, the Japanese pilot was fooled into thinking it to be machine-gun flashes, and likewise broke off the attack.

Not so lucky were pilot Sergeant Ron Downing and his observer, Sergeant Danny Box. Barely eight weeks earlier, they'd almost come to grief during the battle for Wau, when their aircraft had been caught in the blast of a Japanese ammunition dump they were strafing. Luck had been with them that day, and now flying the very same aircraft, Beaufighter A19-53, they would need every ounce of it again.

Both Downing and Box failed to see the approaching Zeros and thus were flying too slow to outrun them. Caught unawares, one Zero managed to close to 100 feet before unleashing its fire. It then pulled up into an almost vertical climb, perhaps fearing return fire from Box's observer position. In those few seconds it shredded the aircraft's elevators, smashed the hydraulics and set the port engine alight. Raking fire also wounded both men, Box collecting bullets through his right shoulder, right thigh and both arms, one round passing clean through his wrist. Ron Downing received lacerations to his shoulder.

Despite their injuries, the men managed to put out the fire in the port engine, turn away from the battle and head for Port Moresby. On the way the port engine failed completely, and with it their chances of making it over the mountains back to Ward's airstrip.

Sergeant Bob Cummins, the pilot who had earlier discovered downed US Marauder pilot Len Nicholson and his crew on a lonely Papuan beach, was himself leaving the battle area after exhausting his ammunition. Cummins found Downing's crippled Beaufighter as it made its way to the small airstrip at Dobodura, nearly 100 miles from Port Moresby, but on the north side of the Owen Stanleys. Staying with him, Cummins offered protection and encouragement, then circled as Downing, despite his own and his aircraft's injuries, managed to put the Beaufighter safely down in a wheels-up landing on the grass beside the airstrip.

Downing gave an encouraging wave, and Cummins, satisfied they would both soon be receiving medical attention, turned for Port Moresby. Both Downing and Box would indeed recover, and their aircraft, despite the damage, would be repaired and back in action by July.

•

The V formations passed diagonally over the convoy, bombing at 10 000 feet but, despite several claims to the contrary, not one of their bombs is believed to have hit any of the ships. Nevertheless, the Japanese pilots fell on them savagely. Captain Crawford's aircraft was 'shredded' with bullets, yet he managed to get it and his crew home in one piece. Meanwhile, Captain Easlon Halcutt suffered a head wound from 20-mm cannon fire and had to be pulled from the pilot's chair, leaving his co-pilot to bring the aircraft back to Port Moresby in time to save Halcutt's life.

Even more dramatic was the fate of Lieutenant Woodrow Moore and the crew of his 63rd Squadron Fortress, *Double Trouble*. Having completed an initial attack, Moore was preparing for a second run when his formation was hit hard by ten Zeros attacking from multiple directions. Moore was struck from below with a steady burst to the centre of the fuselage by a clipped-wing Zero or 'Hamp' before it rolled away.

A fire started in the aircraft as Moore pulled it out of the formation. Soon the radio compartment and the number three engine were ablaze, with flames being seen 'spouting from the windows and tail' as the aircraft lost altitude. Moore managed to dump his bombs and the payload was seen tumbling away as the aircraft burned.

Exactly what happened next is subject to conjecture. A number of Japanese pilots later claimed that Moore's aircraft was at some stage rammed by one of the aircraft carrier *Zuiho*'s most experienced pilots, Chief Flight Petty Officer Maki Masanao. Why he would have chosen to sacrifice himself and his aircraft in such a manner cannot satisfactorily be explained, but several Japanese sources – particularly the eyewitness account of a fellow Zero pilot, Warrant Officer Iwai Tsutomi – insisted that 'both planes broke in two and the four pieces fell jumbled together'.

The ramming theory is doubted by the American airmen who also observed the battle, but the idea of Masanao unintentionally colliding with the bomber is considered possible. Japanese pilots were famous for daringly close interceptions designed to rattle their victims' nerves in the heat of battle. But many distances were misjudged.

What occurred next, however, was never disputed. It can also be definitively stated to have influenced the course and nature of the battle.

Having dropped his bombs, and seeing the aircraft was doomed, Moore ordered everyone out. Seven of the crew of eleven men exited the bomb bay. Almost immediately, though, one man slipped out of his harness – most likely secured in a hurry – and fell to his death. The B-17 then seemed to break up in midair (lending weight to the collision theory) with a wing fluttering down like a falling leaf, as observed by several airmen below. At this moment, the plumes of the American parachutes were spotted by some of the Japanese navy Hamps, who broke off their attacks on the bombers to swoop and machine gun them as they floated down.

Horrified witnesses were initially too stunned to say anything, but then a torrent of profanities flooded the airwaves as news of the killings flashed around the formation.

According to Lex McAulay, 'The effect of this brutality was profound.' Men vomited at what they had just seen, and for the rest of their lives, could not speak of the incident without being overwhelmed with fury. One B-17 pilot stated that 'this more than anything made our boys go out for blood'.

Witnessing the demise of *Double Trouble* from his prime position in the nose of his 64th Squadron Fortress was bombardier Lieutenant Gordon Manuel.

Six of her boys jumped. Their chutes opened and they started to float down. From nowhere, like vultures leaping on a wounded rabbit, the Zeros dove. They had been hiding up above in the clouds. They didn't aim at us or any of the other Forts but at the six men in chutes. They killed them, all right. I watched that, feeling cold and sick, and I said to myself. 'That's all, brother, that's all. Now I know. I know what we're fighting now. Not men – beasts.'

Nearby, three of the most highly regarded fighter pilots in Kenney's air force were flying together as a group covering the heavy bombers, led by Captain Robert L Faurot. All witnessed the demise of *Double Trouble* and the shooting of her airmen. Faurot was one of the 39th Lightning Squadron's most experienced and popular officers, having shepherded many of the green pilots through combat. His aura of invincibility had been further enhanced by an extraordinary encounter over Lae the previous September, when he had destroyed a Zero by dropping his two 500-pound bombs onto it – in midair. The astonishing feat earned him both celebrity status and the US Air Medal, but now, at the end of a long tour, some thought his judgement may have been impaired by fatigue.

Faurot's two wingmen had likewise distinguished themselves in combat. With ten Japanese aircraft to his credit, Lieutenant Fred Shifflet had been one of the few pilots to make it into the air in his P-40 the morning of Pearl Harbor, only to be damaged by flying into the path of friendly anti-aircraft guns protecting Hickam Field. The third of the trio, Lieutenant Hoyt Eason, had claimed three victories on the final day of 1942, making him the first Lightning ace of the war.

Led by Faurot, the three pilots now dived instantly on the Japanese airmen who had committed the massacre, though the strained Faurot may not have been exercising the level of caution required in dogfighting as he failed to notice *another* group of Zeros swooping down from behind.

Fellow 39th Squadron pilot Lieutenant Bob McMahon radioed to warn Faurot that he, the hunter, had now become the hunted. Faurot thanked him for the alert, then seemed to confirm a kill with a verbal 'Got 'em!' before his radio went silent. Each of the three aces managed to account for a Zero before they in turn were set upon, their Lightnings sent spiralling towards the sea.

No one saw them hit the water, but neither was a parachute seen and no one assumed they would have been able to survive with one in any case.

A short time later another Lightning pilot, Lieutenant Jack Jones, was leaving the combat area at low level having exhausted his ammunition, when he saw a Lightning come down below him and skim the water some 20 miles from Cape Ward Hunt. The aircraft twisted, then came to a stop, and from the cockpit emerged the pilot. Jones could not identify him. The aircraft sank almost immediately and the pilot was not seen again. A second Lightning was also then spotted crashing into the sea even closer to Cape Ward Hunt and the pilot observed swimming to shore.

Despite this, nothing was heard of the three men again.

Later, back at Schwimmer airstrip, the 39th Squadron would be in mourning, the success of the battle tempered by the loss of some of their finest.

The killing of the Fortress crew was a moment that considerably changed the temper of the engagement, and the white-hot fury felt by the American and Australian airmen at the slaughter of their comrades would soon rebound on the Japanese tenfold.

The architect of the attack, William Garing, reflected later that this display of Japanese cruelty – brutal and revolting as it was – also made no military sense. 'The shooting down of the pilots and aircrew of the B-17 was a stupid mistake because those seven blokes would have gone into the Bismarck Sea and the sharks would have got them anyway. What was the point in breaking off a fight at a critical time and going down and diving on them?'

One by one, the Japanese merchant ships were overwhelmed. Like trapped beasts sensing their own demise, they thrashed about the ocean in increasingly frantic manoeuvres as simultaneous attacks from multiple angles rendered them smoking, bloodstained wrecks.

Invoking von Moltke's adage that 'no battle plan survives first contact with the enemy', the highly coordinated aerial attack, which supposedly stood or fell on split-second timing between various attacking waves, devolved into chaos. It quickly became a frenzied free-for-all in which pilots, eager not to miss out on the action, grabbed their chance to hit the enemy however they could while limited targets remained.

•

The least effective attacks of the day were those carried out by the four heavy bomber squadrons of the 43rd Bombardment Group, the 63rd, 64th, 65th and 403rd.

284 • THE BATTLE OF THE BISMARCK SEA

Bombing from 7000 feet and crisscrossing the convoy in diagonal patterns, the Fortresses were the first bombers to engage the Japanese ships, and despite many claims of direct hits, none could eventually be substantiated. While claims were not made in bad faith, the bomb aimers undoubtedly confused their own bombs with those of the far more successful medium bombers attacking from lower altitudes. When later tallied, even their own combat reports, which the official RAAF history describes as 'expressively honest', included the comment, '... exact number of hits unknown – at least four near misses observed ... due to interception results were not observed'.

Despite no direct sinkings, the Fortresses certainly served their purpose. If their bombs failed to strike the enemy ships, they undoubtedly broke up their defensive patterns, forcing them to execute wild and panicked manoeuvres, allowing them to be more easily picked off, one by one, by other aircraft. Being the first to attack, the heavies attracted the attention of the Japanese gunners who fired determinedly with their heavy 5-inch mounted anti-aircraft guns, even to the point of ignoring the impending catastrophe being wrought by the Beaufighters and Mitchells.

Even when raking the decks of the ships at mast level, many Allied pilots were surprised to see Japanese gun crews oblivious to their presence, fixated instead on the higher-level bombers, causing them relatively little harm. This is understandable, as the Japanese had yet to experience the devastation of a skip-bombing attack from an aircraft coming at them from just above the waves. By the time they realised the true danger, it was too late.

As Captain WS Royalty, navigator with a 71st Squadron Mitchell, observed:

> It seemed that with so many planes over the target at the same time and at so many altitudes, the Japs didn't know which to shoot at, so their fire never concentrated on a single flight or ship [aircraft]. They didn't even come close to hitting us. Ours was a birds-eye view of a show that was almost unbelievable.

The Fortresses also distracted the bulk of the thirty to forty Zeros which were flying a high-altitude patrol and possibly failed to appreciate the havoc being wreaked on the ships by the smaller aircraft below. By the time they realised what was happening, the convoy was already ablaze.

At least some of the anti-aircraft fire coming up from the defending destroyers was bound to find a target, and one of the unluckiest bomber crews of the day was surely Lieutenant John Smallwood, one of Ed Larner's more experienced 90th Squadron B-25 pilots. Going in to attack a 5000-ton transport, Smallwood pulled away at the last minute to avoid another aircraft, then heard a loud clanging and an explosion, as the cabin was filled with smoke. Opening his bomb doors in case he needed to jettison his two 500-pounders, Smallwood realised the aircraft was still flying satisfactorily, so decided to resume his attack on another ship, which he observed to be listing heavily. Tying himself in with a group of Beaufighters returning to New Guinea, Smallwood approached the airstrip at Seven Mile Strip.

'This was when we realised we had no flaps, no radio and no proper landing gear, nothing', said Smallwood when interviewed later. The damage had taken out the aircraft's hydraulics, and the only wheel which would lower was the front nosewheel, which locked then refused to raise again. Giving his crew of three the option of bailing out over the field or riding out what was going to be a difficult emergency landing, all chose to stay with their skipper. With reduced flaps and a stubbornly unretractable nose wheel, the Mitchell came in fast and awkward, the crew huddled in their crash positions. Upon touching down, the wheel bounced the aircraft back into the air, then followed a series of long hops until it finally settled into a long skid over the metal mesh runway, emitting a shower of sparks and an unearthly sound of metal grating on metal. Had there been even a little more runway, all four men would have walked away from the crash. At the end of the strip, however, a deep ditch caught the nose wheel and flipped the bomber over, instantly killing gunner Sergeant Richard Martin who, unbeknown to Smallwood, had idiotically decided to watch the crash from his top turret. All crewmen were injured, but gunner Bill Blewitt, one of the many Australian airmen flying with the Americans, woke up four days later in hospital in an RAAF hospital, bandaged head to foot. For some reason he was told that he was the only survivor, and he would not discover the truth for another forty years, when he finally reconnected with his old skipper, John Smallwood, who had married an Australian girl and was settled in Sydney.

Sergeant Martin was to be the 3rd Attack Group's only fatality of the battle.

Some of the most vivid images of the battle came from Damien Parer, hanging onto both the plane as well as his camera behind Torchy Uren in Beaufighter A19-5. Later complaining that this day he was 'all fingers and thumbs', Parer at one stage ran out of film just as Uren began a strafing attack. In the middle of clumsily reloading his camera, Parer made a request of the skipper.

'Torchy, can you go over those two burning ships again? I missed them'.

Torchy was happy to oblige. Banking around, he lined up for another strafing run, just for Parer.

Besides providing the world with the most vivid visual record of the battle, Parer would later commit his recollections to paper as well:

You've gone around behind the warships, but they're still banging away with their big guns, pom-poms and ack-ack. You can see tracers whipping by. A cargo ship is in the sights. She is camouflaged and has goalpost masts. She looks blurred at first, but then comes into focus.

The first thunder of fire [from the cannons] gives you a shock. It jars at your feet, and you see the tracers lashing out ahead of you, and orange lights dance before your eyes …

You can smell the foetid stench of gunpowder in your nostrils. Then the plane is banking round again and a fresh target is lining up in the sights. It straightens up and you are in that terrific rush of power again.

You're going in – hard and furious. The great hull of the ship is looming up at you, grey and black and forbidding.

Again the guns begin their violent stammer, again the flashing out of tracers ... You seem suspended in an unwholesome moment of fear and delight as you watch the stream of bullets whang over the decks ... And then you feel that wrench upwards again and the plane sweeps miraculously up. And the ship passes below the fuselage in a dark blur. And all around you, there is all hell let loose and the war is on – is really on.

Summing up the battle, the RAAF official history stated that, 'Soon ships were listing or sinking, their super-structure smashed and blazing, and great clouds of dense black smoke rising into a sky where aircraft circled and dived over the confusion they had wrought among what, less than an hour earlier, had been an impressively orderly convoy.'

From the Japanese perspective, it was as if the world was being torn apart.

•

The hours before the attack saw confidence rising throughout the Japanese convoy as the belief took hold that they had survived the worst the American and Australian airmen could throw at them, and in a few hours would be disembarking at Lae.

Onboard the *Oigawa Maru*, officers assured their sailors lining up on deck for morning parade that during the night, Japanese aircraft had struck Allied airstrips in Port Moresby and that the threat of attack was minimal. However, no sooner were the words out of the officers' mouths, according to signalman Private Tatsue Machida, than two formations of Allied B-17s appeared above, as well as a group of medium bombers approaching from lower level. The parade was drawn to a hurried close by the sounds of army bugles blaring out the air raid warning.

Throughout the convoy, the Japanese were greeting the pleasant turn in the weather, when every sound was drowned out by the noise of hundreds of aircraft engines. Every eye on every ship looked to the sky in dread. Approaching Allied formations were spreading out along all angles and all points of the compass. High above, the outlines of large B-17s could be seen; while level with the horizon, small groups of twin-engine aircraft began circling ominously like birds of prey. On the merchant ships as well as the destroyers, the larger 3- and 5-inch batteries began blasting away at the higher bombers while some of the smaller weapons were levelled at the low-altitude bombers, attempting to lob shells immediately in front of them to throw up spouts of water.

Following Admiral Kimura's orders, many ships turned head-on to what they thought was an impending torpedo attack, unwittingly presenting a strafing Beaufighter with the ideal profile.

Onboard the *Oigawa Maru*, Private Machida was watching the approach of one group of aircraft when the ship was struck amidships by a bomb launched from another. Fire erupted from portholes, landing craft secured to the deck were smashed, and many soldiers were killed instantly by showers of shrapnel or steel fragments torn from the ship itself. A terrible convulsing was felt through the vessel and a panicked officer told Machida that the bomb had penetrated through to the engine room and severed vital steam pipes.

Over on the destroyer *Tokitsukaze*, a junior officer counted some 120 bullet and cannon strikes along one wall as he made his way to the bridge. When he arrived, he found a chaotic mess of dead, dying and wounded with the bridge itself a wreck. 'We've had it,' were the words with which the captain greeted him.

A short time later a bomb struck the destroyer wiping out the engine room along with all twenty of its staff. Looking over the side, the young officer saw the sea turn red. Blood was flowing from the punctured hull.

One of the most detailed and dramatic accounts of the battle came from another of the convoy's destroyers, the *Arashio*. Captain Robert Chatt, one of Ed Larner's 90th Squadron B-25 pilots, made the first frontal attack on the vessel, releasing all of his four bombs simultaneously, three of which scored direct hits.

The result was instant carnage.

Feeling the impact of the bombs from his engineering station below, Sub-lieutenant Masuda Reiji called up to the bridge only to be told it no longer existed.

He raced up and found it destroyed with not a single survivor.

The ship continued to travel at full speed, but with no one left to steer it and a jammed rudder, it slammed, with a sickening screech of bending steel, into the already-ablaze merchant ship *Nojima Maru*, causing more damage to both ships.

Reiji looked up at the larger, burning *Nojima Maru*, whose bridge had likewise been obliterated. Ammunition was exploding all over her decks, which in turn ignited fuel now leaking from hundreds of bullet-ridden drums, and which then began pouring off the decks like a river of fire. Men, some burning, were streaming off the bow into the water.

Unable to take in the picture of horror, Masuda scanned the horizon and saw that all the remaining seven of the convoy's transports were similarly ablaze. Yet another bomb then hit the *Nojima Maru*, which shook and began to sink slowly beside him.

Around the burning hulks, the sea was littered with the detritus of a defeated army: splintered crates; spare truck tyres; small, upturned boats and barges; wooden decking; empty life jackets; biscuit boxes; ledgers of regimental paperwork; and drums of fuel and oil. And everywhere the bodies – and parts of bodies – of Japanese soldiers and sailors of all ranks floating among the still living.

Reiji's account is as vivid as any of the descriptions from the Japanese onboard the doomed ships of Operation 81:

They hit us amidships. B-17s, fighters, skip bombers, and torpedo bombers. On our side, we were madly firing, but we had no chance to beat them off. Our bridge was hit by two 500-pound bombs. Nobody could have survived. The captain, the chief navigator, the gunnery and torpedo chiefs, and the chief medical officer were all killed in action. The chief navigator's blackened body was hanging there, all alone … Somehow, those of us down in the engine room were spared.

Because all the top commanders on the *Arashio* were killed and the ship was heavily damaged, we were ordered to transfer the crew over to my old ship, the *Asashio*. The chief engineer and I were left in charge of the *Arashio*. We decided to stay aboard, because we could still make way at perhaps five or six knots. Then a second air attack came in. This time we were hit by thirty shells – from port to starboard. The ship shook violently. Bullet fragments and shrapnel made it look like a beehive. All the steam pipes burst. The ship became boiling hot. We tried to abandon ship, but planes flying almost as low as the masts sprayed us with machine guns. Hands were shot off, stomachs blown open. Most of the crew were murdered or wounded there. Hundreds were swimming in the ocean. Nobody was there to rescue them. They were wiped out, carried away by a strong current running at roughly four or five knots.

Still aboard were a few sailors, the chief engineer, and I. Eight of us struggled to steer the *Arashio* by hand. Some of those surviving jumped into the sea, saying it was better to take a chance on being saved from the ocean than to remain on such a ship of horrors.

On the *Taimei Maru*, the two operators in the radio room, Kawakami and Suzuki, threw themselves to the floor as a B-25 strafed the deck and bridge. When the onslaught ended, they dashed for a hatchway ladder to seek the protection of the ship's interior. Suddenly, they were enveloped in a flash 'so vivid' recalled Kawakami, 'Suzuki thought it would pierce his body'.

Above them, the bridge appeared to have been blown away, leaving a hole so large that they assumed it had been caused by a crashing aircraft. To add to the horror, several officers and men fell down into it, perishing in an inferno of steam and flame rising from the ship's ruptured bowels.

The next thing Suzuki remembered was the pain of feet running into and over him, as he was roused from unconsciousness on the deck. This, however, probably saved his life. Looking around, he was presented with a nightmarish picture made more surreal by the fact that whatever had knocked him out had also robbed him of his hearing, and so he observed the chaos in complete silence.

The ship was aflame its entire length, with panicked men running everywhere. From the holds, flaming drums of fuel flew out like exploding rockets to land in the sea or on the deck where their contents spilled and added to the inferno. Grabbing a group of terrified soldiers, Suzuki indicated their only option was the sea, into which they leaped. He followed.

Trying to put as much distance between himself and the blazing *Taimei Maru*, Suzuki came across an engineer he knew and pulled him along for a time, but he soon died from blood loss as his right leg had been completely severed. Nearby in the water was the ship's captain, Takiata, delirious from a severe head wound. He soon slipped under the water for good.

Reports began to come in from the rest of the convoy. The destroyers *Shirayuki*, *Arashio* and *Tokitsukaze* had all been hit, with the *Arashio* stopped dead in the water and the *Teiyo Maru* drawn up alongside to rescue as many personnel as possible. One American bomb had struck the *Tokitsukaze*'s engine room, bringing her to a sliding halt, at which point three more bombs hit home.

Other survivors of the *Taimei Maru* were also struggling to live. Having sustained three direct hits, the order to abandon ship came less than twenty minutes after the first bomb struck. A sergeant on gun crew duty who had survived a strafing, then the bombing attack which flooded the engine room and caused the ship's power to fail, began preparations to launch lifeboats. When power was cut to the electric winches, this became all but impossible. In any case, many of the boats had already been holed or wrecked and were useless.

As more explosions rocked the ship from side to side, the sergeant remembered soldiers coming up from the holds like ants emerging from a disturbed nest, looking around briefly at the chaos, then jumping straight into the sea. Below decks it was even more hellish, with men suffering hideous burns and shrapnel wounds, slipping over in blood which was said to be literally sloshing over the floor. 'Panic-stricken members of the crew and passengers ran screaming to and fro in the shambles,' writes Lex McAulay. 'A witness described the scene as a painting from hell.'

Many but not all aircraft carried gun cameras which became activated as a bomb was dropped. The camera's function was to help determine the success of an attack. The images obtained were examined in Brisbane by RAAF and US intelligence staff, including members of the Women's Auxiliary Australian Air Force. They processed and developed the film, then spent many hours staring down into stereoscopes to piece together as accurately as possible the story of the battle, second by second.

Confusion, however, abounded.

The *Teiyo Maru*, for example, was claimed to have been hit by Lieutenant Gordon McCoun (one of the men Larner had told to get off his wing and find his own ship), but attacking the same vessel was Lieutenant Chuck Howe, who recalled it quite differently to McCoun – camouflaged in grey and white – but the result of the four bombs he dropped was uncertain. Nor was it known whether Lieutenant Conn in his 89th Squadron A-20 Havoc dropped his four bombs on the *Nojima Maru* or the *Oigawa Maru*. The written claims of reports of ships damaged and sunk were often contradictory, with some stating to have seen ships break in half while others attest to them floating dead in the water for some time. Many claims and recollections could not be verified by other witnesses.

What was beyond dispute was that the convoy had been obliterated.

In the water, hundreds, possibly thousands of men clung to lifeboats, crates or anything else that could float, and watched the procession of burning, sinking ships around them. One Japanese officer, clinging to the sides of a raft, was one of seventeen doing likewise. A sergeant recalled drifting with others of his regiment, holding onto a box of hard biscuits and singing army songs.

•

High above the doomed convoy, the Allied airmen had begun to run out of targets. With seemingly every Japanese ship damaged or under attack, pilots turned their attention to the barges which had become detached from the larger vessels.

Pilot Walter Lee of the 90th Squadron Mitchell recalled, '... such mass of air power gives one the feeling of invincibility ... I dropped the last 500-pound bomb on a group of barges with only a near miss. I was somewhat disappointed but I still hope that the near miss cracked open a few plates. At 25 feet it should have done something. With our bombs all gone and most of our ammunition spent, we headed back towards land just as fast as we could.'

Finally, the Beaufighters of 30 Squadron broke radio silence. Squadron Leader Ross Little announced briefly over the airwaves to his dozen aircraft, 'Well done, boys, let's go home.' George Drury remembered the moment well. 'We all formed up there, outside the convoy, and went home. Such an amazing victory with so few losses on our side – it was almost unbelievable.'

As they departed the battle area, the carnage visited on Japan's Lae resupply Operation 81 beggared belief. Of the transports, the *Oigawa Maru* was a floating wreck, with over 1200 crewmen and soldiers of the 51st Division dead. She would be finished off during the night by torpedoes from US Navy PT (patrol torpedo) boats. The *Taimei Maru* was at the bottom of the sea having taken 200 soldiers and seamen with her. The *Nojima Maru*, having been attacked multiple times and rammed by the out-of-control *Arashio*, was sinking and would take 400 lives, before being finished off in a later air attack. The *Teiyo Maru*, one of the largest of the fleet, was a smoking hulk, soon to be struck in an afternoon attack with enormous loss of life – over 1900 troops and crewmen, including her captain. The smallest vessel, the *Kembu Maru*, had exploded in a fireball and sunk with twenty onboard. While the *Shinai Maru*, with sixty-five crew and an unknown number of soldiers dead, was another flaming hulk which would soon slip below the waves.

The eight escorting destroyers fared only somewhat better. Admiral Kimura's flagship, the *Shirayuki*, had been lost with thirty-two of her crew after her magazine exploded, blowing off her stern. Remarkably, she remained afloat but would later be scuttled. The *Arashio*, blazing and out of control having collided with the *Nojima Maru*, would later sink with an unknown number of dead onboard. The *Asashio* was badly damaged and would later be torn to pieces by a second attack and sink with a loss of 200 sailors and soldiers. The *Tokitsukaze*, abandoned and dead in the water to the west of the convoy, drifted lifeless with the currents in its own oil slick. She would be the sole ship left afloat in the battle area at the end of the day. Her abandoned hulk would be found by Japanese submarines, who would attempt, in vain, to sink her with torpedoes. Eventually, she too would slip beneath the surface of her own accord.

The remainder of the escorting destroyers, the *Shikinami*, *Yukikaze*, *Uranami* and *Asagumo*, would survive, escaping the catastrophe thanks to their speed and agility, decks laden with survivors. The *Yukikaze* would be the only vessel to escape damage of any sort, and would in fact be one of the handful of the Imperial Japanese Navy's destroyers to survive the war virtually unscathed.

The annihilation of Operation 81 had taken just twenty-eight minutes.

•

Weeks later, a diary fragment of an unknown Japanese soldier who had been onboard the *Teiyo Maru* would be found washed up on a beach on Goodenough Island. It was dated 24 February 1943, a few days before the convoy set sail from Rabaul. The soldier would have been preparing to board.

'Last night,' he wrote, 'I dreamed I saw a dragon rising out of the sea.'

CHAPTER 22

A 'TERRIBLE, YET ESSENTIAL, FINALE'

Earlier, back at Port Moresby, an empty silence had descended upon the various airstrips which surrounded the capital as the aircraft took off and the sound of their engines receded. Hundreds of ground crew and staff who had been toiling non-stop in preparation for what they knew to be a vitally important mission, now had little to do but wait for the return of the airmen and aircraft they served – even doted over – like family.

At Ward's airstrip, 30 Squadron radio operator Bruce Robertson remembered, 'The anxious boys, who had put their all into making sure that each Beaufighter was at her very best, were trying to fill in their time with chitchat to mates on how this special op might be going. It was a time of worry in not knowing what the Beaus were up to.'

Robertson then had an idea which, in his words, 'changed anxiety to yells of delight'. Finding an old Tannoy speaker, he placed it high in a tree. With the help of a couple of mates, he wired it up with a long cable to a radio tuned to the Beaufighters' transmission frequency. Instantly, the extraordinary conversation of the men in the midst of battle was broadcast, loud and clear, to the ground staff.

'All could now hear the battle taking place,' wrote Robertson, 'though the air was filled with Yankee voices, not Aussie accents. The Beaufighters were observing wireless silence, but dozens of the American bomber operators were eulogising those "sons of bitches Aussie Beaufighters" as they flitted back and forth amid the falling bombs.'

Word quickly went around to the surrounding American squadrons and men poured into Ward's. Soon, fleets of fully laden US jeeps appeared and a crowd 3000-strong gathered around the speaker in the scrub next to the runway, as if glued to a live sporting event. But, as one of the Americans observed, 'no ball game ever had a keener listening audience than this'.

Mesmerised, the men listened intently to full and colourful descriptions of exploding and sinking enemy ships, strafing runs and slicks of oil trailing behind wounded vessels. Everyone was thankful, this day, for the American attitude to radio silence. 'You heard the warnings, the curses, the instructions of intrepid flight leaders,' one ground crew member remembered. At one stage, a pilot announced his attack on a ship with, 'I'm gonna make a run on that big fat bastard!' Other announcements were more urgent, with sudden cries of 'Look out, King! Zero back of you! Look out!' Then, in the middle of it all, a calm, surreal enquiry, 'Say, what's the time, Joe?'

The fate of the only Australian casualty of the day would also be witnessed live by the assembled men at Ward's. It was Beaufighter A19-53, flown by Ron Downing with observer

Danny Box, which had been pounced upon by defending Zeros.

'Look out, Ron, your elevator's hit!' interjected a voice with a distinctive Australian accent. The 30 Squadron men looked at one another, and 'Ron ... Ron Downing', was passed among them in whispers. Then another Australian voice was heard over the airwaves. 'Are you okay, Ron? Ron! Danny! Are you all right?'

This was followed by silence.

•

Hours later, the soft roar of the Beaufighters' Bristol engines could be heard returning to the airstrip. Every man stood and rushed to count as many planes as he could see in the clouding midday sky. The two flights, led still by Ross Little and Torchy Uren, approached in double lines astern, then flipped one by one to make a sweeping semicircle over the runway before levelling out to land.

Two aircraft were missing.

Ron Downing's and Danny Box's fate had earlier been revealed. But at that stage, no one knew they had managed to safely land on the other side of the ranges at Dobodura.

The second absent Beaufighter was A19-74, piloted by Bob Cummins and Allan Kirley, who had stayed to see their mate down safely onto the strip. Soon, word of Downing's and Box's survival, despite their wounds – Danny Box in particular, suffering a shattered thigh from a Japanese bullet – would spread like a river of relief through the squadron.

Bob Cummins' whereabouts, however, were still unknown.

Fearing the worst, the squadron began to resign themselves to the loss of a valued crew member when, a full hour after the last Beaufighter had touched down, Cummins roared over the strip and banked to come in to land. Cummins later recalled the atmosphere of his belated – but most welcome – arrival:

> As we made our landing at Ward's, I spied two lonely figures at the end of the strip; my two ground staff Jack Rawlinson and Stan Jeffries had practically given up hope that I had survived the Bismarck Battle. They were genuinely relieved to see Al and I climb out of the aircraft; to the point of tears, in fact.

At the many American bases, similar homecomings were playing out.

At the Schwimmer, Durand, Jackson and Kila airstrips, dozens of B-17s, B-25s and Lightnings were dropping back onto the metal mesh and taxiing to safety, the pilots barely able to contain their excitement at what they had just witnessed. Ground crews too, were filled with anticipation at hearing how their charges had fared. 'How did you go, sir?' they asked, scrambling up to open the cockpit canopies even as the aircraft props were slowing to a halt. 'Super!' the young airmen responded, wild-eyed, or just shaking their heads with a 'Hell, ya shoulda seen it ...'

But there was little time for celebrations. Straightaway, the airmen were corralled into debriefing tents where intelligence officers were waiting to take down their reports while memories remained fresh.

For the American and Australian squadrons, it had been their finest hour. While 30 Squadron had lost not a single man, the combined US units counted one B-17 and a B-25 which had crash-landed back at the base, as well as four P-38 Lightning fighters which were destroyed, claiming the lives of thirteen young airmen. An official and confidential USAAF report compiled soon after the battle stated, 'no irrefutable story or history can be told of this event other than that it represents a complete and annihilating victory'.

As one-sided as these figures were, the battle was not yet over.

•

With an ocean of contradictory and overlapping reports for the squadron's intelligence officers to digest, no clear picture of the current state of the Japanese convoy could be ascertained. It was understood that it had suffered massive losses, but no one knew exactly how many ships were still afloat. As a result, later that day, another strike force was ordered out to attack whatever was left.

Hardly had the crews of 30 Squadron had a chance to submit their reports and grab a quick lunch when they were told they would soon be setting off to do it all over again. This time they would be accompanied by another Australian unit – 22 Squadron – flying their twin-engine A-20 Havoc bombers.

By 1 p.m. 30 Squadron was refuelled and re-armed, but now the ever-fickle New Guinea weather entered to interrupt the proceedings. After taking off from Ward's, the Beaufighters ran headlong into the afternoon monsoon, a sky described by one pilot as 'full of clouds and rocks'. After trying for an hour to push through over the Owen Stanleys, a disappointed 30 Squadron returned to Ward's, their day's work prematurely terminated.

The Havocs of 22 Squadron had already situated themselves on the far side of the ranges at Dobodura and were able to proceed to the convoy unhindered. Here, they were joined by four squadrons of American B-25s, and one of B-17 Fortresses. Their task, they had been told, was to apply the same level of destruction as had been delivered in the morning's attack.

But by now there was little left to destroy.

Arriving over the convoy, the Havoc crews reported four merchant ships ablaze and two Japanese destroyers, one of them the *Tokitsukaze*, low and dead in the water, bobbing in its own oil slick. The other destroyer, the *Asashio*, was damaged but still functioning, at a virtual standstill, picking up survivors. Of these, the astonished airmen noted, there appeared to be many, many hundreds.

Every life raft or upturned boat, every barge, or part thereof, every lid of every crate or any other piece of flotsam or equipment which had yet to sink, appeared to be supporting Japanese soldiers. Scores of others were floating, alone, many face down, while some tried to keep themselves alive on the surface.

For many Allied airmen, this was their second assault on the Japanese convoy for the day.

As a B-25 pilot from the US 71st Squadron recalled:

We took off on the afternoon attack with much more confidence than we had on the morning mission. The assembly point was the same as before but we didn't get together as well and there was some confusion when we finally reached the target. When we arrived in sight of the convoy there were four ships burning and after the attack there were eight fires visible.

Though there were fewer Japanese ships at the time of the afternoon's mission, there were many more Japanese fighters. Without the same number of high-altitude bombers to deal with, the Zeros and Oscars descended low to intercept the Mitchells and Australian Havocs. But their attacks were weak and many Allied airmen were surprised at how the Japanese pilots failed to press home their efforts. One can only speculate as to whether these men, overwhelmed at the destruction of the convoy, were in no mood to protect what had already been laid to waste.

The Japanese fighters may also have been alarmed at the unexpected tenacity of the Australian Havocs. Twenty-eight-year-old Flying Officer Harry Craig, whose occupation before the war was listed as 'jackaroo', was so unfazed by the four Zeros which pursued him as he prepared to attack one of the already crippled destroyers that he turned to face them, opening up with his four nose machine guns and tearing back through at close range.

The Japanese attack was broken up, and not repeated.

The afternoon assault was conducted with a similar intensity to the morning's, but was shorter, lasting barely fifteen minutes.

In that time, several attacks were made on the destroyers *Arashio* and *Tokitsukaze*, the latter of which was already a hulk, awash and low in the water.

Wing Commander Charles Learmonth, 22 Squadron's commander, led his Havocs in to attack at 3 p.m., raining armour-piercing and instantaneous-fused bombs down on the crippled Japanese ships. Circling, each aircraft broke off in a steep dive to attack individually. As Learmonth dropped low, he was confronted by the sight of 'hundreds' of Japanese leaping from the ships into the water at his approach, adding 'some assisted by explosions'. Learmonth later expressed compassion for his victims, but would be one of the few to do so. Most of his fellow airmen, he later said, regarded the next fifteen minutes as 'the time of their lives'.

One merchant ship of around 8000 tons was seen to suddenly explode and further fiery destruction was visited on the *Tokitsukaze*. The *Asashio*, still appearing to be seaworthy, was subjected to a maelstrom of bombing and strafing attacks from both American and Australian aircraft attacking at altitudes both low and high. Again, pilots watched men obliterated before the fire of their multiple guns as they raked the decks.

Incredibly, despite multiple strikes and dozens of near misses, the destroyers remained afloat, defying the best efforts of the Allied airmen to send them to the bottom. Even more surprising was that some of the Japanese soldiers managed to survive the onslaught at all. One machine gunner serving with the Sasebo SNLF, or Marines, having earlier lived through the attack on the *Arashio*, was plucked from the water by the *Asashio*, before surviving the onslaught visited on that ship.

Days later, he would be rescued from the sea for a second time by a Japanese submarine.

Of greater significance than the efforts to sink ships already in their death throes was the observation made by a US reconnaissance B-24 of the four surviving destroyers speeding away from the battle area at their top speed of around 30 knots, apparently laden with survivors. Why they were not attacked at this point is difficult to understand.

Historical sources vary, but most concur that the four remaining destroyers – the *Asagumo*, *Shikinami*, *Uranami* and *Yukikaze* – as well as two submarines which soon appeared on the scene (*I-17* and *I-26*) managed to pluck around 2700 men from the water and spirit them away to safety.

The rescues had begun just as the main morning attack had commenced. Allied airmen reported the Japanese destroyers were trying to pick up survivors while they were still being attacked. After the bombers and strafers had left, the four seaworthy destroyers dashed in among the burning merchantmen and pulled as many men from the sea as their decks could hold.

When the afternoon attack began they sped away northwest, back up through the Vitiaz Strait to rendezvous with two more destroyers which had been sent down from Rabaul. Transferring their human cargo, the four ships would return to the killing zone after dark to search for more survivors.

Hundreds, possibly thousands, of Japanese would be left in the water.

As the pilots, greedy for targets, passed back and forth over the remains of the convoy, they took in the scene of despair beneath them. A seascape of destruction stretching 20 square miles had spread across the surface of the ocean with every piece of it seemingly supporting a desperate clinging survivor.

Leaving the area, the Allied aircraft reported their observations to the busy intelligence officers back at Port Moresby. Realising so many Japanese were still alive, so began – in the words of official RAAF historian Douglas Gillison – the battle's 'terrible, yet essential, finale'.

•

Given the racism of the time, in which all peoples of non–Anglo Saxon heritage were regarded to be inferior, the long list of Japanese crimes, cruelties and atrocities in the Pacific War needed no embellishment and no exaggeration to evoke fear and revulsion among the men of the Fifth Air Force and the RAAF. After a year of intense fighting, it was accepted that this was a world of brutality far beyond the comprehension of young Australian and American men raised in liberal democracies.

In no previous war, nor any earlier conflict, had these soldiers' fathers, grandfathers – or even their brothers currently fighting the Axis forces in Europe – faced an enemy like this. The cruelty and savagery with which the Japanese prosecuted their cause in Asia was, to many at the time, akin to an alien army having landed on earth, dedicated to nothing but extermination.

From the mass slaughter and rape of the Chinese in the years prior to the war itself (300000 in Nanking alone), to the murder of unarmed prisoners and civilians in Malaya and Rabaul; to the execution of nurses, nuns, Dutch and other colonial women, men and girls; to the abominations visited upon the Papuans; to the subjugation of hundreds of thousands of prisoners of war; to the long and lingering deaths forced upon Allied POWs; to the deliberate hunting of Red Cross vessels and the murder of subsequent survivors; to the beheadings, tortures and mutilations, the list of Japanese atrocities was ghastly and endless.

And once again, in the midst of the Battle of the Bismarck Sea, their bizarre cruelty was on full display. Contrary even to the most basic military logic, professional Japanese fighter pilots broke off an attack on an enemy bomber to slaughter men bailing out in parachutes whose fate was almost certainly already sealed.

By early 1943, few Allied servicemen still tried to understand their enemy's motives, or come to grips with the levels of diabolical cruelty to which they seemed to so easily, and quickly, descend. In the absence of understanding, only cold, hard anger was left.

Some time on the night of 3 March 1943, when the reports came in of great numbers of Japanese still in the water hoping to be rescued, it was decided that the Allied airmen would visit them again, the following day, and to a man, wipe them out.

In fact, the slaughter of survivors had begun during the first attack with many of the strafing B-25 pilots firing on groups of Japanese struggling in the water. What was the difference between mowing the enemy down lined up on the deck of a ship, or in the sea?

Large numbers of Japanese soldiers had already been rescued, and no doubt the night would see more rescued as the destroyers returned under cover of darkness to comb the wreckage for survivors. Crowded in lifeboats, or clinging to anything that floated, the tide could easily carry them close to shore, from where they would likely rejoin their armies in New Guinea. All Australian aircrews were given a mantra: every Japanese who managed to come ashore would mean the death of another Australian soldier.

Throughout the night, Allied ground crews worked hard, rearming, refuelling and replacing worn gun barrels. The following morning they took off once again. To suppress enemy fighter attacks, some of the Beaufighters, along with 22 Squadron Havocs, returned to the Japanese airstrips at Lae and Malahang, strafing and bombing them. Once this mission was completed they proceeded to the waters of the Bismarck Sea.

There were far more enemy soldiers than even the intelligence officers had assumed. At dawn, reconnaissance patrols identified up to thirty lifeboats 30 miles northeast of Cape Ward Hunt, all filled with Japanese, as well as many improvised rafts of varying composition and description.

All now became legitimate targets.

One US Mitchell of the 405th Squadron reportedly expended 1200 rounds into the crowded life rafts. Another P-38 Lightning pilot, convinced that some of his comrades had survived parachuting into the sea the previous day, came across a barge with an estimated 100 Japanese onboard or clinging to the side. Making several passes with his 20-mm cannon and

.50-calibre machine guns, he took particular care to kill every single one of them.

Squadron Leader Ross Little, having led his Beaufighters in the earlier mission, returned to attack up to fifteen barges in the area, all loaded with men and equipment. Today there were no falling bombs or drop tanks to worry about, and the pilots lined up carefully and pressed their firing buttons. Flight Sergeant Alf Nelson, flying once again with Pilot Officer Len Vial, looked down and described 'a very bloody show. The water in the bottom of the barges was red with blood. You could see the sea was stained all around.'

US Navy PT boats also took part in the destruction. These fast-moving vessels had arrived during the night from their base at Tufi, 125 miles to the north-west, ostensibly looking for downed US airmen. Finding none, they instead joined in the hunt. Firing off a brace of torpedoes, they finally sank the abandoned *Oigawa Maru*, but in the dark, missed the destroyers. Now they were happy to 'mop up', crosscrossing the water, mercilessly using their heavy machine guns against any Japanese they could find. Some reports suggest they even used their depth charges to dispatch larger numbers clinging to wreckage on the surface.

As the historian Douglas Gillison described it, 'Beaufighters, Bostons and Mitchells swept to and fro over the waters of the Huon Gulf seeking out and destroying barges and rafts crowded with survivors from the sunken enemy ships. It was grim and bloody work for which the crews had little stomach. Some of the men in the Beaufighter crews confessed to experiencing acute nausea.'

Some pilots indeed found the job unpleasant. One unsigned RAAF report made after the battle stated, 'Although the necessity for the strafing of undefended barges was completely understood … the two missions were most distasteful for the crews involved.' Historian Gregory Gilbert even suggests that some men quietly ignored the order, flying back and forth without firing their guns. Some just shot into clear water.

Damien Parer, who eventually found another ride in the back of a Beaufighter, was certainly affected, telling Burton Graham that, 'It was all pretty grim. Poor bloody Japs. They couldn't hit back. They were struggling in the water like drowning rats. It was terrible, but it was necessary.'

Flying Officer Bob Brazenor recalled a somewhat more democratic approach:

We were told that there were lifeboats full of Japanese out in the sea and they had to be got rid of and a few of us who were selected to go out said, 'Well you know, we don't think it's a fair deal, you know.' We didn't refuse to go by any means, but we had it explained to us along the lines of, 'Well look at it this way: for every Japanese that gets on land we might lose a couple of Australian soldiers, so it's your choice. We get rid of the Japs before they get to land or we let them shoot back at us.' So we saw that was a fair point of view, so we went out and we found the lifeboats.

Flying Officer Dick Roe, whose Beaufighter had flipped dramatically under an American bomb blast at the height of the battle the day before, was not nearly so squeamish, quietly telling Burton Graham that, 'Every time I strafed them, I said to myself, "there's one less yellow bastard for the AIF to sweat for".'

Bull Garing, who had ordered the killing of any Japanese survivors, later described an incident at Ward's airstrip where a Beaufighter pilot returning from the slaughter got out of the aircraft, went to the side of the strip, and in Garing's words, '... retched his guts out. Blackjack and I walked over to him and said, "What's wrong with you, son?" and he said, "Sir, I've never seen so many sharks." And I said to him, "Well now, for every one that you sent to the bottom and the sharks got, you've saved one Australian infantryman. Don't forget it."'

In his own recollections of the battle and its bloody aftermath, Blackjack Walker was even more forthright:

Well, it's war and I think war is not finished until your opponent is dead and I don't give a hoot whether they're in the water or whether they're out of the water or in the air or where they are. As far as I'm concerned, from what I've read of what the Japanese did to our fellows during the war, I'm only bloody sorry I didn't get a few hundred more of them.

Most of the airmen that day took to the job with businesslike efficiency. Even three of the large B-17 Fortresses from the 63rd Bombardment Squadron, no longer concerned with anti-aircraft fire from ships, came down to virtual wave height to unleash their forward and rear guns on the survivors. They wanted vengeance for their crewmen who had been slaughtered in their parachutes.

One entry in a US Squadron diary was blunt:

What we didn't get the sharks got. Every man in the squadron would have given two months' pay to be in on the strafing. One gunner expended 1100 rounds of ammunition and burned out two guns.

One strafing B-25 Mitchell pilot actually had to pull up suddenly, as water and wreckage from his many guns boiled up in his path as he attacked a large and crowded barge.

Flying Officer Bob Brazenor recalled:

I've said before, it was pretty gruesome. The sea was red with blood. We sunk the lifeboat and well, I suppose you've got to say there was a certain feeling of helplessness for them, for the Japs that were down there but again at that stage they were enemies to us, so we had a job to do and we had to do it really. It all lasted a quarter of an hour, maybe twenty minutes until there was literally no life left in the area. Some might have had rifles or guns 'cause I had a bullet in my port wing when we came back – but it might have been a ricochet from one of ours.

As witnessed by several airmen, sharks – sometimes in considerable numbers – added to the misery of the Japanese survivors. No firsthand Japanese account of such an attack survives, but many Allied airmen reported schools of them thrashing about in the water, undoubtedly drawn by the blood of the many wounded men. One must presume that no Japanese survived to speak of the horror.

The last signal received from a 30 Squadron strafer that day read:

THREE ENEMY BOATS CONTAINING ABOUT 200 JAPS SIGHTED. OUR ATTACK FINISHED. THERE ARE NO SURVIVORS.

The atmosphere among the returning 30 Squadron pilots this second day of the battle was markedly different from twenty-four hours earlier. There were no 'whoops' and cheers, no sense of elation, simply the grim feeling of a job completed.

That night in his diary, Damien Parer would write, 'I feel very crooked about all this blood and guts'.

•

Incredibly, some Japanese soldiers did manage to survive. Most of them lost none of their aggression, devotion to their cause or absolute willingness to accept death over surrender. PT boat captains who had made their way among the survivors during the night offered food and water in exchange for surrender. Their offers were met with diffidence from some enemy soldiers, while others simply turned and paddled in the other direction.

Entire groups of Japanese drifted out of the battle area. One lifeboat was reportedly borne on the eastern currents all the way to the Solomons, though its occupants' fate is unknown.

The ordeal of RAAF Radar Station 305 can be described with far more certainty. Since the middle of January it had been operating from a hill on the northern side of Goodenough Island. A lonely but important outpost, the small group of RAAF radar operators and Australian Army personnel carried out their vital work in reporting enemy air activity from Rabaul and beyond, but knew little of the wider war going on around them, including the recent Bismarck Sea battle.

On the afternoon of 7 March, a native runner arrived at the radar station and breathlessly reported that 'a great number' of Japanese had landed on the beach at Waibula, just over 3 miles away. The station staff assumed it was an invasion force, come to wipe out the station as well as the men who operated it. One operator, Frank Coghlan, would later write that, 'Due to our isolation we were totally unaware of the Bismarck Sea battle. We were reporting increased air activity at the time but no one in authority bothered to inform us of the reason for this.'

So began a night that could almost be described as comical if not for the gravity of the situation. A perimeter was set up around the radar station and all vital documents prepared for destruction. Even the station itself was set with demolition charges, among which the operators still had to work with a rifle over their knees.

Norm Smith remembers a several-pound charge of TNT sitting beside him, along with an open box of wax matches and a wick, which he was expected to light before bolting to a nearby slit trench. 'The scene was set for a determined assault on the world record for the 50 metres dash!' he recalled years later.

Throughout the night, more and more lurid reports came in. 'In pidgin English,' recalled Coghlan, 'an excited native, under interrogation, indicated that about 2000 of the enemy had disembarked from a large troop transport.'

In the dark, reluctant pairs of airmen – untrained in jungle warfare – were sent forward into the scrub to challenge any activity. Three quick rifle shots was the signal for danger. In reality, the noisy motor-driven alternator which powered the radar apparatus and which had to be kept running, would have drowned out even the most clumsy Japanese approach. As Coghlan recalled, 'The rest of us remained at the ready, trigger-happy and alerted by the slightest sound.'

At one stage, the men took it upon themselves to burn some documents. For some reason, a few spare .303 shells had become tangled up in the mess and they exploded with loud bangs, upsetting others in the party before the false alarm could be reported.

By morning, the only soldiers to arrive were a platoon of Australians who had marched 15 miles through the night to the radar station, and who then proceeded down towards the reported Japanese landing site.

A dozen or so enemy soldiers were indeed discovered on the beach and told to surrender. When they refused, some even brandishing small arms they had somehow managed to hang on to, the Australians opened fire, killing all but three. In a somewhat anticlimactic end to the drama, the men were led blindfolded back up the path past the radar station then guarded in a small area surrounded by fuel drums. They were in a poor state, suffering from the burns of exposure under the tropical sun, but did not complain, believing they were soon to be executed anyway. One who spoke reasonable English even exhorted his captors to the task. 'Hurry up! Hurry up!' he urged. 'All Japanese soldiers want to die.'

Over the next few days, more Japanese arrived on Goodenough Island in dribs and drabs. One barge of twenty-five made it to shore and without food and water, raided native gardens while being pursued by the Australians, who urged them to surrender. Very few did. One Japanese soldier who finally submitted was given a can of army ration pilchards, which he ate, then attempted to slash his wrists with the jagged, still-attached lid.

In a few days, thirty-seven Japanese had been killed or rounded up into reluctant captivity.

The crisis at the radar station averted, the operators were told to remain on the lookout, and for the next several weeks, any night jungle sound was amplified tenfold in dread. On other parts of the island, more Japanese made it to shore, with eighty-five eventually killed and twenty-five captured. On Kiriwina Island in the Trobriands, a party of seven landed and were promptly killed, with fourteen more attacked on the Papuan coast at Tufi.

Some enemy soldiers managed to survive alone. One Japanese private tied his rifle to a plank before jumping off his burning merchant ship. He then drifted for two days before he was picked up by the Australians in a state of delirium, later stating that had he been in his right mind, he would have killed himself before surrendering to the enemy.

It is estimated that just over 800 Japanese soldiers, almost all minus their equipment, supplies and weapons, made it to Lae, courtesy of several small Japanese boats which ventured out to search for them, despite the constant danger of air attack. On 10 March, one vessel brought in 155 survivors and submarine *I-26* rescued fifty-five more. One soldier managed to hold on to several automatic weapons which he proudly presented as he reported for duty after a week drifting on the ocean. It is estimated that of these survivors, several hundred were quickly put back into action. In the following weeks, more barges and rafts were seen drifting among the islands of the Bismarck Sea, most now empty, but others holding a few emaciated corpses or barely living human skeletons who would soon expire. Most still refused to surrender.

Others were more fortunate. One sergeant became famous for diving off the burning *Oigawa Maru* clutching the colours of his 115 Regiment. He somehow protected them for the next several weeks while drifting on barges and life rafts, surviving with a party of a dozen others on fish, before coming ashore on New Britain, where the colours were ceremoniously returned to the army command. Even more astonishing, the sergeant managed to survive the war, putting his survival down to the intervention of heaven, and the warrior spirits of the regiment's dead.

Along the shores of Goodenough and other islands, as well as some parts of the New Guinea coast itself, the flotsam of a defeated fleet continued to wash up for weeks, littering the beaches with debris. Sometimes a Samurai sword or machine pistol was souvenired, but most were simply tossed back into the sea. One sealed cabinet proved to be an intelligence windfall, containing regimental paperwork including orders of battle, strengths, and valuable details of units and commands not previously known to exist.

For weeks after the battle, skirmishes were still occurring, and prisoners still being taken. On 15 April, Australian soldiers reported capturing two Japanese at Tufi, then four days later – nearly seven weeks after the battle – three were killed on tiny Kwaiawata Island in the far east of the Trobriands.

As late as 20 July, the sole remaining survivor of what had been a party of seven which had come ashore on Goodenough Island was taken prisoner. Having lived quietly with a woman and her children in a native village, the Australians eventually found out. Surrendering meekly, he was to be the last Japanese survivor of the battle.

Japan's Operation 81 convoy had been eviscerated, the spark with which they intended to reignite their conquest of New Guinea, extinguished forever. The nearest any of her ships had made it to their destination of Lae was 46 miles.

CHAPTER 23
'NEVER WAS THERE SUCH A DEBACLE'

By sheer chance, on 4 March 1943, the day after the battle, generals Kenney and MacArthur had a trip booked back to the United States, where they intended to press their cause for more men and materiel to be sent to the Pacific in the war against Japan. At the last minute they grabbed the latest, barely filtered intelligence reports filled with myriad repetitions and inaccuracies, accepted them at face value and fired them off in various communiqués.

Now it was not eight but *twenty-two* Japanese cargo vessels which had been sent to the bottom. Fifty-five Japanese aircraft had been destroyed and up to 15 000 soldiers and sailors killed. These ridiculously exaggerated figures were quietly challenged in some circles, but both Kenney and MacArthur retorted furiously, appealing directly to Washington to punish anyone who dared bring the tally back to some level of reality.

Kenney threatened 'action against those responsible' for questioning his assessment of the battle, while MacArthur chose to rail against his old foe, the navy.

> The navy was trying to belittle the whole thing because they weren't in on it ... It's against the rules for land-based airplanes to sink ships, especially naval vessels. It's bad enough for them to sink merchant vessels. They ought to be sunk by battleship gunfire or by submarines. But for airplanes to do it, especially if they aren't naval airplanes, it's all wrong.

MacArthur's tantrum was quietly ignored.

It is understandable that such exaggerations helped bolster levels of public morale, but even long after the war, the two old warriors, MacArthur and Kenney, refused to correct the numbers, their attention no doubt centred on their own legacies.

MacArthur said of the battle, 'We have achieved a victory of such completeness as to assume the proportions of a major disaster to the enemy', and 'the most important air battle of the Pacific War'.

Equally predictably, there was no mention whatsoever of the significant contribution made by the RAAF's 30 and 22 squadrons, those brave men who went in first to suppress the Japanese anti-aircraft guns, paving the way for the grateful US pilots to begin their own work.

For a while the Australian public celebrated the victory, and for the first time dared to believe that the direct Japanese threat to the Australian mainland might finally be diminishing. This was helped in no small part by Damien Parer and the film he released on 19 March 1943, just a fortnight after the battle itself, and which he had filmed standing behind Torchy Uren's cockpit at the height of the battle. Now, in his nine-minute documentary *The Bismarck Convoy Smashed*, awestruck citizens in cinemas around the country could see for themselves the visceral details of the battle fought by their gallant young airmen: the Beaufighters skimming at wave-height over the sea, the burning ships, the Japanese ships whipping under the passing aircraft, every detail visible. Nor, it is interesting to note, was any detail spared of the bloody second day's events and the strafing of the survivors in the water. 'Remember Hong Kong, Manila, Nanking, and a few others, Mister Nippon? You'd better duck', says the stentorian voice-over as footage is shown of a lone lifeboat being obliterated by gunfire. 'Bullseye! And more Japs meet their ancestors ...' Few watching at the time would have had issue with the sentiment.

Historian Lex McAulay states that the exact number of Japanese deaths in the Battle of the Bismarck Sea will never be known, but that 'a reasonable figure would be 3000'. An entire Japanese Division, the 51st, was essentially wiped out.

For almost the first and only time during the Pacific War, the Bismarck Sea saw the RAAF become generous in handing out decorations to its flyers. Despite not even being officially on the battle order that day, Blackjack Walker was awarded the Distinguished Service Order (DSO), as was the CO of 22 Squadron, Wing Commander Keith MacDermott Hampshire, who led his Havocs on dawn attacks on Lae and

Salamaua airfields on 3 March, helping to suppress Japanese fighter presence over the convoy.

Distinguished Flying Crosses were handed out to seven other pilots, including Torchy Uren, who had provided Damien Parer with a platform – literally, in fact, in the form of his head – to capture on film some of the most dramatic moments of the battle.

Despite being the architect of the attack, Group Captain 'Bull' Garing did not resume his old job as head of 9 Operational Group. He was instead sent as far away from the Japanese as possible, to head up No 1 Operational Training Unit East Sale, the large RAAF training facility in southern Victoria. Here, his time was consumed by the deadly riddle of the locally built Bristol Beaufort bombers, which had suffered multiple catastrophic failures and took many young lives before the fault – a poorly constructed horizontal trim mechanism – was identified and rectified. Despite his brilliance, the RAAF were happy to have the forthright Garing thus occupied.

General Kenney, who would go on to be regarded as one of the great heroes of the US Army Air Force, succeeded in turning around his battered Fifth Air Force. The conditions of fighting in the islands, as the war went on, would become no easier for his men, but they had at least proved themselves in adapting to a revolutionary new tactic, with highly modified aircraft capable of delivering shattering blows against the enemy. Ironically, there would be few subsequent opportunities in which to employ it, as the Japanese after the Bismarck Sea disaster refused to sail any more convoys of significant strength.

In August 1943, at the Japanese air base at Wewak on New Guinea's northern coast, Kenney's men once again employed the daring tactics developed prior to the Bismarck Sea battle. In a series of raids, they wiped out Japan's air presence in New Guinea completely, and forever. From then on, Japan's retreat became a tide which ended two years later at Hiroshima and Nagasaki.

Paul Irving 'Pappy' Gunn, the genius tinkerer and architect of many of the new weapons and aircraft modifications which made victory possible, survived the war. He later returned to his beloved Philippines, where he restarted the airline he had begun before the Japanese had rolled in. Having survived numerous near-death experiences at the hand of the enemy, however, Gunn finally succumbed to the power of nature. In 1957 a fierce tropical storm hurled his aircraft into the sea, killing him and all onboard.

•

For the Japanese, the Battle of the Bismarck Sea was a disaster of immeasurable proportions. A few days after the battle, news of the defeat was delivered to an ashen-faced Admiral Yamamoto in Tokyo. He demanded to know what had gone wrong, decreed that no more convoys would set sail to New Guinea, and that all future supplies would be delivered by fast, single ships, barges or submarines – and always at night. This, however – as he knew only too well – would in no way be enough to support even a small garrison, let alone the one already embedded in New Guinea. From this point on the Japanese force would begin to wither away from hunger, disease and a vengeful enemy.

After the war, former Rabaul staff officer Masatake Okumiya described the anguish caused by the battle among the Japanese leaders:

> The effectiveness of enemy air strength was brought to Admiral Yamamoto with the news of a crushing defeat which, if similar events were permitted to occur in the future, promised terrifying disasters for Japan. Our losses for this single battle were fantastic. Not during the entire savage fighting at Guadalcanal did we suffer a single comparable blow. We knew we could no longer run cargo ships or even fast destroyer transports to any front on the north coast of New Guinea, east of Wewak. Our supply operation became a scrabbler's run of barges, small craft and submarines.

Having anticipated another successful convoy supply run, as had occurred in January, Operation 81 had failed on multiple levels. It suffered from poor coordination between air and sea power, no priority given to intelligence, and the spectacular blunder by Admiral Kimura which saw the ships waste their precious cloak of protective darkness.

Little more than a year earlier, Japan had demonstrated to the world the inherent vulnerability of ships to aircraft attack when they sank the British capital ships *Prince of Wales* and *Repulse* off Malaya. Now it was the Japanese themselves who had failed to learn the lesson. The Battle of the Bismarck Sea was a blow from which they would never recover.

At home, Japanese newspapers and radio did not report nor refer to the disaster in any way. But in a grim postscript, the Imperial Japanese Army now quietly instructed that all soldiers would henceforth be given swimming lessons.

After the war, a Japanese destroyer captain was interviewed about his country's long list of defeats following the initial rush of victories after Pearl Harbor. One in particular stood out. 'More shocking to me was the Battle of the Bismarck Sea,' he said. 'Japan's defeat there was unbelievable. Never was there such a debacle.'

•

One of the most lopsided victories in history, the Battle of the Bismarck Sea has been described by one historian as being 'akin to a land battle, fought at sea and won from the air'. It stands out as a peculiarly modern conflict, employing startling new tactics and weapons which somehow fit more comfortably in later confrontations rather than the early stages of the Pacific War.

Despite the drama of its background and setting, the consequences – yet totality – of its outcome, and the astonishing brevity of its main engagement, it has been largely forgotten by those nations whose sons fought with such bravery and daring eight decades ago.

The Battle of the Bismarck Sea represented a high point of cooperation and mutual respect between the young men of the two Allied nations, yet in all but a few American sources the role played by Australia and its airmen is barely mentioned, if at all. On the other hand, the rare Australian commemorations have often been guilty of exaggerating Australia's contribution. On the fiftieth anniversary of the battle in 1993, the national Australian broadcaster produced a feature which included the curious statement that, 'the RAAF pilots were helped … by the Americans'.

In May 2020, just shy of his hundredth birthday, the last Australian airman to fly in the battle – navigator Sergeant Fred Anderson – died. Anderson spent much of the conflict reloading the heavy canisters of cannon ammunition to be quickly expended by his pilot, Bob Brazenor. Perhaps it was enough for him and his now departed comrades to quietly appreciate the truth.

BIBLIOGRAPHY

Arbon, J and Christensen, Chris, *The Bismarck Sea Ran Red*,
    Walsworth Press, Missouri, 1979

Bateson, Charles, *The War with Japan: a concise history*, Ure
    Smith, London, 1968

Bleakley, Jack, *The Eavesdroppers*, AGPS Press, Canberra, 1991

Bradley, Phillip, *The Battle for Wau: New Guinea's Frontline,
    1942–1943*, Cambridge University Press, Cambridge, 2008

Bristol, Randall E., 'The Battle of the Bismarck Sea: Airpower
validated in the Pacific', in possession of the author, Melbourne.

Brune, Peter, *The Spell Broken: Exploding the Myth of Japanese
    Invincibility: Milne Bay to Buna–Sanananda 1942–43*, Allen
    & Unwin, Sydney, 1998

Brune, Peter, *Those Ragged Bloody Heroes: From the Kokoda
    Trail to Gona Beach 1942*, Allen & Unwin, Sydney, 2005

Buggy, Hugh, *Pacific Victory: A short history of Australia's part
    in the war against Japan*, Department of Information,
    Melbourne, 1946

Byrd, Martha, *Kenneth N. Walker*, Air University Press, Montgomery, 1997

Cook, Haruko Taya and Cook, Theodore F., *Japan at War, An Oral History*, The New Press, New York, 1992

Cooper, Anthony, *Kokoda Air Strikes: Allied Air Forces in New Guinea, 1942*, NewSouth Publishing, Sydney, 2014

Cortesi, Lawrence, *The Battle for the Bismarck Sea: War Without Rules*, Nordon Publications, New York, 1967

Day, David, *Reluctant Nation: Australia and the Allied defeat of Japan 1942–45*, Oxford University Press, Melbourne, 1992

Dick, George Turnbull, *Beaufighters Over New Guinea: No 30 Squadron RAAF 1942–1943*, RAAF Museum, Point Cook, 1993

Frisbee, John, *Makers of the United States Air Force*, Office of Air Force History, United States Air Force, Washington DC, 1987

Gann, Timothy D., *Fifth Air Force Light and Medium Bomber Operations During 1942 and 1943*, Air University Press, Montgomery, 1992

Gilbert, Gregory, *The Battle of the Bismarck Sea, March 1943*, Air Power Development Centre, 2013

Gillison, Douglas, *Royal Australian Air Force 1939–1942*, Australian War Memorial, Canberra, 1962

Graham, Burton, *None Shall Survive: The graphic story of the annihilation of the Japanese armada in the Bismarck Sea battle by the U.S. Fifth Air Force and the Royal Australian Air Force: The war against Japan 1943*, F.H. Johnston, Sydney, 1943

Griffith, Thomas E. Jr., *MacArthur's Airman: General George C. Kenney and the War in the Southwest Pacific*, University Press of Kansas, Lawrence, 1998

Johnston, Mark, *Whispering Death: Australian Airmen in the Pacific War*, Allen & Unwin, Sydney, 2011

Kenney, George C., *General Kenney Reports: A Personal History of the Pacific War*, Duell, Sloan and Pearce, New York, 1949

McAulay, Lex, *Blood and Iron: The battle for Kokoda 1942*, Random House Australia, Sydney, 1997

McAulay, Lex, *The Battle of the Bismarck Sea: 3 March 1943*, St. Martin's Press, New York, 1991

Manchester, William, *American Caesar: Douglas MacArthur 1880–1964*, Little, Brown & Co., Boston, 1978

Morison, Samuel Eliot, *Breaking the Bismarcks Barrier: 22 July 1942–1 May 1944*, Little, Brown & Co., Boston, 1950

Null, Gary, *Weapon of Denial, Air Power and the Battle for New Guinea*, Department of the Air Force, Washington DC, 1995

Parnell, Neville, *Whispering Death: A History of the RAAF's Beaufighter Squadrons*, Reed Books, Sydney, 1980

Rodman, Matthew K., *A War of Their Own: Bombers over the Southwest Pacific*, Air University Press, Montgomery, 2005

Rust, Kenn C., *Fifth Air Force Story*, Historical Aviation Album Publication, Temple City, 1973

Spinetta, Lawrence, Bismarck Sea article, *World War Two Magazine*, November 2007

Thompson, Peter, *Pacific Fury: How Australia and her Allies defeated the Japanese*, William Heinemann, Sydney, 2008

Turner, Jim, *30 Squadron, RAAF. Vol 1 March 1942–October 1943*, 2016

US Strategic Bombing Survey (Pacific), *The Campaigns of the Pacific War*, US Government, 1946

Wilson, David, *The Decisive Factor: 75 & 76 Squadrons Port Moresby and Milne Bay 1942*, Banner Books, Melbourne, 1991

INDEX

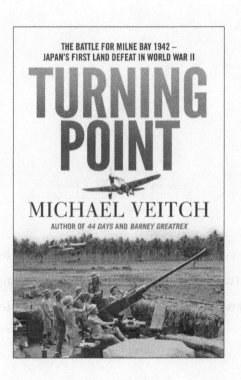

THE BATTLE FOR MILNE BAY 1942 –
JAPAN'S FIRST LAND DEFEAT IN WORLD WAR II

TURNING POINT

MICHAEL VEITCH

AUTHOR OF *44 DAYS* AND *BARNEY GREATREX*

The Battle for Milne Bay – Japan's first defeat on
land in World War II – was a defining moment in the
evolution of the indomitable Australian fighting spirit.
For the men of the AIF, the militia and the RAAF,
it was the turning point in the Pacific, and their finest
– though now largely forgotten – hour.
Forgotten, until now.

hachette
AUSTRALIA

If you would like to find out more about
Hachette Australia, our authors, upcoming events
and new releases you can visit our website or our
social media channels:

hachette.com.au

 HachetteAustralia

  HachetteAus